There Is Only One Road And It Goes Everywhere

KATHLEEN PHELAN

There Is Only One Road And It Goes Everywhere

Journeys to the Land
of Heart's Desires

FERAL
HOUSE

TRAMP
• LIT •
SERIES

Introduction

LIAM PHELAN

Kathleen "Kaye" Phelan would dance into our lives. We lived in a big, white farmhouse halfway up the hill of Howth village, outside Dublin. Kaye was my step-grandmother, married to my grandfather, the writer and tramp Jim Phelan. From the age of about seven, Kaye would appear on our long driveway, a small woman who dressed neatly and who seemed to hover above the ground.

She would sashay up our long, curved driveway, taking small, precise steps, body swinging, often humming some obscure jazz tune, avian in her movements. She carried a small suitcase, or sometimes a little bag. She dressed neatly, maybe in a pair of faded, flared jeans and a flowery top, and she often wore a colourful scarf tied up around her hair.

Once arrived, she would start to talk. And what tales she had to tell. Stories of the road, of her travels across Ireland, Britain or France. She would tell of hitching across Scandinavia, snow on the road and cold bitter enough to knock you dead. Or she would speak of America, that mythical land I had read about through the books of Jack London, Upton Sinclair and John Steinbeck.

For a young boy, Kaye was a creature from another planet. She sounded different to everyone else I met, she looked different and she certainly lived a different life. She had a confidence and a determination that was palpable, even at my young age. Despite having very little money and no regular home, barring a caravan she used as a base without having a vehicle to tow it, she was totally at ease with her place in the world. She moved among tramps and "tinkers" (the common term for travelling people), but also among Lords and Ladies. She told a funny story about hitching in North Africa and meeting a guard at some tiny border crossing who proudly asked her in her finest English: "How is the Queen?" To which Kaye replied in equally melodic tones: "Very well, thank you. I'll let her know you were asking after her."

Kaye would stay in our house for a few days, or sometimes a few weeks. She would always ask what I was reading, and I would relate to her my tales of skateboarding, or venturing out to a nearby island on a leaky dinghy, or getting in fights with local kids because of our politics (left) and religion (none). She was a good listener and always had the right answer or response; she always had your back.

After much pestering and pleading with my parents, Kaye finally took me hitchhiking to England when I was about 13.

We caught the ferry to Holyhead and then hitched through Wales, to Chester, Chesterfield and down to Nottingham. We stayed a few days at her caravan and then hitched back.

It was a rare insight into the craft of being a professional tramp. Much of society looks down on tramps, condemns them for not getting "a real job" or "sponging off others." But travelling with Kaye, it was striking how hard she worked. We would walk miles to find the right spot to hitch—not too straight as cars were going too fast, not too winding as it was difficult for them to stop. Every person who stopped was instantly assessed as a potential mark. Kaye only hitched single occupants, as groups were too dangerous and too hard to penetrate. She would open the passenger door but she never got straight in. She looked the driver in the eye, had a few words and only then decided whether to get in. She told me, "Never get straight in a car. Look at the person first. If they won't look you in the eye, don't get in. If they mumble or look away, don't get in. If they make you feel bad in any way, don't get in."

More than once when we hitched, she would refuse the lift and irate drivers would roar down the road in disgust, furious their offer of goodwill had been refused. But for Kaye, this was life and death, her ability to pick someone who meant her harm or was up to no good in a few seconds. It was the equivalent of a complex psychological profile carried out in a blink of an eye, often without people even realising they were being assessed.

Picking the right person meant the ability to sell a booklet, in which she would write tales about herself and Jim and paint some small watercolours.

Or she might get a few quid or a meal or bed for the night. My instructions were to sit in the back, stay quiet and only

Kathleen imparting vagabond wisdom to American friends during a visit to the States, c. 1970s.

speak when I was spoken to. In hindsight, very Victorian. But I was an eager apprentice and lapped up the interactions in the front seats.

Kaye was able to charm strangers very quickly. She would speak of her life with Jim, her life on the road. She would ask people where they were from, and she seemed to always be able to come back with some story about that town or city, almost anywhere in the world. At some point she would produce her booklets and ask would the driver buy one. It was salesmanship at its finest, and people would hand over money without even realising they had been worked.

We would chat as we waited for lifts, sometimes moving spots or sometimes taking shelter in a café when the rain began to fall.

Later in life, I used her techniques to hitch across Ireland, England, Greece, Australia and Cuba.

Kaye's caravan was tiny, crammed and exceptionally neat. She kept piles of papers, her booklets, paints, Jim's books and a chessboard. I remember getting in trouble for leaving my things lying around, and feeling the sharpness of her tongue.

She was a daily visitor to the bookies, read the form closely and tried to explain her system to me, which essentially boiled down to if you won, you took out your stake and a little more and gambled with the rest.

She taught me to live life in the moment, to trust in the universe, and to always follow your heart. She warned me against mug punters and becoming dreary.

I have lost the letters and drawings she sent me, but still carry her memories wherever I go.

Kaye was a quiet revolutionary, a woman who achieved greatness by living a completely unconventional life that few of us can even dream about.

She was an artist whose greatest creation was her self, and she survived by "selling" her story to anyone she met on her widespread travels across the world.

She came from a conventional middle-class English family, but transcended her background to make the entire planet her playground.

She was also a pioneering woman, living life on the road facing the prospect of sexual assault and death. She was fiercely independent and held her own among rough and sexist men with ease. But she never made a big deal out of it. She shrugged off the danger.

As her best friend and confidante, Gracie Jackman, said of her: "Everything about her was light. She danced her way lightly across the face of this earth."

She helped make me the man I am, and, to quote another, she always carried the flame.

There is only one road. It goes everywhere. That's where she'll be. ⚬

LIAM PHELAN is an Irish journalist living in Sydney.

PUBLISHER'S NOTE

Most books, by the time the reader sees them, have been reviewed and revised by the author and editors numerous times. Kathleen's work here is compiled from found typewritten papers and handwritten pages, and, except for small notes in the margins, unedited. We also suspect that some names may actually be placeholders when one was forgotten, to return later to correct.

We decided it would be unfair to her memory to extensively rework her manuscript without her involvement. So, we present to you her story, very much as we found it. We have included footnotes and images—some found, some from her collection—to assist contemporary readers, but for the most part we have chosen to let her work to speak for itself. We trust you will enjoy the journey.

There Is Only One Road And It Goes Everywhere

What Lamp Has Destiny

Aword to the reader: I like meeting people, and I love talking, and I always want to know how other people live and what they think. Quite simply, I have always wanted to know everything about everything. A tall order, as anyone will agree. But there are people like that. Not many, fortunately, or civilization might fall apart overnight.

Some years ago, young people ran away to St. Ives in Cornwall to become beatniks, or later, in the United States, made for San Francisco to become hippies. My generation hurried to Paris or London to become bohemians. Inevitably, on my arrival in London as a teenager, I drifted to the Speaker's Corner in Hyde Park. There I met Joe Cassidy, a professional hitch-hiker who had thumbed his way all over North and South America, as well as a large part of Europe. He was sampling the roads of England for a few weeks. Until then, I had never thought of vagabondage as an occupation. In fact, I did not know that there was such a profession.

Joe was from California and spent his time thumbing cars and smiling on all and sundry. From him I learned that if you did not like a place, you stood on a grass verge and jerked your thumb. Other people, when things went wrong or when they were being ground down, grinned and groaned and bore it. Joe and I merely jerked a thumb over our shoulder, opened a car door, and moved on to nicer things and more pleasant people. I have been doing that ever since.

Just looking around, trying to find out what goes on in the world, has occupied me for over forty years. In that pursuit I have travelled hundreds of thousands of miles, hitch-hiking in many lands.

After all, you can't ask personal questions of a pilot or a bus driver. Besides, a vagabond generally doesn't have a lot of money for train fares or bus fares. Hitch-hiking is faster, easier, more comfortable, and definitely more pleasant than ordinary travel.

People often ask me how many miles I have travelled. I do not know—or care. It should be borne in mind that I live on the road, have no home or fixed residence. I keep going all the year round, winter and summer alike. I am always intending to follow the sun to a warmer climate. It never works out that way. Usually, I find myself in Morocco when the temperature is over 100 degrees and in the Yukon when it is 50 below.

Sometimes I have been given the hospitality of an old cottage or caravan to house my "possessions"—meaning a typewriter, an easel, some paints, and a few treasured books and letters. At such times I write or paint—and now and then even get a few coins for so doing.

Apart from these occasions I simply go. All day, every day, I just flag a car and go wherever that motorist is going.

From the Sahara desert to the Himalaya Mountains, from Galway Bay to the Golden Gate, Alaska to Argentina. It adds up to a lot of mileage.

No town or city dweller, no normal civilised person, can understand what it means to live plan-less that way. Any city resident who tried to live as I do would be mad. On the other hand, if I tried to live for any length of time in Paris or Pittsburgh, in London or Birmingham, I would be a half-wit, or worse. It takes all kinds to make a world.

This is not an autobiography in the sense of "I was born here, educated elsewhere, and did this or that in the orderly procession of a lifetime." It is just a random telling of anecdotes about my life along the road. After all, the road is my home and I have lived there for a very long time. I am a bridge piece between the old-style tramp with the stick and bundle and the backpacking drifter seen nowadays along the roads of the world.

The tramps of yore took a year to walk from Penzance to Aberdeen (or vice versa) as a professional hitch-hiking vagabond. I think of the Interstate 80 from New York to San Francisco or the road from Scotland to Sicily as just another village street.

Profession: Vagabond. Money: Nil. Address: No fixed residence.

You could say those are my vital statistics.

Thus it will be gathered that I have never had a permanent abode for any length of time. I must also make it clear that I have never had much money for any length of time either. No one should get a picture of a drifter with an income, or a lady vagabond with security. I have never had anything like that, thank God. Mostly I hitch the road without a copper coin. Wherever the first motorist is going, that is just right. Even when it looks all wrong.

Of course, that last statement is founded on the nebulous fatalism of a vagabond. But it works. I mean the way things turn out for the best. So often, the "bad luck lift" turns out to be just right.

For instance: One day I was hitch-hiking out of Wales, just drift-ing, not going anywhere in particular.

Kathleen as a child playing on the beach.

On the outskirts of Chester, I flagged a car, and when it stopped the motorist wound down the window.

"Yes?" he queried. "Aberdeen?" I asked, and hurried on. "Liverpool? Carlisle? Glasgow?" I was naming points north, near and far.

"Garstang," said the motorist. "Hop in!"

I had not the faintest idea where Garstang was. But I hopped. We talked. I never noticed the road or signposts. Somewhere, the driver said something about the East Lancs Road. It goes to Liverpool. Later he mentioned that the road was the A6 going all the way to the Scottish border. Then, in a small vil-lage, he said, "This is Garstang, that's the road north to Scotland. I'm turning off soon for Blackpool. You can come if you like."

Mostly I do just that. Let the road decide to get out or not. A big sign pro-claimed "TO THE NORTH." It was late afternoon, and for a long while, the road was very quiet. I began to regret not having gone to Blackpool.

Then I saw a man sauntering along towards me, on the opposite side of the road. Occasionally he turned back to flag a vehicle southbound. Cars were few and far between in those days, but so were hitch-hikers, so we eyed one another plenty. When he was directly opposite, he stopped and stared across at me.

About six feet tall, he wore a leather jacket and corduroy trousers. A large black hat was pushed to the back of his head and round his neck was knotted a red silk scarf. A duffel bag hung from his shoulder.

He strolled across the road and stood in front of me and grinned. He looked as though he hadn't a care in the world. High, wide and handsome. I had never seen anyone more colourful or alive-looking.

He stood and looked at me while I stared back. Then, in a deep, lilting Irish voice, he said, "And where might you be going?"

I said nothing, just kept on looking.

Then he spoke again.

"You didn't answer me. Where might you be going?"

"Nowhere," I replied.

"I'm going there myself," he said. "Do you mind if I come along a bit of the way with you?"

We turned and headed out of Garstang together.

I'm fond of saying that the road is like a great supermarket. Whatever you need is there for the asking.

Even a husband!

That is how I met Jim Phelan.

He told me that he had no house and no possessions to speak of. A few books, a typewriter, bits and pieces at a friend's place in London. He was a tramp-writer and lived on the road. For a few weeks in the wintertime, he stayed put and wrote a book. As soon as the book was written and sent to a publisher he got out on the road again.

For one nurtured on the works of Jack London and W.H. Davies, there was no need to know more. Here was a carefree irresponsibility to match my own. So I went off with him—and married him—Just. Like. That.

The most important thing was to find a compromise between the road and the writing. For although we both agreed that neither of us could stay in one place for any length of time without going mad, Jim simply had to write.

There is a romantic myth that tramps and vagabonds sleep under bridges or in ditches. Or that tramp authors write their poetry and prose in barns and haystacks. Would that it were so simple.

Our eventual solution was to get a horse-drawn caravan. It became a kind of moveable base when Jim had a writing job to do. After a book was written, the caravan was left on a farm while we hit the road hitch-hiking. It was the perfect answer. We never thought of the wagon as Home: the road was always that. The caravan was just a roof over the typewriter.

But that was way off in the future. On that day of our meeting, we had to think of somewhere to stay, pretty quickly. A book was demanding to be written.

So we went drifting the road, here and there, waiting for something to turn up. ☙

The Back of Beyond

Upleadon in Gloucestershire was a small hidden hamlet on a back road, branching off from a back road, northwest of Gloucester City, and near to Newent. It was truly the back of beyond.

After my road-meet with Jim Phelan, we stayed there in a disused bakehouse that had been converted into quite a livable small cottage. At first, it sounded as if we would have to sleep inside the bakery oven, wrapped in sacks. But the place was furnished with essentials: a bed, a large table, a couple of chairs, a gaslight and a gas ring, and a huge open fireplace. We thought it was marvellous. Exactly what we were looking for.

It was recommended to us by Archie Turner, a well-known citizen of Gloucester. Archie was one of the first vendors of bottled gas. His firm was called Bottogas, and Archie and his wife Jeanne ran their gas business from a little shop in King's Square in the middle of Gloucester City. King's Square was the weekly venue for one of the most glorious open markets in England. It was also one of the busiest. This was because Gloucester was the most famous crossroad city in the country. Nowadays, beautiful bridges span the Severn River. Bridges which carry all the traffic from London and the south of England across into Wales. When we halted in Upleadon no such bridges existed. There was a little car ferry in the village of Aust. Four cars at a time were its limit. But the last bridge over the Severn was in Gloucester.

Anyone going from southern England into Wales—north, south, east, or west—had to cross Glouces- Severn Bridge under construction as viewed from Aust, c. 1962.

ter bridge, and that meant going through the city and passing within a stone's throw of the Gloucester market, so everyone knew it. The Turners' shop fronted onto the market square and they used to boast that everyone in the country visited them.

Archie was from North America and had been a hobo in the States. He had an anarchistic temperament and a soft spot for writers and artists and the bohemian way of life. He was married to Jeanne Berkovici whose family were of Hungarian gipsy origin. An accomplished musician, she had a great follow-ing—literally so—especially on market days, as she strolled up and down the aisles of stalls playing her violin.

I first met the Turners in Hyde Park at Speakers Corner one bitterly cold, snowy Sunday morning. More accurately, they met me. I was standing at the entrance to the Park with George Woodcock[1], trying to sell a paper called *Anarchist Freedom*, when Archie and Jeanne came to buy one. George and I were covered in snowflakes and frozen into statue-like immobility, so the Turners

---

1   **George Woodcock** (May 8, 1912 – January 28, 1995) was a Canadian writer of political biography and history, an anarchist thinker, an essayist and literary critic. He was also a poet and published several volumes of travel writing.

suggested that we give up our attempts to convert the masses and have a meal with them instead. Archie thoughtfully bought up all the copies of the paper, thus freeing us from our guilty feelings at abandoning our post.

We went to a café in Oxford Street, which was a rendezvous for many of the Hyde Park speakers. Owned by a family from Poland, it was always referred to as the 'Polish.' After Sunday morning 'soapboxing' in the Park, Frederick Lohr[2] and his associates of the London Forum gathered there to continue debating amongst themselves. People would not recognise their names today, but back in the forties and early fifties, hundreds of people flocked to Hyde Park on Sundays to listen to them. They were all splendid orators and when heckled, which was all part of the fun, positively sparkled. The hecklers were pretty good too. A far cry from soundbites and spin-doctors.

Archie and Jeanne Turner knew everyone. As a young naïve girl, to be taken along to the 'Polish' and admitted to this dazzling circle was all very thrilling. I thought I was at the heart of the revolution; however, I was not sure which one—several, in fact, because all the speakers had such wildly differing viewpoints and they were all so convincing. Those days were the beginning of my real education. Many might doubt its value, as I turned out to be a vagabond; but, on the other hand, George Woodcock became a well-known writer and wrote a fine biography of George Orwell. Later he was a lecturer at Toronto University.

I became great friends with Frederick and Holly Lohr. They lived in Covent Garden when it was still a real market. They had the flat above the United Dairies in Marchmont Street. I often stayed there at weekends, my regular pad being a room in a commune in Wharton Street near to King's Cross—an extremely dingy room in a dingy street in a dingy area.

We did not call them communes—"communities" was the 'in' word then. They were a hodgepodge of anarchists, pacifists, Trotskyists, and other deviants from the status quo, all preparing to change the world.

Contrary to what most people believed, we were very virtuous—utterly devoted to our various causes. Most people smoked, none drank—not necessarily from virtue—we just had little or no money. Drugs were barely heard of, and as for orgies, we were all too much interested in one another's heads to have much time for one another's bodies.

---

2 **Frederick Lohr** was an 1930s-era political radical. By the time of the outbreak of World War II, he moved to Convent Garden and began speaking at Hyde Park on the side of anarchist politics. He began the London Forum as a salon for fellow thinkers. He remained active in British anarchist and socialist politics until his death in 1960.

I was fortunate to be befriended by Frederick and Holly Lohr and to spend a lot of time with them in Marchmont Street. Their place was a miniature literary salon. Interesting people dropped in continually. I remember particularly the novelist Ethel Mannin[3] and art critic Herbert Read[4]. Plus of course, Archie and Jeanne Turner whenever they were in London.

One weekend, a young man, Dick Connell, came to visit and told us that he had bought a farm in South Wales near to Pontypool and had started a community there. Holly and I would be welcome anytime. We needed no second invitation. We liked the idea of getting out of London for a while, and as we both had bikes, decided to cycle to Wales. We had little money, but we were sure that we could beg food at some farms and do odd jobs on others in order to survive en route.

Consulting a map never entered our heads. We happily took a road out of London with not the faintest idea in which direction we were going. It is true that Southampton is not on the direct road to Wales from London and, generally speaking, there are not many farms there. But, one day, after whizzing through Winchester, we suddenly found ourselves on the outskirts of Southampton city. We discovered a farm at Eastleigh, and promptly applied for jobs!

I have no idea what the farmer and his wife thought of us, maybe that we were a heaven-sent miracle. But yes, they just happened to need a couple of girls for a week or two for a job that had to be done urgently.

The next morning we were put to work. We sat on upturned buckets, in a vile-smelling, sodden shed, sorting out spuds. The good ones for the market, the rotten ones for the pigs. In return, we received board and lodging, which was handy as we were practically starving, plus three shillings each for the week, which was even handier. The work was disgusting but we managed to enjoy ourselves.

---

3   **Ethel Edith Mannin** (October 6, 1900 – December 5, 1984) was a popular British novelist and travel writer who was active in British socialist and anarchist politics. Her writing career began in copywriting and journalism. She became a prolific author, and also politically and socially concerned. Mannin's memoir of the 1920s, *Confessions and Impressions*, sold widely and was one of the first Penguin paperbacks.

4   **Sir Herbert Edward Read** (December 4, 1893 – June 12, 1968) was an English art historian, poet, literary critic and philosopher, best known for numerous books on art, which included influential volumes on the role of art in education. Read was co-founder of the Institute of Contemporary Arts. As well as being a prominent English anarchist, he was one of the earliest English writers to take notice of existentialism. He was co-editor with Michael Fordham of the British edition in English of *The Collected Works of C.G. Jung*.

Are not a couple of adventurous drifters ready for anything?

Never settled anywhere, never learnt anything, never had a steady job, or did anything useful; that, roughly speaking, is what most city folks say about the drifters. Actually, the number of small skills one acquires is astonishing. For instance, the farmers worked with horses, enormous great carthorses. At the end of the first week, we graduated to work with them. I was quite proud to learn how to plough a straight furrow.

Most memorably, one day I was dispatched with a horse and cart piled high with dung, to travel from the farm where we worked at one end of Southampton to a farm at the other side of the city. This meant lumbering along the main street through the centre. It was no mean feat.

I think that ended our love affair with the bucolic way of life. Nor did we feel that we were suited to a spell in a farming community in Wales. We decided to split. Holly opted to go back to London (and to Frederick) by train, taking both bikes with her. I decided to hitch-hike anywhere that anyone would take me. On such a trivial decision a whole way of life can depend.

You might say that destiny went walking, or in this case hitching, because having drifted up through Wales to Chester and eventually getting a lift to Garstang, I met Jim Phelan. And while discussing which direction to take to try to find somewhere for a book to be written, I thought of Gloucester and the Turners. They would certainly know of a place. They certainly did. Upleadon and the converted bakehouse!

The countryside around Upleadon was completely unspoiled. No one ever passed on the narrow lanes. A fox, stalking a cock-pheasant, might pass the bakehouse, not six feet from the window at which we sat, neither bird nor animal taking the slightest notice of us. Jim decided to get down to writing the novel immediately.

Prior to our meeting along the road at Garstang, he had been working as a scriptwriter for Merton Park Films[5], one of several companies owned by Eric Pelly. He had been earning £50 a week plus expenses—a colossal sum of money when a bus driver was lucky to get £3.

---

5   **Merton Park Studios** was a British film production studio located at Long Lodge, 269 Kingston Road in Merton Park, south London. In the 1940s, it was owned by Piprodia Entertainment, Nikhanj Films and Film Producers Guild.
    Opened in 1929, many second features were produced there, and for a time it was home to Radio Luxembourg. Unlike many other studios, it remained open during World War II, producing films for the Ministry of Information. In the late 1940s the studios produced several children's films. In 1958 the first Carry On movie, *Carry On Sergeant*, was made there.

The London office was in West Street, a little back street off St. Martin's Lane, adjacent to the dance practice rooms of the famous dance troupe, the Tiller Girls[6].

Chief of the film company was Harold Purcell, out at Merton Park where the studios were located. Harold was a great film technician and a great songwriter. He wrote some lovely melodies for musicals. One of his famous hits, "The Fisherman's Song," in a show called *The Lisbon Story* was all the rage at the time.

Pelly and Purcell made no demur when Jim said he wanted to quit to write a novel, but put him on a 'retainer' of £5 a week, with Jim having to sign a solemn declaration that he would not work for any rival film company. Surely a vagabond's dream—when they pay a man a fiver a week *not* to work. Jim kept his word!

At about the same time he was introduced to Henry Harben[7], a rich philanthropist who liked giving money to writers with liberal views. He took Jim to dinner at the Savoy and, in addition to giving him an open check for £100 (twice the amount one got for the advance on a novel), agreed to send him £10 a week for the next six months while he was writing the book. That, plus Pelly's fiver meant the money was coming in nicely. Furthermore, Harben said that when the novel was finished, Jim should send him a copy of the script, as he had interests in several publishing firms. He might be able to help.

Of course, while all of this was happening, Jim had no idea that he was going to be at Upleadon, writing a novel about a Gloucestershire village. He was just going to go off along the road with the money and see what fate handed out. So, we were not exactly penniless when we moved into the bakehouse.

As it turned out, Upleadon was a delight. The novel, as Jim used to say, wrote itself. The original title was *Husbandman,* and the story was based on the village and the surrounding area. A lot of the action took place in the Travellers Rest,

6   The **Tiller Girls** were among the most popular dance troupes of the 1890s, first formed by John Tiller in Manchester, England, in 1889. In theatre Tiller had noticed the overall effect of a chorus of dancers was often spoiled by lack of discipline. Tiller found that by linking arms the dancers could dance as one; he is credited with inventing precision dance. Most famous for their high-kicking routines.

7   **Henry Devenish Harben** (b. 1874 – May 18, 1967) was a British barrister and Liberal Party politician who later joined the Labour Party. He was a notable supporter of women's suffrage. In 1910, Harben had joined the Fabian Society, which published his pamphlet "The Endowment of Motherhood." He was elected to the society's executive the following year, and was soon acting as its liaison with Clifford Allen's Inter-University Socialist Federation.

a delightful old-fashioned pub at Malswick. In the novel, it was re-named 'The Ugly Duckling.' The Travellers was a couple of miles from Upleadon, down a beautiful bluebell lane: Hook's Lane. I have heard that the pub has been modernised—I do not know. I have never been back.

The owner, Mrs. Hayward, a marvellous character with whom we were very friendly, appears as one of the principal characters in the book as Mrs. Hawshaw. Bill Phillips, a fiercely independent peasant farmer, appears under his own name. Miss Breame (I cannot remember her real name) was a lady in a nearby village, complete with manicured topiary and cats.

May Hill, where the pagan rites took place, is a famous landmark in Gloucestershire. It is a high hill crowned with a circular forest of trees. The locals used to say that there were 365 of them. Jim and I climbed the hill several times, but we never completed a count. Not surprising, really, as it was always after "closing time" at the Travellers that we went up there.

Upleadon was a cider-apple growing area, and it was the custom each year for farmers to do the rounds of one another's farms for the cider tasting. The nearest farm to our bakehouse cottage belonged to Bill Cox, whose cider was famous. The house was very old and had an ancient underground cider press. One night after closing time at the Travellers, Bill invited everyone to the farm to sample his cider. First, he took us to admire the ancient press. Then the 'tasting' started. The drink was served in pint-sized glass tankards and was a whitish green colour. I had heard that one pint made you blotto and after two you were pole-axed.

Even so, some of the farmers laced it with gin. I thought the taste was horrible, but I managed to drink half a pint and could have flown to the moon. Bill had other ideas. Much worse.

We must all go out to the stable yard, he insisted, to take part in an ancient custom. Only a woman could perform this ceremony, and lo and behold! Here was a woman.

Bill led me to a stable door, opened it, and inside there stood a *gigantic* black bull. Leading me to its head, he took hold of my hand and carefully fitted my little finger into the ring in its nose. I then had to guide the bull out of the stable, take it for one turn around the stable yard, and lead it back to its stall, which I duly did, just as if it was a pet lamb. You see what I mean about the cider!

Everyone cheered. "Goodnight!" "Goodnight!" And we all went home.

The next morning I got up early to go mushrooming. I climbed over a field gate, and halfway across the meadow, I saw a huge black bull approaching.

13

I turned and fled. It was only later in the day that I discovered it was the bull I had taken for 'walkies' the night before. I have never touched a glass of cider since.

We spent a lot of time at the Travellers Rest, counting it as research for the novel. Most of the regulars were local farmers and farmworkers and when the day's work was finished came to the pub on tractors. At closing time we all climbed aboard the trailers and were driven back up Hooks Lane to Upleadon.

I had very pretty curly hair which I wore long, well past shoulder length; and standing on the trailer with my hair flowing back in the breeze, as we sailed up the lane, I thought I looked wonderful. And I preened—mightily.

Many people complimented me on my lovely hair, none more than Mrs. Hayward. She was a small woman, and wore her hair, which was very thick, pulled tightly back from her forehead and knotted into a big bun at the nape of her neck. In the bar, she sometimes reached out and stroked my hair, saying, "You do have beautiful hair, Kathleen." It was always said with a slightly sly, secretive smile, and if I had not known her to be a kindly woman, I might have suspected that one day when my back was turned she would cut off a slice of it.

One afternoon I was brought down to size. I called in at the pub and she was there alone. She came round from the back of the bar to the centre of the room. "Yes, Kathleen," she said, "you do have beautiful hair—but I wonder—have you ever seen anything like this?"

She lifted up her hands and removed several hairpins from the bun at the nape of her neck. Her hair fell to the ground. An absolute shower of it. I gasped. I have seen many surprising things in my life and Mrs. Hayward's hair goes well near the top of the list.

She was completely covered. In fact, she could have walked from Malswick to Gloucester without any clothes, clad only in her shower of hair, and no one would have guessed she was naked. Beautiful hair indeed! I preened less often after that.

And then suddenly, the novel was finished and it was time to leave 'our village' and move on, to wherever.

I have the happiest memories of Upleadon and its countryside. Lush, un-spoilt Gloucestershire, where pheasants walked the lanes and rabbits played in the early morning sunshine. A countryside of bluebells and nightingales and glow-worms. Where the moon was always full, and the sun shone forever. A place for lovers, a perfect Paradise like all those faraway places at the back of beyond. ○ℑ

Literary Lions

We moved to London and took a room in Steele's Road at Chalk Farm. Jim delivered the script of *Husbandman* to Harben, his benefactor, and we sat back to await the millions. No one could have called us mercenary people, but at the same time, we wondered whether we might make forty thousand or a hundred thousand pounds out of the first two or three editions. With a book like that, which might sell, roughly speaking, forever, no one could say what kind of a total might be reached in the long run. We were always optimistic.

In less than a week Harben wrote asking us to call for the manuscript we had sent him. When we called, his butler didn't exactly hand the script out with a pair of tongs, but certainly sniffed prodigiously. We were aware there was a bad odour around.

Harben disliked the book intensely. He never said why. Up till then his praise of Jim's work had been fulsome, to say the least. With more than ten books published, one a best-selling novel titled *Lifer*, countless noteworthy short stories, several scripts for documentary films for the Ministry of Information, plus articles and reviews for all the major magazines and newspapers, his reputation was high!

Indeed, that was why Harben had subsidised the writing of *Husbandman*. Now everything was different. He wrote Jim saying:

"Don't you think you have spent sufficient time trying to live by your pen, and would it not be better to throw it up, while there are still plenty of jobs open for both you and your wife? If I may say so, I think three qualities are necessary for a writer. One is facility. Two is talent. Three is Genius. To be a great writer one needs all three. To be a successful writer needs the first and second. I may be wrong, but I think you have the first and a certain amount of the third, but I do not think that you have sufficient of the second. If you continue trying to write to sell, you are prostituting your third quality unsuccessfully. Why not take a job and occasionally, when you have sufficient time and leisure, write something really worthwhile, because you must. In that case, you might attain success as well."

Jim and Kathleen, the idles of the masses, no less. The clue is in the spelling. We didn't want any jobs. Jim had one. Being a writer was a full-time occupation, even though Harben had decided he wasn't a writer at all. That was the end of our millions. Pity! The money was good while it lasted. But he who pays the piper ...

Harben lived in Cavendish Square, so after collecting the script, it was only a short step to the back bar of the Café Royal to drown our sorrows. Then on into Soho and eventually we pub-crawled our way to Oxford Street and called in at the Feathers, Jim with the script under his arm.

As we entered, the guv'ner took one look at us and I just knew that he had taken an instant dislike and that whatever we wanted, we were not going to get. At the bar, the conversation went thus:

"Two whiskeys, please!"

"Sorry, no whiskey, sir."

"Two brandies."

"Sorry, no brandy."

"Two gin."

"No gin."

"Two rum."

"No rum."

"Two pints of bitter."

"No bitter."

At which, Jim spat. It was a glorious bulls-eye of a spit, which landed "plonk" into the guv'ner's eye. Immediately one of the bartenders jumped over the bar, another followed suit. A fight started, someone screamed "Police!"

Jim and I shot out through the door and ran down a side street into Soho and hid in a phone box in Dean Street. When it seemed safe to do so, we emerged.

"Have you got the script?" asked Jim.

"No, I thought *you* had it!!"

We had left the only copy on the bar counter in the Feathers!

The next morning, posing as Jim's secretary, I went to the Feathers to enquire. My boss had been in there the previous evening and had had a little too much to drink. Had they found a package? No, naturally they had not. Jim had to rewrite the whole of the novel. A most expensive spit!

It was only with the loss of the script and the consequent necessity to rewrite, that I realised that Jim never made carbon copies of anything he wrote. Abbreviated notes in thick notebooks were the only aide-memoire that he possessed. And an incredible memory. I have known very few people who could write a short story, put it aside, and then recite it verbatim. Jim thought that all writers could do that. What was more astonishing was that this was not the first time that he had lost a script, so to speak.

Some years earlier he had written a novel called *In the Can* about the movie industry which was published by Michael Joseph[8]. He was living in Hampstead at the time and set out one morning, with the script under his arm, headed for Michael Joseph's office in Bloomsbury.

A force nine gale was blowing; someone bumped into him; the script fell to the ground (it was in a loose cover), and the three hundred pages flew down Hampstead High Street. Several navvies[9], working on a road job, stamped on various pages, in their hobnailed boots, retrieving as many as they could. Yes, he had to rewrite that one too. Some people never learn!

I decided that I had better take on the typing—plus copies!

It took a couple of weeks to get the script of *Husbandman* ready for the second time and it went off to a literary agent. The agent sent it back within

---

8 **Michael Joseph** (September 26, 1897 – March 15, 1958) was a British publisher and writer, his first book being *Short Story Writing for Profit* (1923). After a period as a literary agent, Joseph founded his own publishing imprint as a subsidiary of Victor Gollancz Ltd. Gollancz invested £4000 in Michael Joseph Ltd. Joseph and Victor Gollancz disagreed on many points and Michael Joseph bought out Gollancz Ltd in 1938 after Gollancz attempted to censor *Across the Frontiers* by Sir Philip Gibbs on political grounds. (Joseph published the first edition in 1938 and a revised edition the following May.)

9 "Navvy" is nineteenth/early twentieth-century British slang for a civil engineer employed in navigational canal excavation, then railway building, but later used to describe a general, unskilled laborer, often in construction. Rarely in usage post-World War II, the word had a brief resurgence in 1983.

a few days. Also, he suggested Jim find another agent—someone bigger—he added tactfully.

We were fast running out of money. What to do? Crisis time had arrived. Our solution in times of crisis was always simple. Run away! Hit the road!

A couple of days later, early in the morning, we headed north out of London. We hitched lifts to anywhere that people were going. Early evening found us miles from anywhere on the borders of Wales, with most of our belongings, plus of course the rejected script. We talked our situation over for a few—a very few—minutes. Jim's solution was very easy. Throw the script in a ditch and walk away and to hell with everyone. Having lost the script once I was a little more cautious.

An hour later, we had taken a room over a little café in Shropshire and sat trying to decide why the novel was being treated as if Jim, and all the characters in the book, suffered from the Black Death. Everyone ran away from it even more quickly than they had run away from his first novel, *Lifer*, written years before I had met him. And yet *Lifer* was eventually published and had been a runaway best-seller. But *Lifer* had first been published to great acclaim in the States. Maybe we could repeat the process. We sent the script of *Husbandman* to New York, giving G.P.O.[10] Charing Cross as our address.

Meanwhile, we would just stay out on the road. As we were up in Cheshire, not far from the Welsh border, we decided to contact Charles Beatty, who was an expert in cubic chess.

Beatty lived at Trelydan Hall near to Welshpool and was married to the novelist Joan Grant[11]. Charles may have invented cubic chess; if not, he was the person who introduced it into England. Jim frequently wrote articles on chess and was well known in the chess world as a very strong player. Charles had sent us an invitation to look in on him whenever we were near. The Beattys had a

---

10 G.P.O. is the British abbreviation for General Post Office. The American counterpart is General Delivery.

11 **Joan Marshall Grant Kelsey** (April 12, 1907 – February 3, 1989) was an English author of historical novels and a reincarnationist. Grant believed she had been reincarnated at least forty times and that her far memory of past lives provided her the base material for her historical novels. She claimed to have an unusual gift of "far memory"—the ability to remember previous lives, and something she referred to as "sensory awareness." Her first and most famous novel was *Winged Pharaoh* (1937). Grant shot to unexpected fame upon publication. The *New York Times* hailed it as "A book of fine idealism, deep compassion and a spiritual quality pure and bright as flame," a sentiment echoed in reviews published elsewhere in the world.

wonderful wine cellar and we had a wonderful few days. And the cubic chess was a great challenge. It was a welcome respite from the road and benefactors and books and literary agents. We left one morning, in torrents of rain, and slept the night in a barn at Tern Hill. One night the manor house; the next night a tool shed. I loved it. We hitched to London. We had not one penny between us. We had no home, no jobs, no income—nothing.

Jim did of course have friends scattered around London. There were also publishers and editors, literary agents, and journalists from whom we could have raised a few pounds quickly. It was also a Sunday, and worse still a bank holiday weekend so every office was closed. We wandered into Trafalgar Square.

Early in the evening when the streets were packed solid with happy people, we stopped being (temporary) city folks and became professional vagabonds again. We picked a good-looking American tourist and fronted him as he had doubtless been 'fronted' many times in the States. Without a second's hesitation, he handed over a pound.

Nearly all of it went for food, immediately. Later in the evening, we stretched out on two seats in the big waiting room at Euston Station. Many other people, passengers or drifters, were spread over the other seats. But on the dot of midnight, the porters and the police turned everyone out into the street and the waiting room was closed. We started to walk towards Fleet Street. Anywhere would do. All we wanted was to get through this bank holiday weekend. Or rather, when you got down to bedrock, what we wanted was a bed for the rest of the night.

I halted suddenly. "Wait a minute," I told Jim. "Let's call it a day. Let's turn in." Jim looked at me curiously. We were passing through a completely deserted street in Bloomsbury—the rear of the British Museum in fact. One might as well have spoken of turning in on the top of Cleopatra's Needle.

Many millions of people must know the place. Half the scholars of the world have passed through that imposing entrance, with its huge bronze gates, and with the two stone lions; one on either side. Jim looked at the deserted street, the gates, the lions, then looked at me. But I led the way, triumphantly.

Two of the lions outside of the British Museum are hollow. No one seemed to know that except the museum janitors—and me. Inside each lion is a long rectangular bench—a comfortable bed for a vagabond—about six feet long and three feet wide.

To this day I have no idea why the sculptor made the lions that way. The benches are not for seats; there is a short seat beside each lion with its back to the animal only a few inches away. Perhaps some genial Universal Mind, who liked vagabonds, made the sculptor, all those ages ago, put the stone benches in. Because one night, far away in the future, Jim and Kathleen Phelan would need a bed. Other people will doubtless think of other explanations. All I know is that the stone bench was just right.

In five minutes we were inside our sleeping bags and settled in. Twice during the night, we heard the rhythmic foot plod of a patrolling policeman and saw

the flicker of his torch as he passed, glancing at windows and doorways. Three or four groups of people passed. One couple sat on one of the stone seats, only twelve inches away. They kissed, and said how lovely everything was, and then went on their way. But no one noticed that the lions had company.

We slept. ○≾

One of the pair of lions carved by Sir George Frampton guarding the northern entrance to the British Museum, London.

Rebels and Poets

One day we hitched through Wales to Holyhead and caught the mail boat to Ireland. The advance on Jim's *Moon in the River* had arrived, so we were in funds. The fare from Holyhead to Dublin was less than two pounds. The boats were ancient; looking like large wooden tubs, floating public bars better describes them. Ladies, on payment of two pence, could sleep on a wooden bench in the hold. The journey took all night and early in the morning an old Irishwoman brought around steaming mugs of tea laced with whiskey, to celebrate that we hadn't sunk. Thanks be to God!

There was something so exciting about sea travel then. The boats were crowded, dirty, noisy, lots of laughter. Everyone drank gallons of booze, which eased the occasional panicky thought that the creaking, heaving mass of wood might start going down instead of across. It was considered a minor miracle each time the boat landed. It all seemed such an adventure.

A far cry from the floating, sanitised shopping precincts of today which have little to do with travel and nothing whatever to do with adventure.

It is unnecessary to say that having arrived in Ireland we did not want to buy, rent, hire or require a house. Nor did we want a furnished cottage, old-world or otherwise. What we were after was someplace like the Upleadon bakehouse. We thought we had found it too.

About twenty-five miles from Dublin, at Killincarrig in County Wicklow, in a tiny village with one shop, one pub, one farm, and twelve houses we got a darling little place. It had obviously been a cowshed, plus a warm comfortable storehouse. A doorway had been knocked into the parting wall, windows had been fitted, a fireplace had been built in and a flex from the nearby pub carried the electric power. Beds, tables, chairs, and cupboards had been installed. It was even better than the bakehouse. It belonged to P.J. O'Connor who owned the pub next door.

However, we discovered that we had acquired a desirable furnished cottage, with all modern conveniences, etc. All for the trifling sum of £5 a week (an enormous rent to pay at that time). Ireland was becoming civilised fast.

1950s-era Royal Mail travel advertisement poster. Mail boats were an inexpensive choice for travel between England and Ireland.

In hindsight, I can see that it was one of the early indications of the end of farming. Cows in cowsheds, how ridiculous, cows can't pay rent! Nowadays this is commonplace. All the beautiful barns that housed the hay and straw and machinery barely exist as storehouses any longer. They are converted to 'Porsche' houses with electric fences all around and the sign saying 'Neighbourhood Watch,' that magnet for vigilantes and Peeping Toms, is everywhere.

Happily, in this country, we have a few houses with flat roofs. Woe betide you if you are sufficiently insane as to walk along the streets of, say, the rich enclaves of Coral Gables in Miami or Beverly Hills in Los Angeles. The owners of expensive houses keep Doberman Pinscher dogs on the rooftops, which leap and snarl at you until you are out of sight. An unnerving experience. We in the U.K. have some catching up to do.

Jim was anxious to get started on writing the next book, so we settled into the cowshed. The book was *Turf-Fire Tales,* a collection of Irish short stories. It was a prolific writing stay in Killincarrig for him. Apart from writing *Turf-Fire,* he wrote for all of the Irish newspapers. The *Irish Times* and the *Independent* wanted articles and the literary magazines wanted short stories. He worked hard and the typewriter rarely stopped. We lived well and spent well.

Our relaxation was to go to Dublin two or three times a week and do the rounds of the pubs. Bus fares from Killincarrig to Dublin were cheap. The journey was interminable but it was the only way to get there. One of the main pubs for writers and journalists was the Pearl Bar[12] near to the *Irish Times* office. Any writer of the day visiting Ireland sooner or later turned up in the Pearl Bar.

There was just one unfortunate thing. The last bus back to Killincarrig left Dungannon Street, only minutes away from the pub, at five to eleven. The Pearl did not close until eleven and it was unthinkable to leave before then. Occasionally we managed to bribe one of the bus conductors to hold the bus for us until after eleven, but when it wasn't one of "our" conductors, it would leave on time and we would be stranded.

We had a good ally in Bertie Smyllie[13], the then-editor of *The Irish Times*, who lived just up the road from us at Killincarrig. Smyllie also spent many evenings in the Pearl Bar. He always left punctually in time to catch the bus and would persuade the driver to wait for us. It was the nights that Smyllie wasn't there that were the problem.

Our solution was simple. If the bus had gone we just walked the twenty-nine miles back to Killincarrig. We used to rest halfway on the seat below the Wolfe Tone[14] monument in Bray. That was usually about 2 a.m. The trek took all night,

---

12 "The Pearl" was located on Fleet Street a few doors down from the offices of *The Irish Times*. This proximity to Ireland's leading newspaper made it the natural yet unofficial tavern for newspaperman, journalists, writers, editors, and literary figures of all types. From 1940 until its closure in 1973, it was the scene of, in the words of documentarians, "monumental rows, literary and otherwise."

13 **Robert Maire Smyllie** (1893 – September 11, 1954) was editor of *The Irish Times* from 1934 until his death in 1954. He contributed to the still ongoing "Irishman's Diary" column of the paper from 1927. He established a non-partisan profile and a modern Irish character for the erstwhile ascendancy paper; for example, he dropped "Kingstown Harbour" for "Dún Laoghaire." He enlisted Flann O'Brien to write his thrice-weekly column "Cruiskeen Lawn" as Myles na gCopaleen.

14 **Theobald Wolfe Tone**, posthumously known as Wolfe Tone (June 20, 1763 – November 19, 1798), was a leading Irish revolutionary figure and one of the founding members of the United Irishmen, a republican society that revolted against British rule in Ireland, where he was a leader going into the 1798 Irish Rebellion. He was captured at Lough Swilly, near Buncrana, County Donegal on November 3, 1798, and was sentenced to death on November 12 by hanging. He died seven days later in unclear circumstances. It has since been theorized and agreed upon by most Irish scholars that he committed suicide while in prison.

but so what! Mad—or maybe just drunk—but certainly not legless, we always made it.

Furthermore, about five miles out of Dublin, near to Stillorgan Church, there was a side road going round by the coast through Blackrock and rejoining the main road further along. Roughly a six-mile diversion. Once in a while we turned off there, putting the extra mileage onto the journey—something about relieving the monotony!

One day we got a check for a hundred pounds, royalties from a previous novel; and we promptly went to the pub next door to cash it and celebrate. Word got around. The pub filled up. At some stage during the evening, Jim started handing out fivers to the local populace who had gathered. Lord and Lady Bountiful, no less! We went back to the cottage with about ten pounds.

Next morning: misery, despair, etc. But this had an unusually happy ending. The local cop had gone round to all the recipients of the fivers and demanded them back. Then, when we were out the next day he had popped them into our kitchen cupboard where I found them later. About seventy pounds! No one locked their doors in those days. And how otherwise could you experience an 'un-burglary'?

At some point during the summer, we decided to walk right across Ireland from Dublin to Galway. Bertie Smyllie thought it a great idea for a series of articles for *The Irish Times*. We were to start from Nelson's Pillar[15] in O'Connell Street in Dublin and end in Eyre Square in Galway, a distance of about 150 miles. We sauntered along about ten miles a day according to the number of pubs along the way. I remember lovely names, the Salmon Leap Inn, the Widda Wogan's, the Fox Covert.

Each evening we had a party in whichever pub we stayed the night. Each morning we got out on the road with the hangover heading for Galway Bay. At every village there would be a few people from the previous night's party who had come on a bit mostly on bikes, to continue the crack[16]! Or there would be

---

15 Nelson's Pillar was a large granite column capped by a statue of Horatio Nelson, built in the center of O'Connell Street in Dublin. Completed in 1809 when Ireland was part of the United Kingdom, it survived until March 1966, when it was severely damaged by explosives planted by Irish republicans. An earlier attempt to destroy it during the Easter Rising of 1922 failed due to dampness. Pressure for its removal intensified in the years preceding the fiftieth anniversary of the Rising. Its sudden demise was, on the whole, well-received by the public. Jokingly, Nelson is often referred to as Ireland's first astronaut.

16 "Crack" is Scots-English slang, widely adopted in Irish slang in the twentieth century, meaning a good time, entertainment, or rousing conversation.

people from the village before that who had come on by train to pick us up. By the time we reached the Shannon river, halfway across Ireland, we were heading a procession.

There is a certain magic about Ireland where things happen which could never happen anywhere else. For instance, one morning we went into the Bridge Inn in Enfield. It was situated beside a packhorse bridge over the main Dublin to Galway railway line. The station was below and the railway signal showed just above the bridge.

The bar in the pub was empty except for the barman and a lonely pint of Guinness standing on the counter. We bought our drinks and as no one appeared to claim the Guinness, Jim asked where the other customer was. "He'll be here directly," said the barman. At which moment a train pulled into the station below the bridge. The driver got out, climbed up the railway signal, stepped onto the roadway, and popped into the pub. Greetings all round, a few items of gossip, the sinking of the Guinness, and then with a "see you tomorrow, Pat," he was off down the signal, on to the train again and driving to Galway.

We were supposed to be walking all the way across Ireland for the purpose of the *Irish Times* articles, but one day as we left Athlone there was a torrential downpour and we were soaked. A car, driven by a priest, stopped to offer us a lift. En route, we confessed that we weren't supposed to be hitch-hiking lifts. He told us that he was going "on retreat" for a few days near Galway. He dropped us off in the next village. When, a few days later, we were in Galway, we went to a large hotel in Eyre Square for a meal. Dining lavishly at one of the tables was "our" priest. On retreat! As he was leaving the dining room he came across to our table, eyes twinkling, and said, "Well, Jim and Kathleen Phelan, I'm not going to mention to anyone that you didn't walk *all* of the way to Galway. Now about being on retreat..."

Some months later we were passing a large church in Bray County, Wicklow. Standing on the steps was someone looking suspiciously like "our" priest, attired in full bishop's regalia. "He's only recently been consecrated," someone in the crowd remarked. "It's Bishop Dunne." As his eyes swept the crowd, they rested on us and I'll swear he winked.

After Athlone and the Shannon river, the Irish countryside starts to get wilder. Ballinasloe, famous for its horse-fair; Athenry, a little walled town, from whence comes the haunting ballad "It's Quiet 'Round Here." There were thirty-seven pubs in Athenry—we didn't have time to visit them all. Eventually, we arrived in Eyre

Square in Galway. The first person we met was the writer Liam O'Flaherty[17]. One of those strange fluke meetings on the road. As we entered the Square at one end, Liam entered at the other. It was very early in the morning and there wasn't another person in sight. Jim and Liam hadn't met for years.

We sat beside the statue of Pádraic Ó Conaire[18], the tramp poet, and I remembered Bertie Smyllie had told me that he had given Ó Conaire his last fiver before he went away to die. It was all a rather strange ending to our pilgrimage. After a couple of nights in Galway we hitched in quick time back to Killincarrig. Jim wrote more stories and we tramped some more in the Wicklow Mountains. A favourite route was to follow the Red

Statue of Pádraic Ó Conaire in Galway, Ireland.

Road to Roundwood. A lonely road amidst the mountains, heather, bogs, and curlews. Inspirational country. Roundwood was quite isolated; a stranger was the event of the year. You were lucky if they let you leave!

After a session in the pub there Jim wrote his story "Johnny the Rag." From the Galway trip came "Quest," "Clio," "And Welcome," and many others, all of which went to make up *Turf-Fire Tales*. Later, many of the stories appeared in

---

17 **Liam O'Flaherty** (August 28, 1896 – September 7, 1984) was an Irish novelist, short-story writer, and is ranked as one of the foremost socialist writers in the first part of the twentieth century, writing about the common people's experience and from their perspective. He served on the Western Front as a soldier in the Irish Guards from 1916 and was badly injured in 1917. After the war, he was a founding member of the Communist Party of Ireland.

18 **Pádraic Ó Conaire** (February 28, 1882 – October 6, 1928) was an Irish writer and journalist who wrote prolifically, primarily in the Irish language. His acclaimed novel *Deoraíocht* has been described as the earliest example of modernist fiction in Irish. A statue of Ó Conaire was unveiled in 1935 by Éamon de Valera in Eyre Square in the heart of Galway City. It was popular with tourists until it was decapitated by four men in 1999. It was repaired at a cost of £50,000 and moved to Galway City Museum in 2004.

magazines such as *Penguin New Writing*, *Argosy*, *Lilliput*, and in a magazine simply called *Story*, edited by Whit Burnett in the States.

Interesting, economically speaking, is that we received more money for the publication of one short story in the States than for the total advance on the whole book in England.

One night we went to the Gate Theatre in Dublin; I don't remember the name of the play. Micheál Mac Liammóir[19] and Hilton Edwards[20] were the principal actors. The cast also included an actor called Noel Purcell[21]. When he appeared on stage, Jim recognised him—or thought he did—as someone from his acting days. Purcell had been 'Joe Moran' then.

The Abbey Theatre was the national theatre, Synge[22], O'Casey[23], etc. The Gate was anything else. There were subtle anti-Irish undertones in whatever we were watching. We were sitting in the front row of the dress circle. Jim started

---

19 **Micheál Mac Liammóir** (born Alfred Willmore; October 25, 1899 – March 6, 1978) was a British-Irish actor, dramatist, impresario, writer, poet and painter. Though born to a Protestant family living in the Kensal Green district of London, he emigrated to Ireland in early adulthood, where he remained for the rest of his life. He co-founded the Gate Theatre with his partner Hilton Edwards. He is one of the most recognizable figures in the arts in twentieth-century Ireland.

20 **Hilton Edwards** (February 2, 1903 – November 18, 1982) was an English-born Irish actor, lighting designer and theatrical producer. He co-founded the Gate Theatre with his partner Micheál Mac Liammóir and has been referred to as the founder of Irish theatre. He was one of the most recognizable figures in the arts in twentieth-century Ireland.

21 **Patrick Joseph Noel Purcell** (December 23, 1900 – March 3, 1985) was a distinguished Irish actor of stage, screen and television. He appeared in the 1956 film *Moby Dick* and the 1962 film *Mutiny on the Bounty*.

22 **Edmund John Millington Synge** (April 16, 1871 – March 24, 1909) was an Irish playwright, poet, prose writer, travel writer and collector of folklore. He was a key figure in the Irish Literary Revival and was one of the co-founders of the Abbey Theatre. He is best known for his play *The Playboy of the Western World*, which caused riots in Dublin during its opening run at the Abbey Theatre.

23 **Seán O'Casey** (né John, later changed to Seán Ó Cathasaigh, March 1880 – September 18, 1964) was an Irish dramatist and memoirist. A committed socialist, he was the first Irish playwright of note to write about the Dublin working classes. O'Casey's first accepted play, *The Shadow of a Gunman*, was performed at the Abbey Theatre in 1923. His depictions of sex and religion were often controversial. A full-scale riot occurred during a production of *Juno and the Paycock* because it was thought to be an attack on the men in the rising and partly in protest in opposition to the animated appearance of a prostitute in Act 2. W.B. Yeats got onto the stage and roared at the audience: "You have disgraced yourselves again."

barracking Purcell-Moran about being a renegade. Then he began to sing "Ó ro! 'sé do bheatha a bhaile."[24]

That was when the ushers moved in to get rid of us. They all knew Jim and were pleading, "Come on, Mr. Phelan, now ... come on ..."

I was shouting, "Don't touch him!" knowing that if anyone tried to remove him forcibly, he'd wallop whoever it was. He left quietly. As usual, I followed. Life may have been embarrassing occasionally, but it was never, ever dull.

We became well acquainted with Kenneth Reddin[25], a famous judge and a well-known writer. *Another Shore* and *Somewhere to the Sea* were two of his best-known novels. Kenneth, his wife Nora, and their children lived at Templeogue, then a separate village on the outskirts of Dublin, now engulfed by sprawling suburbs. The Reddins gave lovely literary dinner parties and we visited them frequently. It was at their house that I first met Maurice Walsh[26]—an absolutely darling man. Small, with twinkly eyes and a long beard, a leprechaun of a man if ever there was one. His books were very popular and made money. He was also very generous, and once sent us a hundred pounds, which was a huge amount to be given as a gift. I don't know for what we were given it, only that we were "between checks" so to speak, and it was a godsend. Maura Laverty[27] was also a

---

24 "Óró, sé do bheatha bhaile" is a traditional Irish song, that came to be known as a rebel song in the early twentieth century. *Óró* is a cheer, while *sé do bheatha 'bhaile* means "welcome home." Since 1916 it has also been known under various other titles, notably "Dord na bhFiann" (Irish for 'Call of the Fighters') or "An Dord Féinne." The latter title is associated with patriot-martyr Patrick Pearse in particular.

25 **Kenneth Sheils Reddin** was the pen name of Kenneth Sarr (1895 – August 17, 1967), an Irish author and judge. His first pseudonym was Kenneth Esser (from "Kenneth S. R."), later shortened to Kenneth Sarr. He joined the Irish Volunteers and was interned after the Easter Rising. Literary figures often met at his father J.J. Reddin's house and Kenneth was associated with the Irish Theatre Company in Hardwicke Street, where his brothers Kerry and Norman acted.

26 **Maurice Walsh** (April 21, 1879 – February 18, 1964) was an Irish novelist, now best known for his short story "The Quiet Man," later made into the Oscar-winning film *The Quiet Man*, directed by John Ford and starring John Wayne and Maureen O'Hara. He was one of Ireland's best-selling authors in the 1930s.

27 **Maura Kelly Laverty** (1907 – July 26, 1966) was an Irish author, journalist and broadcaster known for her work on the Irish television drama serial *Tolka Row*. She published several novels, short stories and critical pieces throughout her career. She was also the author of two classic cookbooks—*Maura Laverty's Cookery Book* (1946) and *Full and Plenty* (1960). Both contain anecdotes and conversation about food, as well as practical recipes.

frequent visitor at the Reddins'. She was well known for her articles on cookery for *The Irish Press*. She was a very funny lady with great stories.

Kenneth knew scores of ballads and after a few drinks sang them lustily. He, too, had a fund of stories—mostly court stories. One evening, he told us how that day he had fined a publican a hefty sum of money for watering the whiskey. Understandably, as it was one of Kenneth's calling places.

The story that I liked best was about an old tinker who got fighting drunk every market day. One morning he was brought up before Kenneth who lectured him and fined him ten shillings. Knowing he had not much money, Kenneth secretly paid the fine. The following month the old tinker was up before him again, on a charge of being drunk and disorderly. Kenneth rebuked him sternly and asked him to explain himself. The tinker said that when he had gone to pay the fine on the previous occasion, he discovered that it had already been paid. So he had had a few drinks to celebrate. Kenneth explained that he was not going to get off so lightly this time with a petty ten shillings. At which the old tinker leaned forward and said quietly, "Don't be too hard on yerself, Judge Reddin. Don't be too hard on yerself!"

Sometimes we visited what still remained of the Liberties[28], where Jim had roamed wild as a youth. Some of the characters he had known were still around. Many buildings had fallen down or were being pulled down, but here and there old places remained.

James Joyce, who knew the Liberties well, wrote somewhere about a girl being given a "fla up the long entry." Scholars studying Joyce used to look for hidden esoteric meanings in such phrases. But *fla* was just the word for fuck, and Long Entry was a small, narrow alleyway not far from the Chalker Doyles pub. Long Entry was still there and probably many a fla was still to be had there too.

The Chalker Doyles was still standing, unaltered. An old man, Johnny Behan, who remembered Jim, was still drinking in the bar. Johnny Behan was his real name, but he was always known as Skibbereen. He was only four feet high and exactly resembled an ape. With long hairy arms with an apelike curvature and tremendous strength, he could have crushed anyone to death with them. I know—he used to greet me with a hug which almost squeezed the life out of me.

---

28 The Liberties is an area in central Dublin, Ireland, located in the southwest of the inner city. One of Dublin's most historic working-class neighborhoods, the area is traditionally associated with the River Poddle, market traders and local family-owned businesses, as well as the Guinness brewery and whiskey distilling, and, historically, the textiles industry and tenement housing.

Pubs in the Liberty had no women's lavatories and rarely any women. However it was unthinkable that honored guests such as myself should squat in the gutter, so whenever I wanted to pee, I was conducted to a nearby house, wherein the main bedroom a huge flowered chamber pot stood ready for me.

An old racecourse habitué, Micksy Collins[29], was still around. He was a wicked old villain and earned his money from performing the "three-card" trick on the racecourses. He taught me how to do this most efficiently, a talent which on an occasional lean period I have found most useful.

One Sunday morning we set off with Micksy in his pony trap to visit Maria Lynch, the queen of the Liberties—who had retired to a posh house in the suburbs—but we never made it. Too many pubs on the way. And the horse, who loved Guinness, got drunker than we did.

Suddenly we felt that we had had enough of Ireland. We had been sent a contract for *Turf-Fire Tales*. We packed up and went to Dún Laoghaire and took a boat back to England.

As we stood on deck watching the Wicklow mountains recede, Jim said, "I will *never* go back to Ireland."

And he never did. ⌘

---

29 **Micksy Collins**: In addition to Kathleen's description, Collins was active in restarting the Irish Republican Army after World War II.

Hiking a Hitch

A word about hitch-hiking.

Nearly everyone takes it for granted that hitch-hiking belongs to the motor era. After all, people couldn't very well hitch-hike a stagecoach or a four-horse wagon. Could they?

As a matter of fact, a person could, and plenty did.

Everyone in any industrial country knows the big furniture trucks which are so numerous on the highways. A huge, box-like structure, with tall double doors at the back, and a luxurious roomy cab in front—there are millions of them on the roads of the world.

Little more than a hundred years ago on the highways of England, a furniture lorry looked almost as it does today. Since 1900 there has been little change in their general appearance.

The only major difference is that nowadays there is a big powerful engine out there in front of the driver. In the past, there would have been three or four horses.

At the back of every big furniture truck and long-distance wagon there was a rope hanging down on either side. This was called the *hitch*. It was fixed top and bottom on a swivel so that there was in effect a rope "hand-rail" on either side of the wagon.

If that wagon passed a person walking up a hill, the person often called out to the driver, "Hitch-hike?" The accent was on the second syllable in those days. One said "Hitch-HIKE!"

The word *hike* (in England, Canada, and North America) meant to hold. It was also a word telling the horse to stop—to hold on there, as it were. Mostly, when asked for a hitch-hike, the driver nodded yes, or waved to indicate "go ahead." Whereupon the walkers moved up the hill on their own feet—but they travelled on the horse's steam, not their own.

Of course, the driver did not always say yes to the would-be hitch-hiker. In which case it would have been very unwise indeed to take hold of the hitch. Because, although the lorry driver was several yards away, he had a twenty-foot whip and could raise weals on the hitch-hiker's legs until he let go.

When the change to motor transport was completed, words like *hitch* and *hike* went out of use in England. But they persisted in the United States, especially in the South and West. In hillbilly songs and in Western cowboy stories, the people talked in a strange attractive idiom. That is how people talked in England, not so long ago, except now it meant thumbing a lift in a truck or a car. In the early movies, the wayfarer always stood on the grass verge and signaled. Then a truck drew up and the hitch-hiker got in. The same thing was true in England. For most people, hitch-hiking meant looking for a lift on the lorries. A marvellous example of the persistence of tradition.

When I first went hitch-hiking it was quite difficult to get a lift. It is true that few people knew what hitch-hiking was and only stared blankly as they drove past. But the real reason was that private cars were few and far between. The majority of cars on the road were those driven by "commercial travellers" as they were known. Most of them stopped to give lifts as they were travelling long distances and were glad of the company. There were no motorways or dual carriageways; even by-passes were almost unheard of.

One of the exciting things about hitching was wondering in which town one would be set down. If someone was going to Preston, they were dropped off in the town centre—ditto Wigan or Warrington or Oxford or Cambridge. This meant walking to the outskirts of the town before it was convenient to thumb again. One got an extraordinary knowledge of every town in the country.

So few people knew about hitching that if one waited on the outskirts of a village for a lift, almost certainly the local busybody would come along and explain that the bus didn't stop there and try to lead you back to the village.

There are no rules about hitch-hiking. Rules are for city people—for planners. Many people give advice to hitch-hikers about what to carry and where to wait for a lift. These are invariably people who have never hitched a mile of the road. Some go so far as to suggest writing a place name on a board and holding it up. There are even books on the subject. But these are strictly for the amateur and happily do no great harm. They have nothing to do with life on the road. We will go anywhere!

Any professional hitch-hiker knows that if you stand on the outskirts of Samarkand thumbing lifts for Wigan, those lifts will come along as surely as people can walk and cabbages can't. Even if the roadster takes along a cat and a dog and a parrot in a golden cage.

With the certainty of that knowledge, when Jim and I left Ireland and landed back at Holyhead we went hitch-hiking straight down Gatling Street, the old A5 road making for Surrey. Somewhere near to Bangor we got a lift with a motorist going to Sunbury, a nice fluke, as we were going to Thames Ditton, only three or four miles further on. We arrived at the house of a friend in time for breakfast. We could hardly have made the journey as quickly if we had taken a non-stop express train from Holyhead to London and a taxi from London to Surrey. I love these lucky lifts—no one ever remembers the other kind—and rightly so.

Our friend had arranged for us the use of a little wooden bungalow, on Thames Ditton island. Stepping into a little boat tied up at the pub, we were rowed over by the ferryman to the island in the middle of the Thames. It was really a wonderful place, a haven for wildlife, where the swans at night almost spoke English. Hardly anyone knew where we were. All of our friends thought we had a big house on the Portsmouth road. Only the ferryman who rowed us back and forth knew whose was the typewriter that rattled and tapped at all hours of the day and night. But the weather eventually took an ill turn.

There was a sudden and savage cold spell. Severe frost alternated with heavy snow. Then when the thaw came things got worse. The Thames over-flowed and everywhere for miles around was underwater. Thames Ditton Island became part of the river, temporarily. We could hardly see the roof of the little bungalow. We had to move in with our friends. Thus, at last, we really did live in a big house on the Portsmouth road—except that it wasn't really a desirable, detached residence with a large garden. In fact, we were only camping out again—in the middle of desirable Suburbia.

The big house was empty and almost unfurnished. We had the use of a large room with nothing in it but a bed, a couple of chairs and a good table. I do not know how we found these places—they just seemed to happen. There was an open fireplace, had we any fuel. Also, an excellent kitchen if anyone had anything worth cooking. How Jim ever wrote a book in these conditions I'll never know.

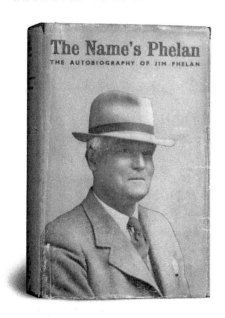

First edition of Jim Phelan's 1948 book,
The Name's Phelan.

In a way, all he ever wanted was a typewriter and a table and a ream of paper so that he could sit down and write forever. As for myself, having thought that life was some kind of a game to take a chance on, I was just happy to be along for the ride.

So in the three months while waiting for the frost to thaw and the floods to abate and the spring to arrive, Jim wrote *The Name's Phelan,* the first volume of his autobiography, and put together a collection of his Irish short stories, *Bog Blossom Stories.*

The two books were sold almost by accident. Fleet Street was then a humming street, and we went there two or three times a week to do the rounds of the pubs. We had met and drank in El Vino's a number of times with Herbert Jones[30], a great admirer of Jim's, when we suddenly discovered that he was on the board of directors at Sidgwick & Jackson's publishing house. When Herbert found out that Jim had two books just waiting to be bought, he immediately alerted the firm, and negotiations were started.

In short, Sidgwick & Jackson published both books and the advance was £250 on each one. They were bought simultaneously so we received £500, and that was the one and only time in Jim's writing life that he received that amount of money as an advance on royalties from any publisher—and for two books. Many writers got much less. Of course, for separate short stories, newspaper articles, radio talks, documentary film scripts and so on he was extremely well paid. That is what we lived on. The money received for what Jim considered "extras" far outstripped what he received over the years for the twenty-two books which were published.

---

30 Herbert Jones was also the editor and selected the works for Sidgwick & Jackson's Jazz Book Club series. Sixty-six titles and various extras were published from 1956 to 1967.

As soon as the scripts were safely disposed of to Sidgwick & Jackson and we had collected the money, we said goodbye to Portsmouth Road and hitched into London.

We had no destination and no preferences. All we intended to do was have a small tour of Fleet Street and Soho, meet a few friends, then make for the next place—wherever that happened to be. Maybe stay for a night or two in Hampstead with friends to get the shape of things to come. That was the program. The typewriter and a couple of suitcases each were stored in the house at Thames Ditton. Everything else we owned fitted into our backpacks or shoulder bags. We owned nothing else whatsoever in the world.

Generally, there would be something in a laundry fifty miles away, and something else in the cleaners fifty miles in the other direction. It helps with the planning of which road to take.

Whenever I go all civilised for a brief spell and work out an itinerary and a working schedule, then I do in fact achieve a competent piece of planning. At such times, I start blithely and in confidence, and I am always delighted on arrival. The next place is always a lot better than I expected. The only snag is that it never, but never is the place for which I started. But no matter—I am only passing through. So having decided on Hampstead, we left Fleet Street and headed for the underground and caught an Edgware train en route there.

For a while, Jim and Dylan Thomas worked together. Dylan was a scriptwriter at Crown Film Unit and Jim was a scriptwriter working for Sydney Box at Verity Films. At the time, Dylan was staying at Staines and we were in Hampstead.

About six every evening, we would meet up in the back bar of the Café Royal to discuss the day's work—or other people's work! A good deal of whiskey would flow. When the back bar closed, we usually moved on to the Gargoyle Club. Eventually, we would get a taxi and take Dylan to the station, to put him on the last train for Staines.

The last train didn't go any further than Reading, but it made one stop on the way, at Staines. Dylan was all right except for one thing—he usually woke up to hear a voice chanting "Reading... Reading. All change please. Reading..."

So Dylan would shiver and freeze for a couple of hours and then depart back for Staines on the early morning milk train, about half-past four. Night after night it happened.

Everyone tried to help with a solution. Many other near-professional drinkers and train-missers all tried to work out some way to have Dylan snatched off that Reading train at Staines—bribing guards and porters at Staines and hiring messenger boys to meet the train and drag Dylan off. Nothing worked for any length of time, Dylan usually woke up to hear that knell of doom—"Reading. All change. Reading." Eventually, Dylan himself solved the problem. Like all great solutions, it was very simple.

He moved to Reading.

So as Jim and I got on the Edgware train that evening for Hampstead— slightly drunk and talking our heads off—we presently heard a man calling out. "Edgware. Terminus. All change. Edgware." It was the last train, but Hampstead was only a few miles back and there were plenty of taxis and we had plenty of money. But—it was only half a mile to the A1 road, the Great North Road.

Well after midnight, we stepped on to a grass verge and jerked our thumbs.

A couple of hours later, we slept at a pub in Biggleswade, about fifty miles from London up the Great North Road. On to the next place!

In the morning, without a word of discussion we turned north up the road. There was no need to talk—we knew one another! South was London, and appointments and business, and work, etc., But we had had all of those things, too much of them, for quite a few weeks. So north it was, naturally.

We stood at a road-junction where a signpost pointed to St. Neots. This signpost was always known to people who lived on the road as "Shaw's Signpost" because George Bernard Shaw[31] lived near to St. Neots. Jim had often called to see Shaw, having first become acquainted with him when he was starting out as a young writer.

Jim and Liam O'Flaherty had shared a place in Camden Town—the young authors in a garret drill. Living on half of nothing and owing their landlady rent, they had the brilliant idea of writing to Shaw who had plenty of money. They told him what marvellous masterpieces they were going to write, and they explained what a tough time they were having. And could Mr. Shaw let them have five pounds, which would help a lot.

The reply came in an envelope addressed to Jim Phelan. The envelope contained a printed postcard which ran as follows:

Mr. Shaw is a writer, not a relieving officer.

It is sufficient that Mr. Shaw writes for you. You cannot expect him to keep you.

---

31 **George Bernard Shaw** (July 26, 1856 – November 2, 1950), was an Irish playwright, critic, polemicist and political activist. His influence on Western theatre, culture and politics extended from the 1880s to his death and beyond. He wrote more than sixty plays, including major works such as *Man and Superman* (1902), *Pygmalion* (1912) and *Saint Joan* (1923). With a range incorporating both contemporary satire and historical allegory, Shaw became the leading dramatist of his generation, and in 1925 was awarded the Nobel Prize in Literature.

If you intend to continue as a writer please remember that in his first six years of authorship Mr. Shaw earned roughly three pounds. No one would ask a grocer to subsidise his competitors. Why should a writer do so?

Written at the bottom in little crabby handwriting was: "Jim Phelan, you should have better sense than to try to get money out of another Irishman."

And pinned on was a five-pound note.

Cut to many years later. Jim wrote a novel entitled *Lifer*, which was a best-seller. The publishers held a party for him and many people asked him for stories about his struggles as a writer. He told the Shaw story. There was a tap on his shoulder and a voice said, "Yes, Jim Phelan, and that's over twenty years ago and you haven't sent the fiver back yet." It was G.B.S.

But, back to the St. Neots signpost on the Great North Road. We hitched a great lift with a man going all the way to Edinburgh. He had given us a lift the year before in Ireland. One of those road coincidences that happen continually. I only use the word coincidence because there is no other available. I am never quite convinced that those things happen by accident. I mean the odds against us hitching that same motorist a second time must be conservatively about a million to one. But the odds against him having decided to visit Edinburgh, as we had done, on a whim, must be about a hundred million to one. My road life is studded with such meetings.

Having arrived in Edinburgh late at night, we checked into the first hotel we came to. It was a temperance hotel! A new experience for us. I hope my uncle Tommy didn't turn in his grave. He never knew there was a bottle of whiskey smaller than a quart. We made up for it the next day.

First, we called at the newspaper offices, where Jim sold an article about coincidences on the road. What else? Then we met up with a few journalists and writers and that evening went to the Press Club. At the Edinburgh Press Club, as at many places in Scotland, there was no accommodation for women in the bar. Surprise! Surprise! Men only was the rule.

I had to go upstairs to a room by myself. The room was the library. I took a glass of whiskey with me. Who needed men?

Presently I called down for another whiskey. One of the men brought it up. He did not go back. I had decided that the library catalog was in an awful mess and had started reorganising it. One of those decisions one comes to when half-drunk. I could use another drink. Another journalist arrived, bringing whiskey. A bottle. He didn't go back either.

About three hours later the Press Club was deserted. In the library upstairs the whole journalistic profession of Scotland appeared to be working on the library catalog. It must have taken a long time to recover. The large library floor was totally carpeted with files and file cards strewn indiscriminately everywhere.

In spite of, or because of, all the good talk and good whiskey, we were away on the road early next morning. We crossed the Firth of Forth on a ferry and arrived on the Hielan side in a slash of rain. A large Rolls-Royce stopped when we flagged it.

A voice from the back called "Sure, sure, come on in," in a beautiful Californian accent. We got in and a tiny man welcomed us. It transpired that it was a hired car, that he was just having a look round. A Rolls-Royce as a taxi, he said, from Bedford to the Firth of Forth just for a look round. The guy was a well-known American jockey, Toner[32] was his surname, and he had been famous in his heyday. He lived in San Francisco, was of Irish extraction, and was looking around for any information about the Toner family. He was in luck. Jim had known the Toner family in Ireland and was able to help with lots of information about them, past and present. We had great difficulty in persuading "our" ex-jockey that it would *not* be a good idea to turn the Rolls around and head for Dublin.

Thus talking we reached Pitlochry, where we managed to extricate ourselves and dropped off to look around. The Highland Games meeting was in progress. The town was packed, not a room to be had, so we stood in the main street and considered which way we should flag the road.

A piper, a tall wild-looking man in a ragged kilt, was parading up and down and started to play. Jim called for a tune and produced a coin or two and soon we were all on very good terms indeed. Then a taxi came along and Jim hailed it.

"Get in there," he told the piper. "Play me a wee bit of the road." We were getting more Scots by the mile! The piper got into the taxi at once, and we told the driver just to keep going and to stop at the first hotel or pub where we would be likely to get a room. We drove slowly out of the town, to the tune of "The Barren Rocks of Laen," the street crowd cheering us on.

Living with Jim was always somehow so public!

---

32 Note: Research shows that indeed, there was a famous American jockey named Toner, but his fame came later than this narrative. We suspect that Kathleen has mixed up his name with another jockey. This is pure speculation based on light research, but we think she and Jim may have encountered the infamous Jimmy Pearson—jockey, art collector, art dealer, hoaxer, bon vivant, and great friend and nemesis to John Huston.

A few miles along the road the taxi driver turned in at the driveway to a fair-sized hotel. We got out and the piper played us up to the entrance. NO room. He piped back down again, we went on. And on, and on.

The countryside was getting more wild and lonely and we were all getting more and more drunk—the driver included. Then we came to a hotel standing high above the road in a big rocky park. The piper played us up again. With a room at last, we paid our musician and the taxi-man and all had a final drink for the road. We signed in. The manageress, when she saw the name Phelan, picked up a copy of the magazine *Penguin New Writing* that she had been reading. She had just finished the story "The Slip" by Jim Phelan.

We were in the Pass of Killiecrankie. It was my first visit there, and to stray into it by accident was lovely. We tramped up the glen the next morning after leaving the hotel, and never paused to flag a car. Because there were no cars! The road was absolutely deserted as were most of the Highland roads years ago. After a long interval, a local farmer came along bound for Inverness. So we went on by Kingussie into Inverness and over on to the Loch Ness road. Down the side of Drumnadrochit, the only point at which the road went away from the Loch for a short distance. Then back to the Loch and on for Fort Augustus and Fort William.

It was only then that I discovered that Fort William was a place that I had known by name since I was a child. The Scots Jacobite ballads were very popular so I grew up singing the words to "Pibroch of Donal Dhu" and similar songs. When the "Pibroch of Donal Dhu" was rallying the clans, Inverlochy was the principal place of the rallying. Indeed, as the poem points out, the war-pipe and pennon[33] would be there. In other words, Inverlochy was the Rebel Army Headquarters. Now there was no such place. Leaving Inverlochy—I mean Fort William, we started to hitch south towards Glasgow. As soon as we pulled out of the town people began calling it the Glasgow road, like speaking of Oxford Street in London or Scotland Road in Liverpool—all of which do in fact go to the places named.

We wanted to meet Paul Vincent Carroll[34] who for some reason tried to write Irish plays although he had such magnificent material at hand in Glasgow.

---

33 pennon: a long triangular or swallow-tailed flag, especially one of a kind formerly attached to a lance or helmet; a pennant.

34 **Paul Vincent Carroll** (July 10, 1900 – October 20, 1968) was an Irish dramatist and writer of movie scenarios and television scripts. Several of his plays were produced by the Abbey Theatre in Dublin. He co-founded the Curtain Theatre Company in Glasgow.

We also wanted to meet David Bone[35], the great seafaring genius who had helped to organise the Dunkirk retreat in 1940. But above all, we wanted to meet James Bridie[36], whose plays were very successful right then.

So, Glasgow. On the way, we crossed Loch Leven on the Ballachulish ferry. We thought of going around the Loch by Kinlochleben, about thirty miles round-trip with little or no traffic, but decided against it. Shame, it would have been a kind of salute to Patrick MacGill[37] and his books *Children of the Dead End* and *Moleskin Joe*.

From the ferry we hitched a lift with a motorist headed for Glasgow, travelling down the whole length of Loch Lomond. Such a wonderful road, such a magical region.

Bridie had a new play in production. So we were to lunch at the Arts Club with Bridie. David Bone would be there too. Then we would go to the matinee of the new show. Surprise! It didn't quite work out like that. Instead, I lunched elsewhere in some women's club for the usual reason. No women were allowed in the Arts Club. We were all to meet later and go to the theatre together. That did not happen as planned either. Bridie and Jim's lunch became a prolonged affair. Matinee time had come and gone, long before they had finished. We never did get to see the play. Not that I minded. I was not exactly in favour of Scots' rules about women and was quite ready to hit the road.

So—we left Glasgow the following morning. Out along the Hamilton road, hitching south... we thought maybe for Cornwall. ಚ

---

35 **Sir David William Bone** (June 22, 1874 – May 17, 1959) was a Scottish commodore and author of nautical fiction. Bone received the Coronation Medal from King George in 1937 for his long association with the Merchant Navy. He also received CBE in 1943 from King George VI.

36 **James Bridie** (January 3, 1888 in Glasgow – January 29, 1951) was the pseudonym of the renowned Scottish playwright, screenwriter and physician whose real name was Osborne Henry Mavor. He was one of the founder of the Citizens Theatre in Glasgow, was the first chairman of the Arts Council in Scotland and was also instrumental in the establishment of the Edinburgh festival. In 1950 he founded the Glasgow College of Dramatic Art, part of the Royal Conservatoire today.

37 **Patrick MacGill** (December 24, 1889 – November 22, 1963) was an Irish journalist, poet and novelist, known as "The Navvy Poet" because he had worked as a navvy before he began writing.

Following the Road

We made it to Cornwall. It was time for the next book. We found an old stone farmhouse called Puckator a mile outside of the little village of St. Cleer on the edge of Bodmin Moor. The house was like a tiny fortress. There was no garden, wall, fence nor ditch. The front door opened straight out onto the flower-spangled moor. Fifty yards away amongst stones that spoke of the Neolithic Age was the black-rock mass, Torra Pooka, which named the place. There wasn't a building in sight. The only sound by day was the skylarks and by night the tinkling talk of streams over stones. A place of magic.

The stone walls of the house were very thick, the windows were tiny, the oaken beams were gnarled and twisted and vast. Across a narrow valley was Trethevy Stone, a tiny structure that could have been one of the first

Puckator Cottage.

houses in England. Only the locals knew its name—nowadays it could well be a National Heritage Monument!

Four giant slabs of stone stood on edge, in a rough rectangle. A fifth slab made a roof. The farmer in whose field it stood probably used it as a cowhouse or sheep shed, but in its day it may have seemed like the White House or Buckingham Palace. Dating back to the time when everyone followed the road it could have been a far distant outpost of Stonehenge.

Stonehenge was one of our sleeping-out places whenever we hitched the road through Wiltshire. Just a lot of old rocks in a field according to the local farmers. In the summertime we walked to it from Amesbury, climbed a fence and crossed the fields, threw down our sleeping bags and slept the night amongst the stones. Times change. There were no electric fences and car parks and underground passages and 2x entrance fees then!

Ruins are great sleeping-out places. I can recommend Carthage and El Djem in Tunisia, Baalbek in Lebanon and Machu Picchu in Peru, to name but a few. Any of these could bear the legend, "Kathleen Phelan slept here."

With ruins in mind, we took a break from Puckator and explored the West country. We hitched through Devon to Corfe Castle in Dorset. Corfe was a village at the foot of the ruined castle with a few cottages and a pub and not much more. On the way, Jim told me a story about something that had happened to him and a couple of his mates some years earlier. This was before culture for the masses became big business and folk were free to wander and explore such places without hindrance. People used to climb up the ruins of the Castle as far as they dare go, then wrote their names or initials at the highest point they could reach. A splendid mental and physical exercise for anyone mad enough to try it.

After a few drinks in the pub, Jim and his friends decided they would have a go. They reached the point where apparently few people had reached before and scrawled their initials. That was about two-thirds of the way up. There were only a few initials at that level. They looked up further. There was in fact a handhold, but it was a few feet away and would have to be jumped for. And it was fifty feet from the ground if you missed.

The three of them decided it was useless to try, but Jim took a second look at it. The beer in the pub must have been very good because ten seconds later he was over the gap. He went on to the top of the ruin. There were only two sets of initials. Jim added his and the date and then...

He had forgotten that you can't jump several feet going down, not for a handhold that isn't there. His friends got poles and ropes but it was no use. Two hours later he was still there, feeling very foolish, with all the rustics in

Widdicombe fair looking up at him, and shouting advice. In the long run, having sobered up considerably, he got fed up and made a dive down towards his mates. It was about ten million to one against his getting anywhere except into a mortuary, but a lucky snatch by his friends saved him. Hitch-hiking to Corfe with this story in mind, on arrival, we looked at the ruin and went into the pub. It was the same as Jim remembered it.

Leaving Dorset reluctantly we hitched back to Puckator. Jim got on once more with writing the book. *We Follow the Roads* was the title. It just flowed off the typewriter. This was a book about the road—mostly about old-style tramps or "sons of rest" as they used to be called.

Cornwall resembled more a foreign country than an English county. The Cornish people did not consider themselves English but held firmly to their Celtic strains; London was far away and the government and its laws had nothing to do with them. All the stories about pirates and smugglers seemed quite in keeping.

Our local pub was in St. Cleer; we joined the darts team, started a chess team, and travelled far and wide within the county to many of the pubs for matches. Hospitality was lavish. Free beer and fresh lobster sandwiches for the visiting teams in Polperro and Looe and Liskeard were taken for granted. Every night was party night. Tourism had not yet been invented.

The historic Jamaica Inn was just up the road from Puckator and in a little hollow on the moor was a place that would have served as a smuggling "den" in any romantic novel. This was the Crow's Nest where Elsie lived, a little twinkling dumpling of a woman. Elsie was a widow and had a few pigs and chickens and goats and lots of good naval rum from her friends in Plymouth. When the pubs closed, many of us would drift over the moor to the Crow's Nest, to drink hot toddy in Elsie's huge kitchen. A huge saucepan would be warming on the stove, Elsie would throw in pints of ale and a bottle of rum. Then, when the drink was ready to serve she plunged in a red-hot poker into the pan. There would come a loud sizzling sound and hot foam would rise to the top of the beer glasses as she filled them with the toddy. Anyone leaving Elsie's kitchen was always slightly better for drink.

A local farmer, Bert Hoskins, drove everyone home in his old truck. Bert had only one eye and racing along the narrow country lanes was a hair-raising experience. Fortunately Bert, too, had always had his share of toddy and this compensated for his driving, which was always erratic, bringing the truck more or less into a straight line.

Late one night, after a heavy toddy session, Elsie told us that she had killed one of her pigs and asked if we would like half of it. We accepted happily, not realizing how big half a pig was. Bert loaded it into the back of the truck and drove us back to Puckator. We hoisted it onto the kitchen table and stared at it. Knowing that we would never be able to face cutting it up and jointing it in the cold light of day, we started right away to demolish it. We chopped and sawed for hours and ended up with a number of hefty joints, all saltpetred and neatly wrapped in greaseproof paper, and stacked them on the kitchen table.

When we woke up the following day with terrible hangovers we couldn't remember anything about the previous night. However, by the time we reached the kitchen we remembered only too well. The place looked like a slaughter-house; bits of blood and bone had flown everywhere as we'd hacked our way through the pig. I hope that I shall never have such a mess to clean up ever again. But we had pork for the whole of the winter, the best I've ever tasted.

Jim finished writing *We Follow the Roads* more or less at the same time as we had finished eating the joints of pork. The script was posted and we said goodbye to Cornwall and hitched to London to find a place to stay while we awaited the outcome.

We found a room in Belsize Park, just down the road from Hampstead. The landlady, Mrs. Gerlach, was an anthroposophist with a huge portrait of Rudolf Steiner[38] hanging in her entrance hall. I had spent a year at Wynstones, a Steiner school in Gloucestershire, which pleased Mrs. Gerlach enormously. She was a very outspoken woman. She said that she didn't really like the "Irish" but was prepared to accept Jim because of my Steiner connections!

With the book finished Jim was free to go back to his real love, writing short stories and feature articles for various magazines. Often the features meant trips to unexpected places. Articles about the Colchester oyster trade and another about beachcombers for *Lilliput* magazine meant a trip to Essex. A feature about boxing booths for *Picture Post* meant going to Barnet Fair.

---

38 **Rudolf Joseph Lorenz Steiner** (February 25, 1861 – March 30, 1925) was an Austrian philosopher, social reformer, architect, esotericist, and claimed clairvoyant. Steiner gained initial recognition at the end of the nineteenth century as a literary critic and published philosophical works including *The Philosophy of Freedom*. At the beginning of the twentieth century he founded an esoteric spiritual movement, anthroposophy, with roots in German idealist philosophy and theosophy; other influences include Goethean science and Rosicrucianism.

We knew the Woods family—Billy[39] and his son Harry, famous in boxing booth history, who set up their stable regularly at the annual fair, taking on all comers.

For recreation, we started going to the White City dog track every week. There was a gas meter in our room, and when we had no money we persuaded Mrs. Gerlach to unlock the meter box and lend us the cash. When we didn't win there was always a frenetic flurry to get the money to pay her back. Of course, she didn't know that she was lending us the money to go to the dogs!

Generally speaking, we were solvent most of the time. *London Evening News* started to buy Jim's short stories about gipsies and tramps. "Wander Girl," the title of the first of many of these stories, started a huge demand for anything he would write about the road. The BBC wanted shorts and talks and feature programs for both radio and TV.

Television was very crude. The storyteller sat staring straight at the camera; there was no movement as only the head and shoulders showed on the screen. Blue shirts had to be worn. As a viewer, it was like looking at a large passport photograph.

BBC TV producers took themselves very seriously, were mostly without humour, and knew little about the person they were "producing." When Jim was doing the run-through for one of his short stories, a young producer asked him if he had had anything extraordinary happen to him, as he was lining up fact stories about interesting experiences. Jim said, "Well, I've been sentenced to death—and sentenced to life." Gales of laughter all round. "I mean *real* experiences," said the producer. Jim did not get a spot in the series. Pity, as it was all true.

Because of all the media attention, people suddenly began offering us arsenic... I mean jobs! What a dreadful world it is, that when a person wants to do you a favour, you are shown into a neat clean cell, to be locked in for life. It is called a profession or career or security and so on. Thus we felt it was time to leave London. Other more sensible people could have the jobs. We would just follow the road. ∞

---

39 **Billy Wood** (unknown) was a fighter who ran a boxing booth, a fairground attraction in which the operator would fight any willing opponent. The winner would win £1 (back then a decent-sized purse). Billy Wood set up his ring at the Durham Miners' gala (also known as the 'Big Meet') in 1919, opening at 7 a.m. and closing at 1 p.m. the next day. In those eighteen hours he fought eighteen colliers, knocking out fifteen of them. Billy became featherweight champion of Scotland and later became a boxing promoter.

Wagon Wheels

Assington and Sudbury, Lavenham and Flatford Mill... it is the Constable country, a lovely part of England, now engulfed by urban sprawl, motorways, nuclear power stations, and waste. When we went there it was quite untouched. Assington was miles from anywhere. It was sometimes hard to find, even when you knew it.

A little cottage had come our way at Assington, by a road fluke. We had seen a news paragraph about a field of sunflowers which were flourishing at Assington and we had gone along to have a look at the miracle—or madness, as the case might be.

Sunflowers had not been grown in England on a commercial scale because of the harsh climate. Sunflowers in Britain meant a few flowers in a garden, which had been raised in a hothouse and set out only when the warm weather came along. That was why the English people paid vast sums annually for sunflower oil from Africa and China and India. Sunflower oil was the major ingredient in (fill in any name you like: artificial honey, natural varnish, cattle feed, car-grease, cooking fat, engine oil, house paint, and artificial suet). I nearly included violin strings, piano keys, and typewriter ribbons, but I am not sure about these. However, it can be taken for granted that sunflower oil could be used for many important things in a civilised country. We, like everyone else, had taken it for granted that the possession of sunflower oil meant handing over millions to people in warm countries. Because everyone knew that sunflowers wouldn't grow here! So we went to Assington "on research."

There we saw a field, nine or ten acres in extent—and it was crowded with ripe sunflowers about five feet high! We sought out the owner. This was Captain Reagan, a "Colonial," as he described himself, who had lived in South Africa and Australia. Reagan talked in telephone numbers about sunflowers and millions, and it sounded so good that we didn't believe a word of it. Then we looked out at the field again and saw thousands and thousands of sunflowers being picked by dozens of gipsy families.

Reagan badly needed "someone who knew his way around" Fleet Street and among the pen-pushers in the government offices. He was willing to pay too, and his ideas of money were far from mean. He had got used to high living as a racing driver before the sunflowers. He indicated the next field to the sunflowers, where a four-room cottage stood empty. We could have it while we looked around.

This, we agreed that night when we had promptly moved into the place, was research par excellence. It was a freelance writer's pipe dream come true, no less. Hastily Jim secured himself a job as a roving agricultural correspondent for the *Farmer and Stockbreeder* magazine. No end to his talents—had not one reviewer described him as an Irish peasant! It was necessary in the course of our work to hitch-hike all over Norfolk and Suffolk.

One day we passed a long line of horse-drawn gipsy caravans near Ipswich, as we went hitching to Felixstowe. Then that night when we got back to Assington, the same rake of wagons had pulled in about half a mile away, and the people were making camp. Next morning we strolled over to the encampment, as we knew that these must be a family called Scampe, who kept to the Suffolk roads, and we wanted some information from them.

Some years earlier there had been a hue-and-cry after an escaped convict from Norwich jail, a gipsy named Wallace Baker. Every morning in the newspapers, the headline read 'Gipsy Baker seen in Lincolnshire,' or 'Gipsy Baker traced to Yorkshire,' and so on. Then one morning the headline was 'Gipsy Baker arrested in Liverpool.'

Two detectives in Bootle had spotted the black-haired, brown-faced man with the gipsy scarf around his neck and had pulled him in. When he refused to tell his name they knew they had their man. At Walton Prison, outside Liverpool, the prisoner was signed in as Wallace X Baker. The 'X' was made by the prisoner, and the warders kindly supplied the rest. *Jim* was the prisoner. The next morning the newspaper headlines were different. (I wonder what the real Wallace Baker must have thought about them?) But at any rate, there was no longer a hue-and-cry after him.

The officials moved their prisoner around from one jail to another. Being at that time a gun-runner, Jim was not too ready to shout out that he wasn't Gipsy Baker, but innocent law-abiding Jim Phelan! Thus he had made an 'X' on the paper and the officials supplied the name. Eventually, he was fetched to Norwich prison. The Norwich warders took one look at him, and said, "That's not Gipsy Baker." So they paid his fare back to Bootle and that was that. The little interlude gave Wallace Baker a chance to get away to Scotland.

Now, Jim wanted to find out where Wally was. The Scampes were relations of the Bakers. Thus they would know his whereabouts. The question was, would they tell a stranger, who looked to them like a city man?

It was early in the morning, and most of the people were sitting around at fires when Jim and I arrived. We picked out the 'sharang' and told our names and asked if they could tell us anything about Wally Baker. A young man at one of the fires looked up at Jim and said, "You're Jim Phelan. Let yourself be plucked for Wally in Bootle, yes?"

He could only have been a child at the time of the Baker incident, but he had the story pat. Furthermore, as soon as Jim's name was mentioned, an old woman turned and called out something in Romani. A small girl came out of a caravan, and the old woman indicated Jim.

"That's Jim Phelan," she said and paused. "Tell the *say*[40] about Wally Baker." The child stood by the fire and recited the story about Wallace Baker and Jim and Norwich jail.

It was from this episode that Jim was inspired to write *Vagabond Cavalry*, a novel about tramps and gipsies, then followed it up with *Wagon Wheels*, a semi-autobiographical book about gipsy lore and tales of the travelling people. *Vagabond Cavalry* was written at the cottage in Assington. As soon as it was finished we were anxious to move on. Especially as the sunflower assignment was completed, sold, and paid for.

Captain Reagan owned a derelict farmhouse in the north end of Suffolk, not far from where Jim's literary agent, Curtis Brown, lived. Reagan suggested he drive us up there to have a look at it and stay there for a while if we liked it.

It was a large farmhouse, empty and desolate-looking, in the middle of a large tract of farmland. The nearest lane was a mile away and led on to another

---

40 Colonial British slang for "boss."

lane and then another—it seemed to be our fate that we always lived in the middle of a maze.

Reagan had bought the whole place, had planted every field with sunflowers, and intended to rebuild the house, which stood empty. But there was water and electricity. If we liked to camp out there for a while... We hardly allowed him to finish the sentence. That night we sat at a wood fire on the ground in a vast fireplace of the huge farmhouse kitchen. It was sparsely furnished with tables and chairs. We had our sleeping bags. It was perfect. Luxury, in fact. (Few writers can have written their books so consistently in such bizarre surroundings.) There were nine rooms to play with.

There was wildlife in abundance. The animals just ignored us. We thought that the cottage at Assington was cut off and lonely. But it was like Piccadilly Circus compared with Redland farmhouse, near Glemsford, Suffolk. Redland was like a desert island and the birds and beasts behaved accordingly. One evening I was standing quietly at a big window. The top sash was lowered and I was watching two partridges frolic in the field just outside. Suddenly I felt something closing down on me as if a cloth had been thrown over my head, but fortunately I did not wince or jump away. Then a second later my face was uncovered and I saw what it was. An owl had come to perch on the down-drawn sash of the window—probably watching the same two partridges as I was doing. He was so tame, so unused to people that he had settled on my head.

Another incident was even more interesting—a lovely lesson in nature lore, and a lesson in how animals can fool us for their survival. The back door of the house opened directly alongside the kitchen where we set up our camp. Straight outside the kitchen door, not four feet away, was a large deep pond, and then another smaller pond another hundred feet beyond that. The main window of the kitchen looked out on the large pond, and then on to the lonely lane that led uphill to *really* lonely places.

Each time I emerged from the back door, a moorhen started flapping about to startle me. I never caught sight of it until the bird was nearly on top of me. Again and again I was tricked—looking about for the bird before taking a step forward and deciding that there wasn't any moorhen on show that morning—then, at the last split second, it would run out like a shot and go skittering across my path making a racket.

Often from the kitchen window I watched the hen and her mate coming and going. I knew there must be a nest of eggs very near, but I could never find it. After a couple of weeks watching the pair, I decided that they had made their nest at the smaller, quieter pond. You could have set your clock by those two birds. The minute I opened the kitchen door, the little bird would flap about the little pond behaving like a lunatic while I watched.

One morning at the crack of dawn, nearly a month later, the moorhen and her mate crossed the deep pond from the kitchen door and went on into the second pond, followed by ten young ones, obviously on their first outing. The nest had been practically under my feet, on the edge of the big pond, mere feet from the kitchen doorstep. The brace of wildfowl must have made the nest before we arrived at the farmhouse, and then made the decision to carry on, and raised their family despite our intrusion. Day after day, the moorhen had sat on the eggs, while her mate stood by to act the fool near the pond, whenever the back door of the farmhouse opened.

Humiliating! But a wonderful example of how by distracting my attention to one place, they had happily got on with their own business right beside me. Just like people, really!

We always seemed to be in touch with the natural world. Finding remote houses along country lanes where cars were unheard of or camping out on remote farms with wildlife all around was normal. Redland Farm was a good place to be for a while.

Two of the Scampe family called one day and told us where the Bakers were to be found. Wally's parents lived in a large beautiful caravan at Reepham in Norfolk. A big powerful old man and a wonderful woman, they gave us a great welcome and arranged to meet us again at Beccles Fair. They had an idea for us which they would tell us about there. They wanted us to meet up with a family of Norfolk travellers—the Kidds of Briston, especially Spencer Kidd.

One day, shortly afterward, Reagan arrived at the Redland farmhouse. He reached into his wallet and handed me an advertisement. "*Times* personal column," he said briefly. "Shouldn't think you'd have any competition. I would write now."

It read, 'Part of an old-world Manor House,' it said, 'available at a merely nominal rent, to pleasant cultured people of intellectual interests. No children. Large garden, paddocks, pastures, etc. Loveliest part of East Anglia. Box XYZ.'

Jim wrote a letter, telling who he was and what he did, mentioning our aimless, drifting habits and indicating that we had no jobs, no property, no income, and no address, only Poste Restante. A couple of days later we got a reply asking us to call. The address was 'The Manor House, Middleton, Suffolk.' I telephoned to make an appointment, and the next day we hitched over to Middleton. We had no idea what to expect. Middleton was a tiny village in a remote part of Suffolk, where the road led nowhere except into the sea.

About a quarter of a mile from the village on a narrow lane was the entrance to a lovely ancient house in a big garden. A crazy pathway under arches of roses led up to a twisted whitewashed house with a thatched roof. Flowers bloomed everywhere. One wall was covered with peaches and another with a grapevine. We followed the path up to a door and rang the bell. Nothing happened. No one answered. Then a very old lady swept round a corner of the house and started aside with a dramatic gesture of surprise, which would have been convincing in a Victorian play. We introduced ourselves.

She opened the door at which we had been ringing, and led the way inside, to a tea table already laid. She rang a small handbell. Then she turned to us again and said "Er..."

Not feeling inclined to repeat our names, we said nothing. A still more ancient lady appeared with a tea-tray, and we relaxed. She looked at us very carefully and said in an ordinary conversational tone, "And how are the peacocks?" Without batting an eyelid, Jim replied, "The white one is very well, but the other—a little off-colour, I think." Everyone sighed with relief.

They were two sisters and they owned the house. The Misses Woolnough. Our hostess at the tea-table was the younger. She was eighty-eight. They had decided it would be a good idea to have a man in the house because of burglars. So they had advertised.

The sisters had had over three hundred replies. With the help of a relative, they had gone over them all, and at last they had picked half a dozen of the most likely. We were fourth of the shortlist of six. But they didn't think it would be necessary to see the other two. Two days later, once again we moved in our 'all.'

The house was a dream residence. The old lady who had given the tea was an artist, and she had painted the house about a hundred times on canvases and small discs and on plates. They were exquisite. There were six rooms apart from the servants' quarters and the place was elegantly furnished. The servants' quarters had a separate entrance and a separate garden. This was the part of the house into which the two old ladies moved, while Jim and I had the main building, at a rent of one pound a week!

There was a public footpath outside the hedge at the bottom of the old ladies' garden. They spent hours pushing wheelbarrows of dead leaves and branches blocking this off. "We *must* have our privacy," they said.

So, out of the three-hundred-odd applicants, the two ladies had chosen two reliable, permanent, civilised types—the Phelans! Jim immediately started to write the book about gipsies, sparked off by meeting up with the Scampes, and with Wally Baker's parents.

We joined Ipswich Chess Club and were invited to play for the Suffolk County team. One of the matches was against Cambridgeshire held at Newmarket. The Penrose brothers, Oliver[41] and Jonathan[42], also Leonard Barden[43], all brilliant newcomers on the chess scene and soon to become chess "notables," played for Cambridgeshire. I, too, was a newcomer to the game, but somewhat less brilliant!

Middleton was quite a distance from Ipswich and we used to hitch back and forth to the chess club. We also became strong supporters of the Ipswich Football team and hitched to all of their matches. They were then in the Third Division. What with the football matches and the chess games and the pubs afterward, we often hitched back to the Manor house in the middle of the night. Occasionally, when the weather was fine, we 'skippered'—the tramp word for sleeping out. It really meant sleeping in a haystack.

People imagine that sleeping in a haystack means lying on top of a stack. That is very uncomfortable. It is not like that at all. Stacks were built with bales of straw like big square stones piled neatly to form a huge square structure. What one did was to pull out several of the bales from the middle of one side of the stack at about waist level and stack them neatly on the ground. That left a spacious cavity in the stack like a little room. Then one climbed in and slept in there. Warm and safe from both wind and rain. Then in the morning, the bales were popped back into place again and only a very shrewd farmer would know that the stack had been tampered with.

One day we hitched to Beccles in Norfolk, where every year there was a colourful horse fair. It was the kind of event that used to happen twice a month

---

41 **Oliver Penrose** (June 6, 1929) is a British theoretical physicist. He is the son of the scientist Lionel Penrose, brother of chess Grandmaster Jonathan Penrose. He was associated with the Open University for seventeen years and was a Professor of Mathematics at Heriot-Watt University in Edinburgh from 1986 until his retirement in 1994.

42 **Jonathan Penrose** (October 7, 1933) is an English chess Grandmaster and International Correspondence Chess Grandmaster (1983) who won the British Chess Championship ten times between 1958 and 1969. He is a psychologist and university lecturer by profession, with a PhD.

43 **Leonard William Barden** (August 20, 1929) is an English chess master, writer, broadcaster, organizer and promoter. The son of a dustman, he was educated at Whitgift School, South Croydon, and Balliol College, Oxford, where he read modern history. He learned to play chess at age thirteen while in a school shelter during a World War II German air raid. Within a few years he became one of the country's leading junior champions. He represented England in four Chess Olympiads. Barden played a major role in the rise of English chess from the 1970s. His column in London's *Evening Standard* is the world's longest-running daily chess column by the same author.

but had dwindled to one day a year. Grooms and horse handlers rushed here and there with horses showing their paces. A man on a rostrum chanted and joked. A large circle of men in breeches and leggings stood around the auctioneer's rostrum and made monosyllabic remarks which meant big money.

Practically all the active jobs were in the hands of the gipsies. We went into the pub, the Black Boy, and there met some of the Scampes and Bakers. In one part of the room around several tables sat about forty people, drinking and talking. They were all members of the same family, the Kidds of Briston. The Kidds were very tough hombres indeed. The late Captain Kidd, the pirate, whose career ended at Execution Dock, was one of the family's forebears. But he was unable to stand the wild life in the caravans of the Briston Kidds. So he ran away to sea—the weakling!

Spencer Kidd, one of the older members of the clan, had a wonderful idea for us. He knew of an old horse-drawn wagon which we could buy for a few pounds. No, it was not exactly fitted out. And no, it was not exactly watertight. But the undercarriage was a hundred years old, built in the time of Queen Victoria, and like iron. A new top could soon be fixed on it.... etc. etc. And no, it wasn't at Beccles, but at Great Yarmouth. The man who owned it had a large workshop and a shack we could sleep in till Jim fixed the wagon ready for the road.

Several drinks later, the money changed hands for a horse-drawn wagon, sight unseen. We went to look at it the next day. It was exactly as promised. The undercarriage was marvellous, the rest was as described.

We moved to Yarmouth and gradually over the weeks, the old wagon turned into a presentable caravan. We had no horse and no car and were not likely to have the latter. But Jim had made a trailer bar, so that the caravan could go behind a Land Rover or tractor out of a muddy field if necessary. The shafts were in perfect condition so that we could go behind a horse if we had one or could borrow one.

We had a gipsy friend in the north of England who offered us a beautiful piebald mare. Up in Yorkshire it was. So one morning we started off along the road across Norfolk, hitch-hiking north. Except it was not exactly a normal hitch-hike.

First, Tom Warnes, an old gipsy acquaintance, harnessed up his horse to the caravan and took us to a lay-by outside of Acle on the Horwich road. After Tom left, we tucked the shafts under the wagon and fitted on the towbar. As we left East Anglia to collect a horse to start the new system of travelling, we had beside us one wagon with no horse or car.

When we thumbed a lift, the important thing was not where the driver was
going, but was there a towage appliance

Traveller friends assisting with Jim and
Kathleen's first caravan.

on the tack of the vehicle, and was the driver willing to tow us along for a few
miles. Of course people loved it, even though they thought we were mad. It
was best described by a local journalist who wrote, "As far as hitch-hiking
goes, the Phelans have done everything. Right now they are standing outside
of Norwich hitching lifts not only for themselves but for their gipsy caravan as
well. We only wait for the day when they thumb not only for themselves and a
wagon but also for a horse."

Small wonder that I insist: There are no rules for hitch-hiking! ೮ঽ

Roaming at Random

Casterton was a tiny hamlet tucked away among the Westmorland Fells near to Kirby Lonsdale. It is famous through Charlotte Brontë, Casterton Hall being the setting for the school which the young Jane Eyre attended. Westmorland, of course, no longer exists, being lumped with Cumberland to form Cumbria.

It was the end of civilisation, that is for anyone coming from Lancaster and making for Durham. From Lancaster, the house groups dwindled. City and town, village and hamlet tapered off one by one. Then came Casterton and Barbon, the last of the house groups. After that the traveller plunged into the lonely, lovely waste of the fells, covering miles without ever seeing a hen-hut, let alone a town. This was our first halting-place for any length of time after leaving East Anglia.

It was time for the next book to be written. With no horse and no towage vehicle, our progress had been slow—a real Alice in Wonderland gamble. Sometimes we fixed the towbar on the front of the wagon and hitched a Land Rover. Other times we borrowed a horse for a few miles and then I walked it back to its owner in the night-time. On barren moors and in lonely pastures, the old gipsy caravan pulled in and the typewriter was busy—turning out newspaper articles and short stories. Now, once again, it was book time.

After leaving Norfolk, we spent a considerable amount of time in Lincolnshire. We had pulled into the paddock of the rectory at Kirby Laythorpe, a tiny village outside of Sleaford, while we hitched to London for a few days. It was the Festival of Britain and Jim was invited to do an interview on a giant television screen in the Pleasure Gardens in Battersea Park.

It was a celebrity program hosted by Valentine Dyall[44] who was famous as "the man in black" on a popular radio series. After the show, he asked Jim to sign his own private celebrities book. There were three names already on the page: M. Henri Spaak, United Nations Legation, Brussels. Queen Juliana, The Hague, Holland. Margaret Truman, White House, Washington. To this, Jim added: Jim Phelan, No Fixed Residence.

On reaching Casterton, we pulled the caravan into a little field high on a hillside at the edge of Casterton Fell. We had a view of Barbon Castle on one side and a glimmer of the river Lune on the other. During the winter months there, Jim wrote *Underworld*.

One day a car pulled in and a man called to pay his respects. He said he was the famous Tschiffely[45]. We had to laugh, as Jim had known Shiff years earlier. He had met him with artist Nina Hamnett and this man resembled Shiff as much as I resemble Tom Thumb. But he had been passing himself off as the great Shiff for years.

Aimé Tschiffely was a famous horseman who wrote a lovely book called *Tschiffely's Ride*. It was an account of a journey he had made on horseback from Buenos Aires to the States. A tremendous journey considering the state of the roads and the bridges at that time.

After *Wagon Wheels* was published Jim received lots of letters about it, many of them from women who asked him outright to marry them, others saying that they had always wanted to hit the road and could they be his companion. We

---

44 **Valentine Dyall** (May 7, 1908 – June 24, 1985) was an English character actor. His distinctive voice made him especially popular as a voice actor, and he was known for many years as "The Man in Black," the narrator of the BBC Radio horror series *Appointment with Fear*.

45 **Aimé Félix Tschiffely** (May 7, 1895 – January 5, 1954) was a Swiss-born Argentine professor, writer, and adventurer. A.F. Tschiffely (as he was better known) wrote a number of books, most famously *Tschiffely's Ride* (1933) in which he recounts his solo journey on horseback from Argentina to New York City, an epic adventure that still marks one of the greatest horse rides of all time. Tschiffely was a household name in the United States during the 1930s, meeting with President Calvin Coolidge and appearing in *National Geographic* Magazine, and earning a living from his popular book sales.

always read these letters hoping one might be from a stray millionaire, before consigning them to the garbage. Only once did Jim send a reply.

The letters were always sent to Harrap's publishers to be forwarded to wherever we were. At Casterton, a letter arrived from a woman who said she was miserable with her doctor husband and would be very happy to run away with Jim if he would name time and place. Unfortunately, she lived in a nearby village and naturally had no idea that the man she was after was practically on her doorstep.

Thinking we might run into her unawares, Jim wrote her a friendly letter, saying how complimented he was by her admiration for his lifestyle and that he and his wife would be delighted to meet her sometime for a drink. She did not reply; it must have been quite devastating for her. However, I don't remember any suicides among doctors' wives...

Speaking of wives. One evening in Cambridge after Jim had given an interview with Dick Joice[46] on Anglia TV, we were wandering along the high street when two women stopped Jim and told him gushingly that they had seen the program and would he like to spend the evening with them. Jim introduced me—his wife. "Wife?" one of them screamed. "You said nothing about a *wife* on television." They hurried away into the night.

When *Underworld* was finished we left Casterton and headed off with the wagon into the Lake District. This was when we first became acquainted with Kay Callaghan[47] and her family at Skelwith Bridge.

Skelwith Bridge is a hamlet three miles from Ambleside at the start of the Langdale valley. The bridge itself is an ancient packhorse one, spanning one of those talking, turbulent rivers of the Lake District. The river flowed through Kay's garden. One of the most beautifully situated houses that you could wish for. The house itself was nothing. A large, long one-storied wooden building, more like a log cabin than anything else, bought for Kay by her mother when

---

46 **Dick Joice** (1921 – 1999) was a British regional television presenter renowned in the East of England for his Anglia Television programs—particularly the *Bygones* show that ran from 1967 for twenty years. He was a director of Anglia TV in the company's infancy and its head of local programs.

47 **Kay Callaghan** (May 3, 1917 – November 29, 2005): After her divorce from her acting partner, Dan Callaghan, she moved to the Lake District in 1950 and bought Rosewood at Skelwith Bridge, near Ambleside, a home for both her family and the rescue animals she took under her wing. Kay started a café, shop and B&B business at Rosewood which became a magnet for a varied cast of artists, climbers, musicians and rovers. As her children grew up Callaghan started the charity Animal Rescue in 1971.

Kay decided to quit the stage, marry a fellow actor and bring up a family in the country.

We pulled the wagon onto some farmland just opposite Kay's house, at the riverbank. I went to the house each day to get a bucket of water. There was no mains water, it was pumped up from the river.

So we had a wonderful pitch beside a singing river. There were trout and otters and wild ducks in the stream, curlews overhead calling mournfully. Wild geese coming from nowhere and going to the same place and hares and rabbits and deer cavorting in the fields. It was the exact opposite of a zoological garden—what higher praise is there? It was a dream and reality together, and

Jim (standing), Kathleen (sitting in doorway), and friends posing with caravan.

that is the best of life. From Skelwith we moved only a short distance to Crowe Howe, a farm near to Rydal Water. Huge fells dotted with sheep rose behind us. There was also the occasional bull. Bulls were let out to roam the fellsides. Apt to be a bit savage too. Our farmer's own two bulls were in their stalls, so as long as we kept inside his boundary line, all was well.

Twenty-five hundred acres is a good bit of tramping ground. However, one morning Jim crossed the boundary without noticing that he had done so, and out in the middle of the lonely fell, rounding a rocky bank, he met a big bull walking towards him. It didn't see me, so I scurried away. Jim tried to stroll quietly away too, but the bull wasn't having that and came on at an increasing trot. Then Jim turned to run; there was a wire fence about two hundred yards away and he hoped to reach it before the bull got him. Then he found that he was on the bull's pathway, with a sheer wall of rock on one side and a steep drop on the other.

The bull was steadily gaining ground when to my amazement Jim took off his hat and ran back to meet it. In fact, he slapped it in the face, stuck his fingers in one of its eyes, then ran and crawled under the wire fence. When we got back to the wagon he wrote a letter to Roy Campbell[48], in Spain, telling him what had happened. Roy Campbell was a famous poet and well-known on the radio. He had also been a professional bullfighter. So Jim wrote and told him about the bull incident and the escape and asked Roy if he would like his autograph.

Those Spanish matadors? Pfft... They had to have lances and swords and things like that. But in the Lake District in England, the real bull-fighting mob? They took on the bulls with their bare hands. Jim claimed it was the nicotine on his fingers that had really bothered the bull. Roy answered saying that in the bullring, the pros used a nicotine preparation exactly as Jim had done to deal with a similar emergency. I think that was only a load of bullshit.

But it is an ill wind, etc. There was another sequel to the bull episode. Jim had written a short story called "The Bull." It was about a sadistic farmer who tortured and tormented a prize bull he had on his farm. The sadist's technique for torturing the poor animal was clever. In a big pasture, there was a small shed with a feeding rack inside, where hay would be stored in winter. The sadist used to walk the field and let the bull chase him. Then when the bull had nearly caught him, he used to slip into the shed and get behind the feeding rack. The bull couldn't harm him there, but of course it would always try. So the sadist could catch hold of the metal ring in the bull's nose. Then he turned and twisted and jerked until eventually, the bull was screaming with pain. In the end, he would slip away through a loose plank at the end of the shed and be safe before the bull came round to the shed door.

That went on for weeks until one day the sadist's younger brother nailed up the loose plank, and when the sadist lured on the bull and ran for the safety of the shed—that was the end. The older brother got his just deserts.

After the incident with the bull on the fell, Jim rewrote the story and sold it—this time making the guy who punished that nasty bull the hero! Villainy and heroism are largely a matter of chance.

---

48 **Ignatius Royston Dunnachie Campbell** was a South African poet and satirist of Scottish and Scotch-Irish descent. Despite being lavishly praised at the beginning of his career in the 1920s, Campbell's subsequent conversion to Roman Catholicism, and his poetic attacks against The Bloomsbury Group, Sigmund Freud, the Soviet Union, and the Second Spanish Republic during the Spanish Civil War, caused him to become a very controversial figure during his lifetime. Despite Campbell's attacks against both racism and apartheid in his native South Africa and his outraged refusal of Sir Oswald Mosley's efforts to recruit him into the British Union of Fascists, Campbell continues to be labeled a fascist and left out of poetry anthologies and college courses.

Underworld was sold to Harrap's while we were at Rydal. As soon as we received the advance we decided to leave the wagon there and hit the road south for France. We hitched to Folkestone and took the ferry across to Boulogne. Our first lift was with a commercial traveller who trafficked in champagne. This was my first time in France. I even remember the man's name, Jacques Lansoy. His car was filled with bottles. We all stayed at a lovely little hotel called Les Sept Étoiles in Montreuil.

M. Lansoy insisted we sample his champagne to celebrate my entrance into France. A great start. Two years later we were to hitch with Jacques Lansoy again. One day a car stopped and the driver wound down the window, and said, "Is this as far as you've got in two years?" But that was in Sweden, between Gothenburg and Stockholm. He was still in champagne. So were we!

It was this trip, the first of many, which gave me my passion for France. If I am out on the road at sun-up, just drifting along quietly, very quietly, while people are still sleeping in the towns and villages, I have nostalgia and a longing for those French roads. Getting up in the grey of the dawning, waiting for the sun to rise, while a clock in a village church strikes the hour, I saunter and smile and love all the world. And so we drifted down the road to Abbéville long before there was any stream of traffic. An elderly man gave us a lift and said he would take us there.

Abbéville was badly shattered, having been bombed by both sides during the war. The rebuilding of the city had begun, but only just. Piles of rubbish lay everywhere, most of the sidewalks were still broken up, and there were a thousand gaps, like broken teeth, between the shops on even the busiest streets. Our driver knew every inch of the district, both in peace and war. He had been an officer in the Engineers in the French army, had taken part in many of the battles in and near Abbéville. Thus we had a real conducted tour of the city, or rather of the ruins.

After Abbéville he took us along the Paris road, and went out of his way to show us the site of an ancient battlefield—"Long past—long past," he said, "but famous." It was hard to understand his accent and we said we had never heard of the battle. The old Frenchman was badly disappointed. One of the places—the few places—his tone implied, where the English had beaten the French. Sad, sad, that we should not know the name of that place.

While I was trying to think of Mons, Verdun, Armentières, and other places that couldn't possibly be the right one from his pronunciation, we came to a narrow road with a signpost. The motorist halted and pointed. "There! That way!"

And see, there was the name all right—Crécy. Definitely before my time. We parted from the ex-major after leaving the Crécy battlefield and got a lift right to the heart of Paris. In the early evening, we were walking down Rue Vavin. Vavin was one of those ancient streets which are really separate little villages, surviving practically untouched in the midst of the city's rush and bustle. Clear to Rue Raspail and less than a hundred meters from the Luxembourg gardens, Rue Vavin led its own life and went its own way. There were few foreign visitors in the area. A couple of hotels and small cafés; it was an oasis. Jim and I fell in love with it from the first minute. We stayed at a tiny hotel, Hotel L'Espérance—and in all

Kathleen, focused on her chess game, c. 1970s.

63

the years we stayed in Paris, sometimes for weeks or even months at a time, we never lived anywhere else.

I visited the street not so long ago and it was still more or less the same, except that it was impossible to walk along the pavements, as residents' cars were mounted on them at either side.

No longer was one able to see the street. When we lived there none of the inhabitants possessed cars, except for the doctor and the nightclub owner. It is pleasing to think back and remember that I was lucky enough to know the place and myriad other small streets when they were exactly as they must have been when Utrillo[49] painted them.

In Paris, we became acquainted with Marcel Duhamel[50] and met Sartre[51] and Raymond Queneau[52] and others of the Gallimard[53] gang. It was also a time

---

49 **Maurice Utrillo** (né Valadon, December 26, 1883 – November 5, 1955) was a French painter who specialized in cityscapes. Born in the Montmartre quarter of Paris, France, Utrillo is one of the few famous painters of Montmartre who were born there.

 Utrillo was the son of the artist Suzanne Valadon (born Marie-Clémentine Valadon), who was then an eighteen-year-old artist's model. She never revealed who was the father of her child; speculation exists that he was the offspring from a liaison with an equally young amateur painter named Boissy, or with the well-established painter Pierre-Cécile Puvis de Chavannes, or even with Renoir. In 1891 a Spanish artist, Miguel Utrillo y Molins, signed a legal document acknowledging paternity, although the question remains as to whether he was in fact the child's father.

50 **Marcel Duhamel** (July 16, 1900 – March 6, 1977) was a French actor and screenwriter, founder of the Série noire publishing imprint. He played The Foreman in Jean Renoir's 1936 *The Crime of Monsieur Lange*. In 1953 he was credited as screenplay writer for *Cet homme est dangereux*, a French film adaptation of Peter Cheyney's novel of the same name.

51 **Jean-Paul Charles Aymard Sartre** (June 1905 – April 15, 1980) was a French philosopher, playwright, novelist, screenwriter, political activist, biographer, and literary critic. He was one of the key figures in the philosophy of existentialism and phenomenology, and one of the leading figures in twentieth-century French philosophy and Marxism. His work has also influenced sociology, critical theory, post-colonial theory, and literary studies, and continues to influence these disciplines.

52 **Raymond Queneau** (February 21, 1903 – October 25, 1976) was a French novelist, poet, critic, editor and co-founder and president of *OULIPO ("Ouvroir de literature potentielle")*, notable for his wit and cynical humor.

53 **Éditions Gallimard** is one of the leading French book publishers. *The Guardian* has described it as having "the best backlist in the world." In 2003 it and its subsidiaries published 1,418 titles. Founded by Gaston Gallimard in 1911, the publisher is now majority-owned by his grandson Antoine Gallimard.

when chess was very much part of my life. There was a chess café in a small back street called Rue Ciseaux. I always called it Scissor Street. It was not far from cafés Flore and Deux Magots, just off Boulevard St. Germain.

The two cafés were popular with the literati, or so the tourists thought. They had been, but by the time we arrived on the scene they were flooded with visitors trying to guess with which of the famous people they were mingling. Meanwhile, Sartre and others had moved on to less well-known haunts such as the café in Rue Ciseaux.

A funny thing happened there one evening. I was quite a good chess player and women chess players were rare in Paris and indeed anywhere else. Naturally, the chess habitués of the café did not know that the "pretty little Irish girl" (their description) had qualified for the U.K.'s women championship as one of the twelve best of the contestants, plus having played for numerous county teams all over England and Ireland. (Of course I didn't have much competition to get to that—but I certainly had novelty value.)

Consequently, in the Rue Ciseaux café the regular chess players "played down" to me. God help them! I was mopping up opponents in quick time. But, oh dear, how slight was the male confidence in their superiority. Suddenly all the chivalry for the pretty little Irish girl went out of the window. When ordering their food and drink, they joked and demanded "Deux rosbif! [Two roast beefs!]" Soon *we* were the 'deux rosbif.' No longer were we their Irish allies. Time to move on from Paris.

One morning we took the metro to the southern terminus and hitched a lift to the roundabout at Fontainebleau. The Rhône road was black with hitchhikers. Many of them looked as if they had been there for days, thumbing the road by day and retiring to camp out in the woods at night. There was an unbroken stream of traffic going on for the French Riviera and the southeast, but all the vehicles were packed solid with people and luggage. It was the beginning of what is now commonplace. The start of "le camping"—the camping era.

Every car had camping gear on the rooftop. (Soon this would follow the same pattern on the roads from everywhere in the U.K. making for Cornwall.) It was the beginning of the changeover from a two weeks' family holiday at the seaside in bed and breakfast accommodation, to the litter of families and chattels strewn all over the countryside. Tourism had begun in earnest. Sufficient to say that up to that time there were few, if any, caravan sites in the whole of the U.K. I am in favour of the abolition of all such places. Let those who sold out their birthright for a mess of Birmingham, Pittsburgh, and Clermont Ferrand, stay in those places—forcibly if necessary. And leave the road for those who belong on it!

The throng of hitch-hikers, German, French, Dutch, Belgian, Danish, American, and British, waved and signaled to the long line of passing cars. Some showed placards. We walked on for a couple of kilometers and waited. We hoped for a champagne salesman; many of the cars carried their name and trade on the outside of the vehicle.

Presently we had luck, a car passed all the other hitch-hikers, stopped, and took us to Auxerre. Of course, it all depends on what you call luck! By the time we reached Auxerre it was falling dusk and the town was packed out. Night arrived, and a dark night at that; we left the town to walk south along the Route Nationale. This was not easy walking. There was no surface on the French roads as we know surface. No pavements (naturally), single-line traffic, and the road was broken in many places. Apart from which, the French truck drivers, who ruled the roads, tore along at a furious pace; the last thing they thought of was a pedestrian—except as a huge joke. Nevertheless, the trucks looked beautiful, because they were festooned with little red, green, and white lights like Christmas decorations.

At last we reached a side road which turned away from the main to a little place called Champs, and we breathed a sigh of relief as we started down it into the darkness. Before we reached the village we were nearly eaten alive by a dozen wild dogs. We stood them off and cursed them loudly in English and Irish and Romani and bad French. Then someone else shouted at them, and a moment later we were surrounded by a dozen wild-looking men. We had strayed into a gipsy camp. The men looked very tough indeed, and they sounded most menacing.

We called out who we were, in Romani, and they started to ask questions. Having allayed their suspicions they became embarrassingly friendly. We were offered a share of any one of their caravans for the night. Then one of the men told us that the people who owned the little bistro in the village belonged to this family and offered to take us there. The patron insisted that there was no room, but our gipsy took all that in his stride.

"Jetez-deux," he ordered and jerked his left thumb over his shoulder. "Throw out two."

It was the simplest and most sweeping billet order I had ever heard. Throw out two and then there would be room for the gipsies from Ireland. Simple!

Next morning we were off on the road at sun-up. We had just turned in to the main road from the little lane and were ready to flag a car when a girl rode up on a bicycle. She was from the bistro and she was plainly relieved to have caught us up. Gravely, she handed me a small parcel. "You forgot this," she announced triumphantly.

We had been eating some peaches in our room and I had wrapped up the peach stones in a paper bag. The folks at the case weren't going to take a chance on mislaying any of *our* property. Had we not been introduced by the sharang of the gipsy encampment?

Hitching further and further south, it was becoming perceptibly warmer when we reached Avignon. Avignon was like a place out of Grimms' Fairy Tales. The tall, polygonal, loop-holed town walls, the medieval fortifications, the fantastically narrow streets all made it look like a theatrical set.

We met a young journalist, Raymond Duclos[54], who was from Madagascar. He had read dozens of books about Ireland. His conversation was loaded with quotations from Irish literature and Irish history. One in particular I remember—a quote from Fintan Lalor[55]. Every now and again he would say, "England's difficulty is Ireland's opportunity." For him, it was a slogan for all the incipient rebellions against colonialism. For many years he wrote to us. Eventually, he returned to Madagascar. Like so many of those wonderful people we met while drifting, we never saw or heard from him again.

An Indian prince, or he might have been a Maharajah, driving a gleaming Mercedes, speaking English with a cultured accent, gave us a lift to Marseilles. We sat and drank wine in a waterfront café and looked out across the bay to the Château de l'Île. A wonderful, remarkable view, which has long since disappeared.

Memories of Marseilles flood back. It is one of the cities for which I have a secret passion. In the days when ports were ports and to be there made anywhere in the world seem accessible. Sizzling heat. Sleeping in the shade on the pavements during the afternoons with the rest of the Marseilles population. We lived in a small hotel down beside the port, in Luili Street. It was really a brothel—used mainly by cops. We gave it respectability.

---

54 As Kathleen notes, there are many people whom she befriended and kept contact with throughout her life and travels that were dear to her, yet their stories are lost to history. Raymond Duclos is such a person.

55 **James Fintan Lalor** (March 10, 1807 – December 27, 1849) was an Irish revolutionary and journalist. A leading member of the Irish Confederation (Young Ireland), he was to play an active part in both the Rebellion in July 1848 and the attempted Rising in September of that same year. Lalor's writings were to exert a seminal influence on later Irish leaders.

The Château d'If was already a tourist attraction, made famous by Dumas in *The Count of Monte Cristo*. Above the cell doors were the names of various characters from the novel. Edmund Dantes, Abbe Feria, etc. I wondered who the real convicts had been.

There was a café in the prison yard. When the waiter came for our order, Jim requested bread and water for two. When they brought it, the waiter indicated a man who wanted to talk with us. We invited him over.

He was the advance publicity man for Pinder's Circus, which was in town. On hearing that Jim was a writer, he said that he would recommend him to his boss, M. Spiessert, for a job. *HIS* job. He was quitting.

We joined the circus entourage and travelled with them for a while along the Côte d'Azur, as far as Fréjus. We took part in all of the town processions. The first one, in Marseilles, was spectacular. Like a Cecil B. DeMille movie. I sat on a float with ten Indian women as we drove around the city. The Indian girls each had a leopard on a chain attached to their wrists. I merely sat, sans leopard, in petrified silence, while pretending not to be petrified at all. At midnight, our procession ended by travelling down the whole length of the Canebière. It was a truly amazing sight.

Lining either side of the boulevard were all the African soldiers from the French Foreign Legion—the Headquarters was in Marseilles. They were about nine feet tall and carried flaming torches to light the street. It is a wonder that the city did not disappear in a ball of fire. It was just sensational.

The next day there was a big recruiting meeting up at the Legion Headquarters, on a hill above the city. The procession in which we had taken part was to advertise it! We went to the meeting but did not enlist. The following morning we headed out along the coast road. As we passed through the market we saw someone bowing and waving and smiling at us. It was our Indian prince of the Mercedes, now speaking in perfect French—selling carpets.

We drifted through the beautiful fishing villages of the Mediterranean, Le Lavandou, Cassis, La Cavalière, playing boules, sipping bouillabaisse, drinking pastis, and sleeping out on the lovely beaches. All now unrecognisable, engulfed by tower blocks, campsites, motels. Full marks for destruction. We were making for Cannes, hoping for mail at the Post Office. There we settled into a little hotel, Le Chanticleer, beside the church of that name. Here the circus caught up with us. I knew they had arrived when I walked out of our room one morning into the narrow alleyway. I was confronted by a huge lion, roaring its head off. Fortunately, it was behind bars.

But we were not destined to move on with our circus friends. A telegram from Harrap's told us that publication day for *Underworld* was looming near. This meant that we would get the remainder of the advance money. It seemed the moment to turn in our tracks and start back. We took a train to Nice and hitched across the Alps for Grenoble and Lyons, to head north.

One night we fetched up in Ivry, a small village where we tried to find a room. There was a distinct anti-British bias. Some incident from the war, we surmised. No one would give or sell us anything. No coffee, no wine, no cigarettes, no food, no room.

At each place, they said the same thing.

"Anglais, hein? Non, pas de chambre. Complet[56]."

At our last attempt, we managed to explain that we were Irish, and the old woman looked us over.

"Irlandais..." she said dubiously. Then she had an inspiration.

"Vous connaissez la chanson, 'Long Way to Tipperairee,'" she demanded of me.

"Oui, madame," I said. She pushed her face almost into mine.

"Alors, chantez!" she ordered. So I sang 'It's a Long Way to Tipperary' on the doorstep of her house in Ivry. She beamed and said, "Mais oui. Une vraie Irlandaise." And she led the way inside.

The next morning we headed for Boulogne, Folkestone, London, the Lake District, and the wagon. We picked up the mail. The major item was that Harrap's had sent us the cheque, *Underworld* was published, the first edition had already sold out and a second edition was planned.

Just right for a welcome back to England.

It was the early fifties and things in the publishing world were changing. Jim was taking stock of what he wanted to do literary-wise. During the years that we had been together, he had written many top-rate short stories, many well-paid feature articles, and nine books. But gradually the radio work was taking over, broadcasts of short stories, talks about vagabondage, the road in general, documentary features for radio such as *Lorry Harbour* with Denis Mitchell[57] and another about the East End of London with

---

56 "English, eh? No, no room. Full."

57 **Denis Mitchell** (August 11, 1911 – 1990) was a British documentary filmmaker, renowned for his innovative radio and television documentaries. His radio and television career can broadly be characterized by the constant interest Mitchell displayed in "giving voice to the voiceless" and in the rhythms and prosody of everyday vernacular speech.

R.D. Smith[58]. There had been a break into television following the interview with Valentine Dyall at the Festival of Britain.

TV series were spreading everywhere. The number of publishers was decreasing. The shape, the size and the contents of books were changing fast. The paperback market was growing. Short stories in newspapers—one of our main sources of income—were almost nil, as were short-story magazines.

Short-story slots were now on the radio, not in newspapers. Vagabond gossip about the road wasn't a feature article anymore; it was a TV interview. Racy anecdotes about the characters you met on the road? That wasn't a vagabond book; it was a radio series and so on. What to do? Decision time.

So there we were, back in the Lake District, considering our future. It will be no surprise to anyone when I say that we did what we had always done in such circumstances: run away.

Within days, we were back on the road, hitching south for France again. Marcel Duhamel, when we met him in Paris, had implored us to visit with him in Antibes. "Soon," he had said. This was soon!

Once again we were making for the Riviera; this time we decided to take the Route Napoléon through the Alps calling at Sisteron and Digne and so on. We also visited a small village called Lurs. The weather was heavenly, blazing hot days and beautiful soft balmy nights. Most of the time we slept out. After leaving Digne we decided to hitch through the night and get to Cannes in the early hours of the morning.

Somewhere during the day, we were stopped by the police, only to have our passports checked. This was all normal. Tourism had barely been heard of, there were few vehicles on the road, so the village cops, being bored to death, naturally stopped any strangers they sighted, just for a chat. Jim had had a letter from BBC Manchester about a program he was to do later in the year inside his passport, knowing that sometime he was bound to see it and remember. The cops, seeing the envelope with the BBC logo printed on it, were naturally curious and duly impressed.

We hitched all day and on into the night and made it into Cannes about four in the morning. The Mediterranean coast looked beautiful. There was a deathly hush at that hour and we sat on a seat overlooking the sea. A soft warm night, not a breath of wind, not a sound save the *clonk, clonk* of the fishing

---

58 **Reginald Donald "Reggie" Smith** (July 31, 1914 – May 3, 1985) was a teacher and lecturer, BBC radio producer, possible Communist spy and model for the character of Guy Pringle in the novel sequence *Fortunes of War* written by his wife, Olivia Manning.

boats, and the occasional chiming of a church clock. Over all hung the heavy lemon scent from the sea, which folk think was only a bit of poetic writing from Homer; but years ago, before pollution took over, it pervaded the morning air.

When the town began to stir, we went to the rail station and caught a little train along to Antibes. We arrived at Marcel's house at about eight o'clock. How had we got there so early, he wanted to know. Well, we'd hitched through the Alps, hadn't we? Lurs, Digne, Cannes, etc. "I hope you have a good alibi," he joked and handed us the morning paper. The headline news was that a British scientist and his family had been murdered somewhere along the road that we had just travelled. Sir Jack Drummond[59]. And that, roughly speaking, was that. The Drummond murder and the Dominici family who were involved became world-famous; the Phelans passed a pleasant summer at Antibes.

Antibes was just a small fishing place with a few luxury villas scattered about and a few luxury yachts in the harbor. Unrecognisable with what it is like today. It was also a haven for writers and artists from Paris on vacation. Our main

---

59 **Sir Jack Cecil Drummond** (January 12, 1891 – August 4/5, 1952) was a distinguished biochemist, noted for his work on nutrition as applied to the British diet under rationing during the Second World War. He was murdered, together with his wife and ten-year-old daughter, in what became known as the Dominici affair, on the night of 4–5 August 1952 near Lurs, a village in Southern France. On the evening of August 4, 1952, while on holiday in France in their green Hillman estate car, the Drummonds stopped by the side of the N96 main road, less than 200 meters from a farmhouse called La Grand'Terre. A footpath leads from the site down to the banks of the river Durance.

La Grand'Terre was the home of the Dominicis, a family of Franco-Italian peasant farmers: the patriarch Gaston, his wife Marie, their son Gustave, Gustave's wife Yvette, and their baby son Alain. It was Gustave who claimed to have found the three dead bodies around 5:30 a.m. on the morning of 5 August, and who flagged down a passing motorcyclist, Jean-Marie Olivier, telling him to fetch the police.

Anne's body was found near the car. Jack's lay on the other side of the N96, covered by a camp bed. They had both been shot by a Rock-Ola M1 carbine. The body of ten-year-old Elizabeth was found 77 meters away, down the path leading to the river, on the other side of the bridge over the railway. Her head had been brutally smashed in by the stock of the rifle. The barrel of the murder weapon was soon found in the river, with the stock a short distance downstream. It is likely that the force of the blow or blows used to kill Elizabeth had also broken the stock off the rifle.

Gaston Dominici was convicted of the murders in November 1954 and sentenced to death by guillotine. However, both the police investigation and the conduct of the trial had been widely criticized and, after two inconclusive inquiries, President René Coty commuted the sentence to life imprisonment. Coty was succeeded in 1959 by President Charles de Gaulle, who ordered Dominici's release on humanitarian grounds, but did not pardon him, nor grant his request for a retrial.

rendez-vous was a small nondescript shack of a café on the beach where everyone congregated in the evenings. One evening, we met a man from Southampton. A Cornishman, Josh Billings. He was captaining a yacht from San Remo around the Mediterranean. As the owner was not there, he invited us aboard to meet some of his mates.

They had wine. Very good wine. I remember dancing the Cornish Floral dance with Billings. In the brilliant full moon of the Med. We danced up and down the deserted streets of Antibes, and in spite of—or because of—the myriad bottles of wine, never put a foot wrong.

One of the group was a yachtsman called Cremey. He spoke no known language, except to say 'Cremey de Menthe!' at each round of drinks. Cremey dressed in fur-lined sea-rig, so he may have come from Lapland or Finland or even Siberia because the *night* temperature in Antibes was around 80 degrees.

Each evening, we dined and sat around, oh, so elegantly, with Marcel Duhamel, at his villa 'Fin-lande,' with wife of the Deputy French Interior Minister, Helene Bokanowski; Anouk, then just starting out on her acting career, and later to become famous as Anouk Aimee[60], and others of the artistic set, discussing books and plays and paintings until late in the evening. Then they would all disappear to their various villas and we would drift down to the waterfront to a sailor's 'dive' and

15-year-old Anouk Aimée in Marcel Carné's unfinished film *La Fleur de l'âge*, 1947. Photo by Émile Savitry.

---

60 **Anouk Aimée** (born Nicole Françoise Florence Dreyfus, April 27, 1932), a French film actress, has appeared in 70 films since 1947, having begun her film career at age 14. Although the majority of her films were French, she also made a number of films in Spain, Great Britain, Italy and Germany, along with some American productions.

Among her films are Federico Fellini's *La Dolce Vita* (1960) and *8½* (1963), Jacques Demy's *Lola* (1961), George Cukor's *Justine* (1969), Bernardo Bertolucci's *Tragedy of a Ridiculous Man* (1981) and Robert Altman's *Prêt à Porter* (1994). She won the Golden Globe Award for Best Actress - Motion Picture Drama and the BAFTA Award for Best Actress, and was nominated for the Academy Award for Best Actress for her acting in *A Man and a Woman* (1966).

drink with Billings and Cremey until the early hours. As I recall, the arts were never in those conversations. Fun times!

Happily, we always knew when it was time to quit a place and hit the road. One morning we were once again thumbing lifts north; eventually, we were heading up the A6 in England making for the Lake District and Rydal Farm. It was time for a wagon move. We wended our way with the caravan up across Dunmail Raise, the hump of Helvellyn, over into the vale of St. John, then along the narrow roads around Skiddaw.

On a tiny rock farm at Blencow, not a hundred yards from a singing river, there was just one patch of green to site the caravan. Curlews called high above. The river talked loudly, in a Cumberland accent. Twice in the black before the dawning, wild geese went honking high overhead. It was a long way from Marseilles and the Mediterranean. This was the next place.

High Roads
and Holidays

Blencow was a small village near Penrith. We had not intended to stay there for very long, but to head for Hadrian's Wall and the Border country. However, it froze every day for two months; we were ice-bound. Jim decided to write a second volume for his autobiography. *Tramp at Anchor*. An easy book to write. It opened with a short summary of *The Name's Phelan* as a lead-in, followed by the material from *Jail Journey*, which had been a great success when first published, but out of print for years.

While Jim hit the typewriter, I snared rabbits! Roast rabbit became our staple diet. This was before the plague of myxomatosis; since then I have never touched it. After the script was finished and sent off to Harrap's, we moved to Warwick on Eden, just outside of Carlisle.

One dark winter's evening there was a knock on the caravan door, a detective from Carlisle. He understood that we had spent much of the summer in France, hitch-hiking through the Alps, and would we call next morning at Carlisle police station to answer a few questions? We went.

The questions were all about our trip along the route Napoleon, especially on the day of the murders. Well, we had heard and seen nothing. What we wanted to know was how, after all those weeks, they had managed to trace us to a horse-drawn wagon on the moors along the Scottish border.

The cop who had interviewed us on the road through the Alps had made no note of our names, but he did remember that it was someone from BBC Manchester. So the Yard had got in touch with the Beeb, who had said, "That can only be the Phelans... they were travelling horse-drawn along the road to Scotland. Their mail goes to Carlisle post office." And the grapevine did the rest.

We kept on creeping with the caravan just south of Hadrian's Wall. It was a strange place where the ghosts come crowding with every wisp of mist, even before darkness falls. We pulled in at Walton, a small hamlet; the name speaks for itself. There was just one farm beside the ruins of the Wall. Looking away from the farm up the narrow road that leads to Newcastle and the borders of Scotland it was easy to see the ghosts.

They come from medieval times, and from the days when the Danes held all of the north of England. Also, there will be a few foreign-looking ghosts, from the earlier days of the Roman wall. Walton in those days would have been a kind of gipsy camp, peopled by runaway Roman legionaries and escaped Gaulish prisoners—and a few drifting girls of the Picts and Scots.

One doesn't have to look far for strange happenings for a song or a story in Walton, on the Newcastle road. Even today the magic rubs off. The farm at Walton where we pulled in the horse-drawn caravan was owned by a family called Beatty. Father, mother, and David, their eleven-year-old son, who was their pride and joy who would one day inherit the farm.

The caravan was way down at the bottom of a field and it seemed a good place to leave it for a while, so we decided to head for Scandinavia.

Jim had a literary agent, David Grunbaum in Copenhagen, selling lots of translations of his short stories to magazines such as *Hjemmets Sondag* and also Radio Denmark. They were extremely popular. It seemed a good place to head for.

So one morning we hitched south to Harwich and caught a boat to the Hook of Holland. We drifted north to Rotterdam and Hamburg, took a train across the Kiel canal, and eventually arrived in Copenhagen. Two novels, *Lifer* and *Moon in the River,* had been published by Carit Andersen[61]; David Grunbaum had a lot of money for us.

As the exchange rate was heavily against the pound, we had let the money accumulate and had £800 worth of kroner to collect. Grunbaum had fixed

---

61 **Poul Carit Andersen** (March 23, 1910 – September 29, 1982) was a Danish publisher and author. He attended the Danish bookstore school and bookstore school in Leipzig and was on a study stay abroad 1930–31. In 1940 he founded Carit Andersens Forlag and ran an independent publishing business.

several interviews with newspapers and radio, so we were able to earn a fair bit of money while we were there.

We stayed with Jim's translator, Kurt Kreuzfeld, and his family who lived along Oster Sogade, not too far from the city centre. It was April, not really the time of year to be hitching through Scandinavia.

Ice and snow were everywhere. It was freezing cold most of the time out of doors, cold enough to kill anyone. If it didn't kill you, you got a second chance indoors, where the central heating in the apartment was enough to roast you alive. That is if you hadn't been killed by the food first.

We ate endless stews, made with meat so bright red and coarse, that I had difficulty in deciding what it was. I discovered after a few days that it was *horse!* That was the end as far as we were concerned, and we left. Otherwise, we had a fantastic time. The Kreutzfelds were lovely people and did everything possible to make our stay enjoyable. They could hardly be held accountable for the weather, and the fact that to eat horse was something approaching cannibalism would never have entered their minds—nor to any other of the Danes that I met.

Jim's publisher, Carit Andersen, threw a great party for us as did several editors and radio folk. We also spent a great evening pub-crawling with Tom Kristiansen[62], that great writer and great drinker. Several articles appeared in newspapers and magazines. As we could not speak Danish, we had no idea what was being written about us. Recently I had someone translate one of the articles for me. Jim was described as a wandering thief. He would have loved that.

Carit Andersen's wife was both beautiful and elegant and spoke English impeccably, so conversation was easy. Only once was I taken aback, to everyone's hilarity.

Many Danish words are almost the same as words spoken in the Gorbals or Gallowgate in Glasgow or on Tyneside in England, e.g., *gan*/to go, *hyem*/home and so forth. Knowing no Danish I was unaware of this.

As we were leaving, Mrs. Andersen came to say goodbye and lapsed into Danish saying "Ye gan hyem?" I could not stop laughing. As far as I was concerned,

---

62 **Tom Kristensen** (August 4, 1893 – June 2, 1974), was a Danish poet, novelist, literary critic and journalist. In 1930 he published perhaps his most well-known work, the novel *Hærværk* (literally: *Vandalism*, published in English as *Havoc* in 1968). *Hærværk* is the story of Danish journalist Ole Jastrau who is driven to self-destruction by drinking himself to death. Apart from its presumed autobiographical character, it probably reflects the intellectual, political and personal crises of many writers and artists between the World Wars. The book is also considered one of the best literary Danish-language depictions of alcoholism.

her beautiful English had flown out of the window and she was speaking in the street speech of the North country.

We left Copenhagen reluctantly and set out for Elsinore and the boat across to Sweden to hitch to Stockholm and repeat the process. *Lifer* had been translated by a Swedish journalist, Else Kleen[63], whom we hoped to meet. However, Ms. Kleen had married the Swedish Foreign Secretary (Gustav Moeller[64]) by the time we got to Stockholm and was not particularly interested in passing tramp-writers. We stayed in the city for a while selling stories and giving newspaper interviews, picking up valuable kroner, then we headed out of the city hitching north.

We had a contact at Uppsala University; Jim was to give a talk there. Uppsala was famous for anyone interested in studying philology. After the talk, we all went to a restaurant for a meal. A man from a circus joined us, he had travelled with Pinder's Circus in France at the same time as we had, and was a friend of M. Spiessert, the manager, our erstwhile boss. One of those curious road coincidence meetings. He had travelled with circuses all over Europe and boasted that he was illiterate in seventeen languages. Just the right person to join in a discussion about philology.

From Uppsala, we kept heading north. Hitch-hiking was unknown, so every car stopped to discover what we wanted. I say all, but there was hardly any traffic on the roads—if they could be called roads. Cart tracks better describe them. Although it was late May, it was bitterly cold, the snow piled high on either side. Not a house, not a village, only mile after mile of pine trees. All the way to Lapland. Crossing mighty rivers on high spindly bridges. Far below, ocean-going ships sailed along. Huge rafts of timber floated down to the sea a thousand miles away.

Late one night, watching from a high bridge, a motorist showed us how the rafts of lumber came down and were carefully "riffled" away so as not to break

---

63 **Else Kleen** (1882 – 1968) was a Swedish journalist, author, and social reformer. She was a well-known participator in public debate in the Swedish press for sixty years. As an author, she is perhaps most known as a fashion journalist, advising women on how to dress elegantly and practically at a small cost. As a social reformer, she is known for her advocacy for humane treatment of inmates, both criminal and insane.

64 **Gustav Möller** (1884 – 1970) was a prominent Swedish Social Democratic politician, credited as the father of the social security system and the Welfare state, also called Folkhemmet. He was a Member of Parliament in 1918–1954 and Member of the Government in 1924–26, 1932–36 and 1936–51.

down the bridge. It must have been eleven o'clock, but the sun was only just going down as we were so far north. We watched it set.

We crossed the road and looked at the swirling river below, with the island-like rafts of lumber looking like packs of floating cigars far below, except that they weighed about twenty thousand tons. Suddenly the motorist exclaimed, "Oh, look, it's sunrise. We've been talking all night." And there was the sun coming up again. *Very* strange.

Harnosand, Sundsvall, we pressed on for Umea. We hardly ever slept, because night never came. Just endless days. Occasionally there was a gap between the pine trees to show a wild pasture with reindeer grazing.

There were no signposts—every car had a compass. One day a farmer gave us a lift. He had long white hair and a long white beard and resembled Father Christmas. On and on we rode with him through the pine forests. Distances were hard to gauge. One Swedish mile equalled ten English. Our farmer explained his farming.

The life cycle of the pine trees was about a hundred years. The life of a reindeer about twenty-five years. In Lapland, if you were a farmer, you sold the pine trees that your grandfather planted. And you sold the reindeer that your father bred.

Meanwhile you threw in a few handfuls of pine cones here and there—that was for your grandson. And you let the reindeer get together in the pastures—that was for your son.

"Nice, easy farming," said Father Christmas, and laughed as he dropped us off and drove away.

The cold was terrifying. We lived on coffee and aquavit. We were supposed to be heading for Kiruna and the Land of the Midnight Sun. But it was so cold one morning that when we stepped out to hitch further north, we looked at one another and shivered, and without speaking a word crossed to the other side of the road and started to hitch south.

We were like ghosts, cold, hungry, and tired. Tired, because as it was light for twenty-four hours we had just kept on—waiting for night to fall. It didn't! Also, there was the fact that Jim had a date to give a talk on the radio at Manchester BBC. We had lost all track of time and days and dates but it seemed like a good idea to try to get there. Everything added up to heading south.

One day a man gave us a lift and told us that he had a friend who spoke perfect English and he was sure that he would love to meet us. He would take us. We drove for miles to a small wayside café. The owner was the English-speaking friend. We were introduced and our driver waited for the conversation to start.

The proprietor looked a little discomfited but led Jim over to a wall and pointed to a huge poster of a ship of the Cunard line. Then he shouted out triumphantly, "Liverpool!" It was his only word of English. He had been kidding his friend for years that he was a great linguist. Then there was silence.

Jim, realizing the situation immediately, winked at the owner and the two of them proceeded to talk a lot of gibberish to one another, occasionally throwing in the word Liverpool. The friend was satisfied and the owner's reputation was safe. It transpired that he had made one trip from Gothenburg to Liverpool as a deckhand forty years earlier!

On our way back through Copenhagen, Jim sold an article about our travels in Sweden— mostly about pubs. Liquor laws in Sweden were very strict. A man could have two glasses of beer and a woman only one.

Kathleen sitting under a signpost, c. late 1960s.

Outside of every café, where liquor was served, stood a uniformed policeman with a huge sword. As one entered the café, the cop barred the doorway with the sword and leaned over to smell your breath. Any beer fumes and there was no getting in. There was an interesting side issue. To buy drink for the home was rationed. A householder was limited to a certain number of bottles a month. Consequently the puritans and temperance people were the black marketeers. They purchased their rations of liquor and sold them at astronomical prices to the depraved!

The Danes, who were great beer drinkers, had a nice "out" for the drunks who lay about the pavements. They always explained that they were Swedes over for the beer.

We arrived at the Hook of Holland to find that Jim was due in Manchester the following day! We arrived in Harwich in the early hours of a summer morning.

We started hitching across Essex, and presently got a lift in a small truck going to Chesterfield. The driver was so excited by our mammoth hitch-hike that he insisted on driving us all the way to Manchester.

We arrived outside of the studios in Piccadilly about midday. The driver, much to his delight, was given lunch in the BBC canteen and a tour of the building.

"Where have you come from?" asked Grahame Miller, the producer.

"Lapland," Jim told him, and Grahame roared with laughter. After the program was finished, Grahame asked again, "Now, Jim, where did you *really* come from?"

I sometimes wonder myself.

Back to Walton the next day and time to move on again. The night before we were to leave, David, the farmer's young son, who drove a tractor very competently about the farm, asked if he could tow the caravan up to the farm lane the next morning and help us to harness up. For him, it was a great thrill. The family gathered and waved goodbye until we rounded a bend in the road. We left the Beattys' knowing David's future as a farmer. But life never works out exactly as planned, Fate plays curious tricks. For instance, thirty years later I was hitch-hiking from Devon to London, a man gave me a lift and as we chatted, I asked where he came from originally, and he told me Carlisle. We discussed our shared liking for that city and the surrounding area. Then he explained that he came from a much smaller place, Brampton, about twenty miles from the city. I, too, knew Brampton. We discussed Brampton. Presently I asked him if, as he knew Brampton, he also knew Walton and the Beatty family. I told him about our stay there with the gipsy caravan, about young David, and did he ever know them.

"Oh, yes," he said. "I can tell you about the Beattys. Mrs. Beatty died and Mr. Beatty now lives in Brampton. And as for David, well, you are talking to him!"

He went on to ask me if I realised how much my way of life influenced people. That morning, all those years ago, when he watched our caravan disappear round the bend in the road, he made a private resolve never to be a farmer, but to go off along the road himself.

When he left school, he told his father that he didn't want to be a farmer. Instead, he and a school friend got apprenticed to an engineering firm in Carlisle. For seven years, they saved all their money and when they finished the apprenticeship they took off for Canada, bought a small truck, converted it to a living van and for two years travelled all over North America. Then, having indulged his wanderlust, he married happily, had children and was now a commercial rep for a big engineering firm—still travelling.

That is my favourite coincidence story of the many I have had down the years. ○ॐ

Drifting South

After getting back to Sweden from Walton, we decided to drift south again. Winters were so cold in the north country that Scotland was out of the question. It was late summer and we took the high road over the fells to Alston, the highest town in England. We found a farm a couple of miles outside of the town where we could pull in. This was known as Swinburn Walton's place.

Swinburn Walton was a famous sheep farmer, his black-faced sheep fetching high prices at every market in Cumberland, Northumberland, Yorkshire, Ayrshire, and Midlothian.

It is no offence to the present-day population of the modern world to say that generally speaking, strong personality, individualism, integrity, strength, and pride are not of much use to a person. In the average industrial city, such things are severe handicaps.

But Swinburn did not move or live in a modern city. He lived in the wild hill country of Cumberland, and he dealt with people more or less like himself, from Scotland and Lakeland and the Border country.

Thus, his writ ran, in any sheep market from Ilkley Moor to Ayr. He and his wife Ethel took us all over the Border country to sheep markets and cattle fairs where we met the most stimulating personalities. One such was Harrison Rudd. Harrison was a kind of market loafer, helping to give a prod to a wayward bullock or hold down a fretful horse. He would be rewarded with a pound or two which he immediately spent in the nearest pub. He had done little else all his life. Even as a child he had helped to drive the shoed geese from Carlisle to whichever market they were bound for. Little leather shoes used to be fixed to the feet of the geese before they set off for a trek over the hills to Lazonby market under Harrison's care.

Staying at the Waltons' place was fortunate for us. We had decided to buy our own horse for the caravan while we were in the North Country instead of continually borrowing one and then having to return it in a horsebox. Or worse still walking it back to its owner when we didn't have the money for the horsebox. I remember once walking a huge black stallion fifteen miles from Scotch Corner to Brough in the middle of the night.

To have a horse of our own would save us considerable expense, but also it would save us much time and trouble in the finding and fixing of pitches and the next horse to borrow. And of course, we both liked horses.

Swinburn had been a horse-breaker in his young days, had several horses of his own, was a great judge of hunters, working horses, and show-ponies. We bought a horse at Carlisle market, for $45. We learned that his name was Hobo, which we thought was a good sign. He was a beauty.

So we hired a horsebox and had Hobo transferred out to Swinburn's farm. Then we bought a set of harness with our last ten pounds, and we got Swinburn to test the horse for us. This last was very important—some horses will just not pull a caravan.

Hobo wouldn't. It was a dreadful shame, but it was no use. If either of us had been in charge instead of Swinburn Walton, on that first test, not only would the caravan have been kicked to ribbons, so would we. He just refused to go forward. Backward seemed to be all he knew—into a stone wall.

We ended up by offering Hobo to a horse dealer in Carlisle, to sell for us. Meanwhile, Swinburn lent us a mare of his own, named Jewel. She was happy to draw a caravan or a baby's pram or an invalid's cart.

Two days later we set off on the high road over the tops for Scotch Corner and the south. It was a wonderful trip, over the narrow hill road from Alston to Middleton-in-Teesdale. It was a hard road; the horse-drawn gipsies used to go twenty miles round to avoid it. We, in our innocence, went over the top. It took us four days to do eighteen miles.

We followed the river Tyne, from Alston, right up to its source, where it was a stream a foot wide. Then we crossed the watershed, a lone, bare mountain top, for three miles until we met another tiny stream a foot wide. We followed that one downhill until it became a mighty river, the Tees.

From the tiny village of Romaldkirk, we hired a horsebox and sent Jewel back to Swinburn. We would have loved to have bought her from him. She was not half as valuable, moneywise, as Hobo, and was eighteen years old. But Swinburn wouldn't part with her; she had been the children's pony and was family.

I'm sure Jewel was sad to go. Adventure had come to her. She had been brought up on the fells where the grass grows short. At first, when we turned her in to a field at night, she ignored all the long beautiful grass and made her way to the edge of the field to eat around the thin border. She soon learned though.

Another thing which saddened me was that, as it was great horse country, whenever we trundled past a field with horses, they would run alongside the caravan on the other side of the fence. Then when they could get no further, they would gang up in a group and watch us continue down the road, with the most mournful expressions on their faces, until we were out of sight.

The horse trader in Carlisle sent us a cheque for £50 for Hobo, so we had gained a few pounds if anyone wants to count things that way. As I saw it we had lost a lovely horse.

We bought a piebald mare for thirty pounds from Jerry Pollard, well known in the north country. She was accustomed to traffic, having pulled a milk float for a few years. Her name was Melody. So we set off again for Scotch Corner and Yorkshire and the south.

It is an interesting thing that people who live on the road are of every creed and denomination to start with. And after a few years, each one still holds to his or her original beliefs. In every case, something has been added. And that something is what I call faith in the road. It can't be learned from other people. And it can't be learned out of a book. It can only come from the road itself.

Only a handful of the population in the U.K. lives the life of a vagabond or tramp nowadays. The number keeps dwindling. But it is only they who remain who have a complete unquestioning faith in life—a belief that everything will turn out all right.

Lots of people say they have that kind of faith. But they don't really. People in cities cannot and dare not trust their lives to any such belief. How could they? People cannot walk out into a crowded street and hope the cars will miss them. They cannot leave their rent unpaid, trusting that the landlord won't mind. And they cannot walk away from the office or factory or shop, hoping for the best.

But, that's how people on the road live. And that is how everyone in the world used to live at one time. Living in towns and cities is a very recent affair.

Thirty thousand years ago there wasn't a town or city in existence. The world was populated by nomads. They lived as the blackbirds and rabbits lived—taking no thought for the morrow and having no great possessions. They lived like drifters live today, just going along, and knowing that everything would be all right.

"Ask, and thou shalt receive." There it is in five words. Everyone believed that at one time. But nowadays only the roadsters will trust their lives to such a fatók. And that's true for *all* the vagabonds.

I happen to be able to read and write. The next tramp may not be able to write his or her own name. But they know, as I do, that whatever they need most will come their way.

This is a very handy philosophy. All you really need is the time to wait around!

So there we were one early morning travelling along the road from Barnard Castle to Scotch Corner. Melody was a lovely high-stepping pony and it was a tough road for a horse wagon. Suddenly, on a lonely twisting bit of the road, the breeching broke. That's an important piece of the harness anywhere. On a hilly road, it is vital. And with a spirited horse waiting to kick everything to bits, that break meant trouble. I grabbed Melody's head, and Jim tried to repair the breeching. But he had no real gear—no leather strap or copper rivets and so on. Only the laces from his shoes and a belt.

But there he was working furiously against time, and both of us wishing we had what was needed. We didn't want a purse of gold. Only a leather strap about twelve inches long, and five copper rivets to fasten. But on a lonely moorland road at six in the morning in the north of England, we might just as well have wished for a purse of gold, for all the hope we had of getting anywhere. And then a voice said, "Harness broken?"

I mean, here was I wrestling for my life with a wicked pony and Jim trying to fix a busted breeching and this man comes along to make a bright conversation. "Harness broken?"

I could see Jim take a deep breath before he exploded with a few choice words. But then he didn't. The man was small, about fifty or sixty, cheerful and friendly, and you could see he meant well. So Jim just said, "Uh-huh. Broken is right."

"I used to be a bank manager," he told us next. Now I drew a long breath, intending to say, "Thanks for your most interesting autobiography. And now—will you kindly go away." But he looked so concerned I just couldn't hurt his feelings. So I just said, "Oh, good for you."

"I know nothing about horses or caravans," he went on. "But my son used to have one." I murmured something polite and hoped against hope that Jim would get the thing patched before Melody kicked everything out of sight.

"I'm going now," the man said. "I only live down there," pointing vaguely along the road. He went off, while Jim went on with the patching and I hung on to the mare, wishing I had—

And at that moment a girl got off a bicycle.

"My father sent these," she said. And she handed over a leather strap about twelve inches long and half a dozen copper rivets.

There's the faith of a vagabond—a complete and unquestioning reliance on the road. When you need something and wish for it in complete faith, it comes as surely as a child getting toys off a Christmas tree. Living in towns and cities seems to make it impossible for people to understand this.

And yet, every great teacher in history—everyone has told the same thing, often in words of one syllable.

Have no great possessions. Take no thought for the morrow. Ask and thou shalt receive. Cast your bread and it will return unto you a hundredfold.

Perhaps it is only the drifters, owning little in the way of material goods, spending long hours alone, tramping the roads and hills, it is only they who have the need, and the urge, and the leisure, to meditate on such things.

Managing a horse and travelling with the gipsy wagon became a full-time job. Not much writing was getting done. Eventually, we pulled in at West Tanfield, near to Ripon. A wonderful pitch. West Panfield was a little square stone village built around a single field. Harper's Field it was called because it belonged to Mr. Harper. Our caravan was in the middle of that field, in the middle of the village, with the church outside the left side window and the village shop outside the right window and the village pub almost

Jim posing with caravan, c. late 1950s.

within reaching distance of the door. We were in the heart of civilisation so to speak.

We did not intend to stay long, so one morning we harnessed up and took the road, and Melody went lame as we pulled out of the field. We unharnessed and sent for a vet. Put the horse out to grass, the vet advised, for at least a month. There was nothing radically wrong. But if she was worked within the next few weeks, she would break down. To grass for a month or so. We phoned Jerry Pollard, our horse dealer, and gave him Melody to look after. That was better than hiring a grass field, and waiting around, and perhaps having no horse at the end just the same. So we were free to move on somehow, somewhere, the next day. But the best-laid plans often go amiss.

That night the typewriter rattled and clattered till about four in the morning. Jim had started to write the next book, *Tramping the Toby*. When we looked outside at sun-up there was three feet of snow in the field. So we ended up staying at West Tanfield for the winter and the book got written.

When it was finished we got a tow with a farm tractor along the road to York. Having to pick somewhere for the tractor to take us, we used a map to pick out a place, which was very unusual for us. We told the towage man to take us to Acomb, which looked an excellent possibility, a small village very near to York city, certain that we would be able to halt at one of the farms there.

The driver halted three or four miles before the city and asked us which part of Acomb. We were in the middle of a big wide busy street, with bus stops and shopping centres and taxi ranks. Not at all the best place to discuss a possible pitch in a possible village.

So I said rather curtly, "Oh, anywhere, anywhere. Stop at the first farm in Acomb." The man didn't move and we held up a line of traffic while we glared at one another. "Sir," he said to Jim and stared open-mouthed. "Didden' thee know? This here is Acomb."

So it was. Taxis, bus stops, chain stores, and all—Acomb was now part of York city. So much for using maps. Ours was a recent publication, but completely out of date. Maps often are. I have a theory that map-makers copy from generation to generation so that the maps are always out of date. We told the driver to take us round the outskirts of York and stop outside of the first village pub, along the open road. We stopped outside of a little inn at Nether/Upper Poppleton. The landlord said yes, we could pull in alongside. It was far better luck than we deserved.

We had luck work-wise too. Jim sold an article to the local paper and the *Yorkshire Post* bought the serial rights of *Tramp at Anchor*. The money was very good, so we did not stay long around York. There were lots of gipsies, relations of the Baker family in the area, and they towed us to another pub outside of Doncaster. We were in good racing territory so we spent a lot of time and money at race meetings seeking our fortune.

Still heading south we stayed for a few days at an attractive farm in Kirklington in Nottinghamshire. The countryside was beautiful. Early summer. Ancient pastures were bounded by tall, still more ancient hawthorn hedges in full blossom. We travelled down one of the small roads which went alongside a tributary of the river Trent and ended in the Vale of Belvoir at the village of Branston. We pulled into a beautiful apple orchard. Belvoir was as beautiful as its name suggests. We were there during Derby week and backed the winner, Never Say Die. Ridden by a fifteen-year-old kid, Lester Piggott.

A farm lorry towed us next to the village of Glaston in Leicestershire. Glaston was a lonely place although it was on the east-west road. Our wagon was in the loneliest part of it, on the very edge of the village.

Years earlier, a huge mansion had fallen into ruins or had been burnt down. The ruins had been overgrown and the place was now a farm. The farmer lived in the village but gave us permission to pull in beside the ruins. Part of the demesne wall had fallen down so we were able to drive through the gap and pitch right inside, tucked away among the ruins of the forgotten mansion. All the main east-west traffic, Leicester to Grantham and Lincolnshire, passed within ten feet of the gap in the wall, yet no one knew there was a caravan with people there.

It was summertime and Jim had a program to prepare for BBC Manchester, so I decided to go strawberry-picking each day. The farmer suggested a place about a mile away—he would speak with the owner. How boring! There were strawberry fields about fifty miles away in East Anglia, around Spalding. My idea was to hitch the fifty miles each day from Glaston to Spalding, pick fruit, and hitch back again.

Each morning I set off about 4 a.m. and started throwing my thumb. Picked fruit in East Anglia, then left about four in the afternoon with the money earned that day and got back to the wagon around seven in the evening. I've often thought this trip could make an interesting mystery story.

I would arrive in Stamford at about six o'clock, pick up a newspaper and cigarettes, then hitch on. After a week the newsagent saw me as a regular and would have sworn blind that I lived and worked in the environs of Stamford—I couldn't possibly have committed a murder in either Glaston or Spalding!

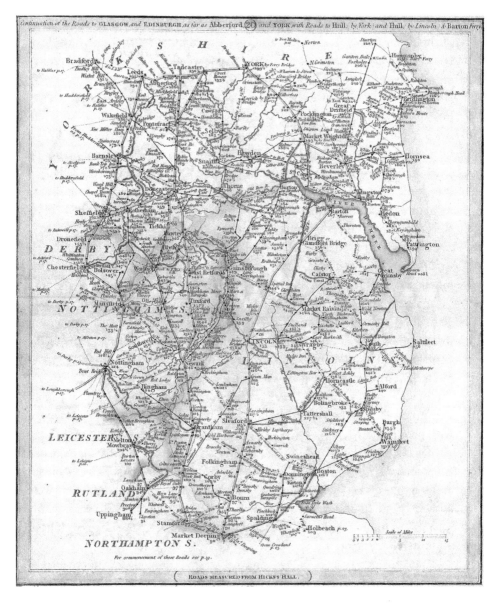

Market Deeping road to Leeds and York, published 1815.

Leaving Stamford I would hitch on to Market Deeping, getting there around eight o'clock. Market Deeping was a lovely racing village. I waited there to watch Vergette's string of racehorses walk down the village street.

The jockeys used to wave to me and call out the name of a likely winner. They would have sworn I lived somewhere around Market Deeping. As for my fellow fruit-picaroons in Spalding, I was always waiting in the Square ready to jump on the truck with them and ride out to Glenny's fruit fields, returning with them about three in the afternoon. I *had* to live somewhere near to Spalding.

So that summer, Jim and I lived on strawberries and cream and other goodies bought from the proceeds of the picking fields. I loved the atmosphere and camaraderie out in the fruit farmlands and was truly sorry when the season finished. But Jim had also finished the writing job for radio and it was time to go further south.

A lucky tow with a passing gipsy put us several miles into a wild, deserted place, covered with bull-dozers and heaps of dirt, with deep holes in the ground, with names like Greenfields Road and Gipsy Lane stuck up on signposts in the middle of nothing. The best was in the centre of a leveled space, a circle of three hundred yards diameter, consisting of dirty yellow clay. That sign said 'Bus Stop.' It was Corby New Town—but not yet. We left there as soon as possible to the district known as 'The Spire' among tramps and gipsies, and all road folk. The spire is the church at Hanslope, but the name covers a wide stretch of country, between Northampton and Wolverton. The people there, for generations, have always been known to the road-going population as the friendliest in the world.

We pitched at the rear of the Rogue and Crown pub in Yardley Hastings, a small village in the middle of the Spire. Tramp marks abounded in the village. We had good luck with selling a few short stories, so we went into the pub for a few drinks. On occasions like this, inspiration always struck.

When we got back into the wagon, Jim had a brilliant idea. We decided to hitch-hike to Trieste! I wasn't sure that I knew where it was... ଔ

Trieste Trip

have no clear idea why we decided to go to Trieste. Certainly not for any specific purpose, except that it happened to be at the top of the Adriatic and we had often thought of hitch-hiking there.

We thought we might like to visit Central Europe. There were still problems, subsequent to the war, about getting visas. But Trieste, being adjacent to Yugoslavia, seemed like a good jumping-off place. We could not state what country Trieste was in, because no one knew at that time. It had in fact four governments: English, Russian, Italian, and American. But bureaucracy was satisfied and so were we, and we got the necessary clearance papers. How wonderful it must have been when a person could just go down the docks and get on a ship and go wherever it was going.

For anyone living on the road, form-filling about where you are coming from and whither bound is just meaningless mumbo-jumbo. Generally speaking, I do know where I am coming from, but as to where I am going? If I knew that, I would have to turn round and go in the opposite direction.

One morning we left Yardley Hastings in Northants, Trieste-bound. We did not get there as quickly as we expected. As usual, we stopped off in Paris for a while in our customary Hotel L'Esperance in Rue Vavin.

One night we were making our way back there on the Metro, when a fight broke out as we got off the train. We found ourselves in the middle of a gang bashing one another, when suddenly they started in on us. We gave back!! Then one little man screamed for the police. About a dozen cops appeared from nowhere. Several respectable Parisians screamed that we had walked on to the platform and assaulted the harmless little monsieur. Then had kicked him, gouged him, spat on the French flag, etc. etc. We were still listening to the etceteras when the cops slung us in the Black Maria[65].

We said nothing at all and were presently brought in to the gendarmerie of Saint Sulpice.

We were lined up in front of the inspector's desk and the little innocent man told the story of his innocence again. It didn't sound so good that time, especially as the several respectable witnesses who had egged him on had somehow faded away.

By the time the cynical and very curt gendarme had rapped out a few questions, the little man began to stammer a bit and demand his legal rights and police protection and so on.

Halfway through the repetition of his wrongs, the inspector crumpled up the sheet of paper listing the myriad charges and threw away the charge sheet. There was a general laugh from the roomful of gendarmes and the situation eased.

But as the little man *had* made a definite charge against Jim—grievous bodily harm—Jim was theoretically locked up, although he stayed there gossiping with the cops. The little man went away, to return the following morning if he still wished to press the charge.

It was arranged that I go to the Rue Vavin and bring our hotelier to bail Jim out. All was going nicely and I was sure bail would not be required and that Jim was going to walk out of the gendarmerie presently and everything would be forgotten.

Then suddenly the guardroom door opened and another gendarme came in. He looked like the most villainous person, and Jim was immediately reminded of Robert Browning's poem "Fra Lippo Lippi."

In the poem, Fra Lippo Lippi has climbed over the monastery wall one night and has gone off round the taverns for a night out. Then, on his way back, the watchmen caught him trying to get over the wall again into the monastery and he was fetched to the guardroom.

Not that it mattered; Lippo knew the police, and was standing there, joking with them, when the guardroom door opened and a villainous-looking guard came in. Fra Lippo turned to the captain of the watch.

---

65 British slang for a vehicle that transports prisoners.

"He's Judas to the life," Lippo says and demands a crayon or a piece of chalk to sketch the man. We were in a similar situation when the French flic came in. Jim turned to me; "He's Judas to the life," he quoted.

Unfortunately, the gendarme understood English but had *not* read Browning. He was only about five feet high, but he kicked Jim under the chin and nearly knocked his head off. Jim grabbed him by the throat. That was the end of the "Entente Cordiale" and l'amitié and the joking.

Six or seven of the cops clubbed him, kicked him and slung him in a cell. A police doctor examined him. Eventually it transpired that Jim had fallen down, twice, on the Metro platform, before beating up the little innocent man. The police had had to fetch us to the gendarmerie for our own good so that we could rest for a while.

We were then free to leave if I would pay the nine-hundred-and-sixty-franc expenses, and sign a statement that Jim's injuries were accidentally acquired.

Somehow I felt we were lucky. I paid and signed, happily. A taxi got us to the Rue Vavin. There was a wonderful doctor, Dr. Worsier, a Swiss, who had been a medical officer of the Paris resistance during the war, living opposite our hotel and who came to administer whatever was necessary.

It was a wonderful mixture of ancient and modern medicine. On the one hand, a nurse came with a strange iron contraption, metal cups, and a flaming gas jet and 'cupped him for pleurisy.' Shades of Charles Dickens. Dr. Worsier gave him the newest thing in modern medicine which had hardly been heard of in England: penicillin tablets called Terramycin.

So we hovered around in Paris for a month spending most of our money, waiting for Jim to be fit to travel. Then one day we were all set to go again and were back at Fontainebleau roundabout hitching towards Italy via Dijon and Lyon and eventually Milan.

In Milan we stayed in a little pensione, and in the restaurant met a Venetian who gave us addresses of people to see when we should eventually reach Venice. The most important one was that of the owner of a lovely café, Tre Rosé, just off San Marco Square. In those days there were few tourists and strolling around in an almost deserted square was sheer heaven. Venice is the only place I know that looks even better in reality than it does on a picture postcard.

The owner of Tre Rosé was a fat, smiling, benign-looking man rather like an Irish bookmaker or a Tammany Hall politician. He provided a wonderful meal and gave us an address nearby where we could stay for a week or two. It was in fact the headquarters of the gondoliers' syndicate, so we had free transport up and down the canals. Our own fleet of taxis! Somehow we had fallen on our feet again.

Venice remains a dream place for me, a dream place of brilliant colours and good food and good wine and tolling belfries and musical street calls. And canals and gondolas.

Even a small boy calling to another makes the language sound like a snatch of grand opera when he calls from a canal alley, "Lorr-ren-zeen-no. Lorr-ren-zeen-no."

After a few days, we made our way to Mestre. We knew we were only about fifty miles from Trieste. We waited for hours on the side of the road. Not one vehicle passed in either direction. I went back to check the signpost and then we started walking. Almost immediately a car showed up and stopped. Two Italian cops got out. They asked questions very politely. Then they asked questions, still more politely.

It is better not to lose one's temper. But it was rather trying after saying forty or fifty times that we had no particular business in Trieste. When the official then asked brightly, why, in that case *were* we going to... then we surrendered. I said, rather feebly, that we weren't really particular and that Venice would probably be just as interesting. The cops immediately agreed, so they watched us turn back for Venice.

Somewhat later we left Venice again, for Trieste. But this time we went on a train. It seemed preferable to dying of hunger by the side of the road while answering millions of questions.

The train journey along the top of the Adriatic was breathtaking, the scenery was so magnificent. Occasionally there were glimpses of a vast mountain range ahead. Sometimes, a big smoky seaport was visible, which might have been Par Cathay but was probably Trieste.

The conductor of the train came along to chat with us. Then the Customs and Passport men came along and the conductor went away. The passport men went too—and took all our papers with them. (I always find that a bit scary—I just know I'm never going to get them back.)

The conductor came back to gossip again. We asked him why they had taken away our papers. With a perfectly straight face, he said they were probably copying our signatures in case we had to sign a confession of murder later. We'd never committed a murder, had we? he asked facetiously.

He had a set of very cheap false teeth. They looked like tin. Also, he wore an enormous brass tie pin, and several imitation gold rings on his fingers. Apart from these decorations he had a large cheap wristwatch on one wrist and a huge brass bracelet on the other. There was a kind of lunatic gaudiness about him.

The train arrived at Trieste station and as we made for the door to get out, our passports came in, with the train conductor. He handed them over, smiled and waved goodbye, saying he hoped to see us again.

Trieste was a curious city. It was a kind of buffer state, half Italian, half Yugoslavian. Looking back I think it must have been mostly inhabited by spies. Nobody seemed to be what they said they were or doing what they said they did. There was a theatrical air to it. Any minute there was going to be a flourish of trumpets and a rhythmic drum-tapping and the beginnings of a military march and then the Puritarian lifeguards would parade on stage to the strains of "Yankee Doodle" or "The Red Flag," singing, "small profits and quick returns" or some other of the great slogans for which good men live. And die, of course. Trieste might look like the setting for a play, but the play would eventually be a bloody tragedy.

We had difficulty finding a room. Here were two people who had no story to account for their movements, with no genuine documents to prove that they were a legitimate business, who had nothing to sell and wanted nothing to buy, who were not going anywhere, nor doing anything. Eventually we found one. The owner of the place was Russian. He had several stock sentences, in each language. He turned on his smile, spoke the sentence, turned off his smile, and waited. Just like a mechanical toy.

There were some streets which had notices in large block letters on billboards like 'OUT OF BOUNDS TO U.S. PERSONNEL.' Or an inscription in Russian, presumably saying the same thing. 'NOT ADVISED FOR BRITISH TROOPS' or 'ITALIANS KEEP OUT.'

Naturally, as we did not belong to any of these categories we entered this enclave. We found a bistro and ordered a drink. The owner spoke in Italian—with a Lancashire accent! Jim asked him if he came from Bolton. He was presumably 'one of our men in Trieste.' It must have been devastating to have his cover blown by a couple of tourists after only a couple of sentences.

One night we went to the opera, held in the Roman amphitheater. I like to think that some of the Roman legionaries who had been stationed there might also at some time have seen service along Hadrian's Wall. It had been the headquarters of the same legion.

Presently we decided that it was time to drift back to the U.K. The same conductor was on the train. His false teeth were real gold now. His wristwatch was gold. The heavy tie pin was gold as were the bracelet and rings. Three trips a week he made—even allowing for rake-offs. Not bad!

So back to Yardley Hastings and the wagon in the Spire. Trieste was swiftly a dream, gone into the mists of memory, where it has remained. Except for the entry in my passport, I would never believe I had been there. ⌑

Roaming at Random II

After getting back to Hastings from Trieste we decided to make for Oxford. We found a farm outside of the city, at Headington. En route there we lost a hubcap from one of the wheels of the wagon. The caravan had patent wheel caps, little brass oil boxes screwed on which kept the axle permanently lubricated. We went to an engineering firm in the city to see if they could make one for us.

No one at the firm had the faintest idea of how to do it. But they had a forge. Jim, ever adaptable, asked if he could use it, and made the hubcap himself. Crowds gathered to watch this feat of engineering.

The place was quite near to Oxford University Press. We were owed some money by the firm for a couple of articles Jim had written. So with the new

The Bear Inn, Oxford

hubcap fixed, we drove the wagon around and up the high street and stopped outside of the entrance. Jim went in and collected the money over the counter. Nobody could say we didn't do things in style.

We had a happy stay at Headington. With Oxford only four miles away and lots of interesting people in the city, it was a fun time. Dan Davin was a director at Clarendon Press, and he and his wife Winnie became great friends of ours. Most nights we spent in the pubs. The Bear Inn[66], run by Alan Course, who was the cartoonist on the *Oxford Mail*; the Lamb and Flag where Louis MacNeice[67] and Bertie Rogers[68] were frequent visitors; and the Eagle and Child where C.S. Lewis and Tolkien held court.

We moved on down the Thames valley to Wallingford. *Tramping the Toby* was published while we were there. It was a time when we always seemed to have

---

66 The Bear Inn is one of the oldest pubs in Oxford, England, dating back to 1242. Its circa-seventeenth-century incarnation stands on the corner of Alfred Street and Blue Boar Street, opposite Bear Lane in the center of Oxford, just north of Christ Church.

   The earliest mention of the lands and buildings subsequently occupied by The Bear Inn are found in the Cartularies of St Frideswide. Christina Pady, who was part of the ruling group of burgess families in Oxford at this time, is recorded as having inherited these properties from her late husband, Laurence Kepeharme, the first Mayor of Oxford (died circa 1209), and from her uncle, John Pady.

   The main text states that the inn came, under the name of The Bear Inne, into the possession of brothers Richard and Roger Taverner following the dissolution of St Frideswide's Priory. Richard Edes, later Dean of Worcester, records the proprietor of The Bear in 1583 as a Matthew Harrison, who had a pet bear named Furze.

   The present building was built in the early seventeenth century as the residence of the coaching inn's ostler. It was converted into a separate tavern, The Jolly Trooper, in 1774. The Bear Inn's premises at the High Street was rebuilt and converted into private housing in 1801 and its business name transferred to the former Jolly Trooper.

67 **Frederick Louis MacNeice** (September 12, 1907 – September 3, 1963) was an Irish poet and playwright from Northern Ireland, and a member of the Auden Group, which also included W.H. Auden, Stephen Spender and Cecil Day-Lewis. MacNeice's body of work was widely appreciated by the public during his lifetime, due in part to his relaxed but socially and emotionally aware style. Never as overtly or simplistically political as some of his contemporaries, he expressed a humane opposition to totalitarianism as well as an acute awareness of his roots.

68 **William Robert Rodgers** (1909 – 1969), known as Bertie, and born in Belfast, Northern Ireland, was probably best known as a poet, but was also a prose essayist, a book reviewer, a radio broadcaster and script writer, a lecturer and, latterly, a teacher, as well as a former Presbyterian minister.

lots of money, so we were never far from a racecourse. We went to Cheltenham for the whole of the jumps festival. We had lots of luck with the horses and made lots of money. We backed the winner of the Gold Cup, Gay Donald, at fifty to one! Happy, happy days.

When the jumps season finished we followed the flat. We drifted down through the Berkshire villages of Theale and Thatcham just outside of Newbury. Thatcham, now commuter country, was a pretty sleepy village. We had the caravan on the grounds of a big house owned by Colonel Neville, a keen race follower. We all went to the Grand National and had another good winner, Quare Times.

From Thatcham the wagon wound down the lanes to Kingsclere, to the estate of Gilbert Way. This was the first person I knew to own his own helicopter; I don't suppose there were too many around at that time. A couple of miles away were the racing stables of Peter Hastings Pass. In the early hours of the morning, we went up there to watch the horses go out to exercise.

This was *Watership Down* country. And there really were hundreds of rabbits. Each morning there were dozens of them playing around the caravan. I loved to steal quietly up to a nearby warren at sun-up and see all those rabbits playing in the dew. One stamp of my foot on the ground and every single rabbit would freeze-frame, then with a lift of their little white butts, they would dash to the warren and dive down into the rabbit holes. In a couple of minutes they would all be out and back nibbling again. Miraculous. They must have driven the farmers wild.

After the myxomatosis syndrome that became a rarer and rarer sight. But it's coming back. As I sit writing this I can look out through my window and see several playing on the edge of "my" wood. But I'm not telling anyone where that is.

One day at Newbury races we met a jockey, Peter Bristowe. He was recovering from a broken leg and he spent the afternoon with us. He promised to send us the name of a fancied horse whenever he knew there was something good. It was customary with someone like Peter not to give him money for the 'info'—but when the 'tip' ran to put a few pounds on the horse for him, then send him his winnings.

He sent us the name of a horse, Torrid Zone. From the morning papers it certainly looked like no winner, not even likely to get over the fences. But we backed it and put something on for Peter. It won at ten to one. I have never forgotten the feeling I had when I heard the result. It was like magic. This name coming from nowhere and producing manna from heaven. Money from winning on the horses is always magic money as far as I am concerned. As a lifelong gambler, I have never lost the wonder of it. For a while we had lots of luck via Peter. Tragically, however, the source of good fortune dried up. Peter, ever a mad driver, took one bend too sharply one night, crashed his car and was killed. Such a waste of such a lovely guy and a delightful friend.

It was a hot dry summer that year as we wound our way through the lanes south of Basingstoke, then a quiet sleepy town, unrecognisable today. We stayed for a while on a farm a couple of miles outside of the town. This was Hatch Warren, owned by Rex Patterson. Rex was a farmer and an inventor of agricultural implements—he invented the Patterson buckrake. He also wrote articles on farming for the *Sunday Times*. Before the farming, he had been a lorry driver a short while with Ryan Price who went on to become one of the most famous of horse-trainers.

Rex owned several farms in the lovely area in North Hampshire called the Candovers. Preston Candover and Brown Candover lead down eventually to Alresford and Alton.

It was while we were there that we began a long acquaintance with Frankie Durr, who became a well-known jockey. One day we were bus-hitching to Salisbury racecourse and Frankie stopped to give us a lift. He also gave us three winners. Of course he didn't know that. We decided to back him in all of his races. He had the three winners. At that time he was at Arundel riding for John Dunlop's[69] stable. Dunlop trained for the Duke of Norfolk and had some beautiful horses. The Dunlop dynasty still goes on, still producing winners!

We spent all summer drifting through the Candovers stopping off at each of Rex's farms. The weather was glorious. Jim was telling many of his stories on radio and TV and used to rehearse them in the field. It was very funny, as there was a large herd of cows in the pasture and Jim would walk down to where they were grazing, waving the script as he went. The cows would come and gather round him and he would tell them the story. They never moved an inch until he had finished, just standing there staring at him. When he came to the end and stopped they would let out a chorus of mooing.

---

69 **John Leeper Dunlop** (July 10, 1939 – July 7, 2018) was an English race horse trainer based in Arundel, Sussex. He trained the winners of seventy-four Group One races, including ten British Classics, with over 3,000 winners in total. He played a pivotal role in the establishment of Middle Eastern influences in British horseracing, training Hatta, Sheikh Mohammed's first winner as an owner at Brighton in 1977.

By September we were just outside of Alton, at Chawton. It was hops-picking time, so it was a great Romany festival. Alton was like a scene from a Western movie the afternoon that the gipsies arrived for the picking. A huge policeman was on duty in the middle of the town. His job was to get the Romany caravans to their various pitches before darkness fell.

"Where for?" he called out as a picturesque caravan with a high-stepping piebald horse came along the main street. The gipsy called the name of the farm and the cop promptly waved him into the caravan line for that particular farm.

Meanwhile, the motorists from east, west, and centre cluttered up the streets all around Alton waiting and hoping for the best turn away to take a by-road. It was a Romany concourse! Most of the pubs had signs in the windows saying: 'NO TRAVELLERS SERVED'!!

Happily, over the years, one or two of the gipsy families had gone into the pub trade. So, as the Romanies would say, 'The gav was kushti!'—meaning those pubs would welcome the travellers. In those pubs the evenings were wild.

We were not far from Selborne, where the naturalist Gilbert White[70] had lived. Some friends, Bill[71] and Kitty Gaunt, were the curators of the house. We took them along to meet our gipsy friends who were most impressed. Bill drew sketches of them and handed them around. Bill was a well-known art critic and a fine artist. From Alton we moved to the Meon Valley, never going far each day, never staying long anywhere, except at East Meon, a little village tucked under the Hampshire Downs. Winter had arrived suddenly and there was a hard black frost for many weeks. Not a single race meeting was held during

70 **Gilbert White** (July 18, 1720 – June 26, 1793) was a "parson-naturalist," a pioneering English naturalist, ecologist and ornithologist. He is best known for his *Natural History and Antiquities of Selborne*. White is regarded by many as England's first ecologist, and one of those who shaped the modern attitude of respect for nature. White's influence on artists is celebrated in the exhibition *Drawn to Nature: Gilbert White and the Artists*. The OED gives White credit for first having used 'x' to represent a kiss in a letter written in 1763.

71 **William Gaunt** (1900 – 1980) was a British artist and art historian, best known for his books on British nineteenth-century art. Gaunt was fascinated by the Pre-Raphaelites, at that time undervalued as Victorian. He published in 1942 his most enduring title on that subject, *The Pre-Raphaelite Tragedy*. He completed an M.A. in 1926. In 1930 he published a collection of his drawings, called *London Promenade*. 1935 he married "Kitty" Mary Catherine Reilly Connolly (died 1980). The years 1930–39 were spent writing various literary and artistic criticism, including *The Pre-Raphaelite Tragedy*. The Gaunts lived in a country cottage near the Surrey Hampshire borders.

the whole of February because of the hard ground. But the radio and TV work was still in demand so we were kept busy.

We left East Meon at the first hint of spring and soon we were at the Sussex border, outside of Petersfield. We stayed in the orchard of a manor house. The owner, Admiral Bonham Carter[72], had lots of good liquor and each day we went up to the house for a lunchtime aperitif and listened to his tales of the Navy. Another enjoyment of drinking there was not just that he was a wonderful host, nor that the liquor was excellent, but the drinks were served in his library where Gibbon was reputed to have written part of his *Decline and Fall.*

The racing took over again and we went to lots of race-meetings. So many racecourses were near to hand. This was the year that Devon Loch did *not* win the Grand National. The class society produces some strange behavior. Lots of people did not mind losing their money because it was the Queen Mother's horse!

There was a beautiful old Tudor café in the middle of the main street in Petersfield, where all the upmarket people went for coffee. The woman who owned the place asked me which horse I had backed. So I told her Must which was quite a fancied runner. Her lip curled disdainfully as she said, "Of course all of my regular customers backed the Queen Mother's horse. *Must!* Why, every little corner-boy backed that horse!" I loved it!

We kept moving through Sussex, Midhurst and Petworth, Billingshurst, and Fittleworth. The A272 road wound its way through these places. Some of the prettiest east-west roads in the country at that time, and one of my favourite roads through beautiful, beautiful Sussex. Quiet lush meadows, bluebell woods, and nightingales. The quiet part of the county, of which Belloc[73] and Chesterton[74] wrote so well. Searching for the place of mythical Roundabout, of Chesterton's poem.

---

72 **Rear Admiral Sir Christopher Douglas Bonham-Carter** (November 3, 1907 – June 3, 1975) was a Royal Navy officer and Treasurer to the Duke of Edinburgh from 1959 to 1970. He is a great-uncle to actress Helena Bonham Carter.

73 **Joseph Hilaire Pierre René Belloc** (July 27, 1870 – July 16, 1953) was a British-French writer and historian and one of the most prolific writers in England during the early twentieth century. Belloc was also an orator, poet, sailor, satirist, writer of letters, soldier, and political activist. He was a noted disputant, with a number of long-running feuds. His widely sold *Cautionary Tales for Children* included "Jim, who ran away from his nurse, and was eaten by a lion" and "Matilda, who told lies and was burned to death."

74 **Gilbert Keith Chesterton** (May 29, 1874 – June 14, 1936) was an English writer, philosopher, lay theologian, and literary and art critic. He has been referred to as the "prince of paradox." *Time* magazine observed of his writing style:

To find the town of Roundabout
The pleasant town of Roundabout
That makes the world go round.

Fortunately, Chesterton died before the M1, M2, MXYZ were built. Although he would doubtless have written an excellent poem about them too.

We moved to Bolney. A pretty little place only a hundred yards from the London-Brighton Way. We were hidden in a paddock with a couple of race-horses. At Bolney, it was still the fourteenth century.

The paddock was owned by Josh Fearly. A former racehorse trainer, his house was filled with all kinds of racing memorabilia. There were several beautiful statuettes of horses, which he had won as prizes for certain big races. It was a miniature museum.

One day, hitching down the Brighton road from London, a man gave us a lift who said he had a cottage in the Sussex woods, not far from Brighton. We were welcome to take our caravan over and winter there in his large orchard. We went the next day.

His "cottage in the woods" was a large house with lots of parkland near Hurstpierpoint. The man was Cornish, Bill Penhaligon. His wife, Jean Mickle-burgh, had been a well-known actress. She came from Bristol. Her father had been a pianist and started life as a piano-tuner and ended up founding the huge music store which used to dominate the centre of the city.

This was a lovely wintering place for us. Bill and Jim got on famously as did Jean and I. Although we were sleeping in the caravan we spent a lot of time up at the house, especially at weekends. Bill and Jean loved entertaining, so weekends were party time. They had two young children, Susan and Michael. Susan had great ambitions at seven years old to be an actress, and as her 'party piece' every night sang "There's No Business Like Show Business." Knowing what you want out of life and going straight for it requires a lot of dedication.

Years later, I was walking along the Strand one evening and there was the name Susan Penhaligon[75], up in lights. She was playing the lead in a Tom

---

"Whenever possible Chesterton made his points with popular sayings, proverbs, allegories—first carefully turning them inside out."

75 **Susan Penhaligon** (July 3, 1949) is a British actress and writer. She is known for her role in the drama series *Bouquet of Barbed Wire* (1976), and for playing Helen Barker in the sitcom *A Fine Romance* (1981–84). She also appeared in the soap opera *Emmerdale* (2006). Her film appearances include *No Sex Please, We're British* (1973) and Paul Verhoeven's *Soldier of Orange* (1977).

Stoppard play. I love it when someone realises their childhood fantasies. A rare occurrence.

When winter ended we moved away from Hurstpierpoint to a farm on the outskirts of Brighton. The address was 'The Field.' Very apt. One day we hitched up the Brighton road to London. A car stopped, the driver was going there. A little farther up the road, we passed a crossroads where some children were playing. After about twenty miles the driver stopped the car and, apologising, said he had forgotten a call he had to make and if we would continue along the road and hadn't got a lift by the time he came along again he would pick us up. We got a lift to the outskirts of Croydon and sure enough, after a little while along came our original driver. After a lot of talking he suddenly said to Jim, "You seem to be a very understanding person, I wonder if you could help me with a problem. Actually I didn't have a call to make when I turned back. I just had to go back to that crossroads where those kids were playing—and expose myself to them."

I was astounded—he looked like such a normal man! I can't remember what advice Jim gave to him. I do know that we had one or two copies of *Tramping the Toby* with us, which we were trying to sell. Jim was *sure* it would be of help to him—so the man bought one. When I reprimanded Jim later, he said, "Oh no, it was too late to do anything about the kids—but I had to make him pay somehow!"

During the winter Jim had written and sold a book of crime stories called *Fetters for Twenty*, so with the arrival of spring, it was back to the races. As we were pitched near to the London-Brighton road we were within easy distance of so many racetracks: Kempton Park, Sandown Hurst Park, Epsom, Ascot, Newbury—to name but a few. We scarcely missed a race meeting. We got to be as well known as the signposts on the Brighton road. All the Southdown coach drivers knew us and stopped to give us lifts to wherever we might be hitching. We spent the summer travelling through Sussex. Steyning and Storrington, Ashington and Washington.

We pulled in at Walker's farm just below Chanctonbury Ring. Chanctonbury is a famous place, a hill that might have been a holy place back in the Stone Age—perhaps before Stonehenge was built. The hill is crowned with a large circle of trees and is a beacon for miles around. Unfortunately, it is a bit misshapen now, as during a terrible storm a few years ago a lot of the Chanctonbury trees were uprooted.

While at the farm below Chanctonbury, a number of wagons pulled in and set up a fairground. All kinds of sideshows and roundabouts and swings. This was a family fair owned by the Harris family. The Harrises were known in every town and village in Sussex and beyond, having travelled the Sussex roads and set up a fair for generations. They were thrilled to have our gipsy wagon incorporated into their outfit and invited us to travel Sussex with them throughout the summer. So for a while we became fairground folk—a continuation from when we had travelled with the Pinder's Circus from Marseilles to Nice. When I was a child I used to run away to fairgrounds. There was a booth I always headed for. A table marked out with squares, with a groove down which you rolled a penny (my gambling fever started at a very early age!) If you managed to get the penny to settle in one of the squares clear of any of the lines you got your penny back plus another one.

Once I had a lift with a man who described himself as an amusement caterer. Plugging all the sideshow stuff to fairground managers and the like. He showed me some advertisements for the things he sold. They were all telling how difficult it was to win—'COMES UP ONE TIME IN 500' and so on. A sobering thought. The other side of the coin. There was a booth in the Harrises' fairground for winning the pennies—so full circle. I was allowed to be in charge of the 'penny-lark.' I enjoyed surreptitiously edging a kid's pennies onto the squares so that they won one. Perhaps I turned on a generation of gamblers. Happy thought.

After leaving Sussex we started off across into Hampshire. Jim was to take part in a radio series with Rene Cutforth[76], called *Tinker, Tailor*. It was to be made at Romsey, so we had to get the caravan moved over there.

We had a curious tow. We met a man who owned a fleet of road maintenance gear. It was a well-known firm, Hills of Botley, near Southampton. So we got the wagon ready for Hills' tow. When the vehicle arrived it was a piece of machinery as big as a block of flats! We crawled along the road at about ten miles an hour—ideal for us, as the caravan had iron tires, but at the same time infuriating for the long line of drivers who had to follow us nose to tail for about twenty miles. On arrival at Romsey after such a tow, we realised that the days of the caravan and the way we travelled with it, either behind a vehicle or horse-drawn, were numbered. The wagon was not going to last forever, and the increase in cars and the widening of roads were making it more and more difficult. We would have to change it for a better one or a more modern one, or something!

---

76 **René Cutforth** (February 6, 1909 – April 1, 1984) was a British journalist, television and radio broadcaster and writer.

A chance meeting with Dudley Forwood[77], a large landowner at Barford Park near Salisbury, gave us a breathing space. He invited us to take the caravan to his place for a while. It seemed a good idea to go and winter there. It was to mark a turning point. ⌘

---

77 **Sir Dudley Richard Forwood, 3rd Baronet** (1912 – 2001) was sole equerry to the Duke of Windsor after his abdication in 1937 until the outbreak of war in 1939. Forwood first met the Duke, then Prince of Wales, in 1934 in Austria at the Grand Hotel, Kitzbuhel, where the Prince and Wallis Simpson were taking a skiing holiday.

Far from the Madding Crowd

Wood's huge farm, Barford Park, about six miles south of Salisbury. It was a great place to spend the winter. Dudley had a magnificent herd of pedigree Hereford cattle. He also had the river Avon flowing through the property. It was wonderful to see the herd plunge into the river and swim across from pasture to pasture, the cows carefully tucking their young calves to their upstream side so that the current wouldn't sweep them away. Dudley's wife Mary bred King Charles Spaniel dogs. She also had several beautiful Arabian horses, given her as a gift by King Ibn Saud. These beautiful silver-grey horses used to visit us at the caravan. It is all like a fairytale in my head—some other life, some other time.

While we were at Barford, Dudley bought the old house, Burley, in the middle of the New Forest, from Lady Lucas. The house was magnificent. True, it was in need of much repair, but the roofs and walls were intact, massive old fireplaces in all the rooms with the chimneys in working order, no water or electricity of course, but there was a well twenty foot deep. There were ancient sconces in all the rooms, the place could be lit by candlelight. The whole was surrounded by a large parkland, plus New Forest.

The demesne wall was broken down here and there, so the ponies and deer wandered freely through the grounds. It was much too isolated to have been vandalised. Three miles in one direction, a forest logging road led through Oakleigh plantation to Burley village.

There was a stony track which wandered across a moor bright with heather and gorse, for three miles the other way. Strings of the forest ponies ambled lazily, and herds of fallow deer grazed gently by day. At night, a nightjar called out from every bush.

The moorland track eventually emerged onto the A31 road, in the middle of nowhere, between Picket Post and Cadnam roundabout. It was actually the main London to Bournemouth road. At that time it was unfenced and the animals wandered about quite freely from one end of the forest to the other. At night you could hear the roar of speeding cars. The cops used to do their one-hundred-miles-an-hour speed practice because it was such a long, lonely straight stretch of road.

Dudley drove us over to show us the Old House. He intended to renovate the place in a couple of years or so. Meanwhile, if we wanted to have our wagon there and use the place, he would get his workmen to put the caravan on a low loader and drive it down the moorland track to install us. We could stay as long as we liked.

Without a thought for the practicalities we instantly agreed, and by the end of the week the wagon was on the lawn in front of the house. Dudley and the workmen drove off and we were truly on our own, far from the madding crowd.

Burley Manor and its deer.

It is not easy to describe the peace and loveliness of that lone glade in the heart of the forest. Sometimes I felt I knew every deer, badger, pony, fox, rabbit, woodpecker, and squirrel for miles. When winter came, one of the hardest for years, there was deep snow and ice everywhere. We were totally isolated.

A white world—the only bit of green was the patch underneath our caravan where the heat from the paraffin stove filtered down and melted the snow. Word must have gone out among the forest animals that there was green grass growing because the deer came trying to get at it when we were sleeping.

One day we managed to walk the three miles down through the woods to Burley village to contact the Foresters. They broke trail with a tractor, hauling up sacks of deer cake and bales of hay. For a few weeks, I fed the animals. They came from far and wide for breakfast!

What I liked, especially, was that when the spring came and the snow melted away, the mares who had been in foal came to visit us bringing their offspring to be admired. Even the fallow deer came through the broken fence morning and evening to show off their fawns.

We were adopted completely by the forest animals. There was one particular wild rabbit who used to come a mile down the moorland track every night to see us. He stayed nearby, grazing on the best of the grass, would lollop quietly away if I opened the wagon door, then steal back to halt by the wagon shafts. In the dawning, when the owls had mostly made for home, the young rabbit would set off up the track again. I knew where his warren was and I always hoped that the hawks and owls wouldn't get him before he was big enough to look out for himself.

People we met in Burley commiserated with us because of our lack of modern conveniences, but we had the last laugh. During the severe winter with everything frozen up, the locals had stories of burst pipes and no water; we smugly lowered a bucket into our twenty-foot-deep well and drew up as much water as we liked. Its electricity lines came down so low that people had little or no heating; we lit our large candles and made a beautiful log fire in one of the huge fireplaces in the old house and wallowed in the warmth, and played at being Lord and Lady of the Manor. Jim would sit down below composing a story while gazing into the flames. I—wearing a long dress, my hair flowing down to my waist, sat up in the gallery, playing my harp. So romantic.

Occasionally during the winter when there was a meet of the New Forest Buckhounds, horses and dogs would career across the parkland. Lord and Lady of the Manor indeed! King Louis and his lady love and his cohorts more like. Dudley was Master of the New Forest Buckhounds and traditionally the opening meet—in early November—was held on the lawn of the Old House. Our caravan was the centrepiece this year. Everything circled around us. Lots of excellent fruit cake and fine sherry was handed out. We feasted!

The caravan stayed in the Old House clearing for a couple of years or so. We saw it occasionally, coming back to it from the road after long spells of hitch-hiking, to check that it was okay and to live amongst the trees and animals for a while before setting off again. Each time that we returned the caravan was a little more the worse for wear; it was slowly deteriorating. We had no idea what we should do about it or without it. But the road solves everything.

One day we hitch-hiked to Dorset. A man gave us a lift and told us he had once been a publisher and knew Jim's books very well. Nowadays he owned a caravan site at Charmouth. He was sure his wife, who was Irish, would love to meet us, and would we go to lunch? This was Fred Pricknell and his wife Tara.

Tara was from Tipperary and owned Kiltinan Castle, near Clonmel. She had been brought up there, and her house at Charmouth was filled with paintings of the castle and photographs of Tara, as a young girl on horseback, at the Dublin horse shows.

She had been a show jumper; there were cabinets filled with the trophies she had won as the Irish champion. Now she owned a few horses which went racing over the jumps.

She adored Jim, not least because the I.R.A. had not burned down the family castle during "the troubles." When we told them about the gipsy wagon in the New Forest and that it was falling apart at the seams and that it would never get up across the moorland track again, the Bricknells promptly offered us one of the caravans from their site. We could stay there with it for a while and if we liked it, move off with it whenever we liked.

"Money? Payment? What nonsense! Think of it as a fair exchange for saving the family mansion all those years ago!"

So I began another of my weird peregrinations across the countryside akin to my trips to the strawberry fields in Lincolnshire.

It was roughly eighty miles from Charmouth to the New Forest, plus the three-mile walk each way across the moor. We needed to transfer our goods and chattels from the old wagon to the new. Jim had started working on a program for BBC Wales and had a deadline date. So he just *had* to stick to the typewriter.

For two weeks I was up every morning about 4 a.m. With a large empty suitcase I hit the road, hitching across to the forest. I walked down the track, loaded up the suitcase, then hitched back to Charmouth. The following morning I repeated the process. This went on day after day for about a fortnight.

At last I had the old wagon emptied of all that we wanted to keep. I have no idea now what precious scripts or letters were left behind—but quite a lot. That was all normal to us!

On the last trip, I threw a gallon of paraffin into the caravan and lit a match or two. In half an hour there was only a circle of ashes, with a couple of wagon axles, four wheel bands and a trailer bar lying in the dusk. The feeling of exhilaration as the whole thing went *whoosh* remains with me to this day. I have had a secret sympathy with arsonists ever since. Lucky I didn't start on the Forest as well! There was something truly awesome about the whole event.

I think that whatever changes there may be to that part of the Forest, the ghosts of the Old House and the gipsy caravan will still be hovering around there.

We stayed at Charmouth all through the summer. Well, the new caravan stayed there. We were everywhere else. Two gipsy programs, *Boney Bosivel* and the *Raggedy Rawnie,* produced by Cynthia Pughe[78], meant several trips to the London BBC. Wales got on the bandwagon and we were hitching back and forth to Swansea and Cardiff and Bangor. A BBC radio producer in Cardiff was anxious to do a series of vagabond programs with us. Six weeks for wandering up and down the lovely Welsh roads, plus a hefty fee at the end, was our idea of heaven. With a nice car—complete with one of those old huge recording vans following behind—we trundled the high roads and by-roads of Wales, setting up various venues to be used for the program. We started in Newport, South Wales, and ended in Bangor. It meant we travelled hither and over along the Usk Valley, the wild west coast, the mountains of Snowdonia, and Anglesey island.

After the series was finished we returned to the caravan in Charmouth and decided it was time to move on. We found a farm at Colyford near Axminster in Devon. Westward TV decided to make a series of small films of Jim to be shown throughout the autumn. We found a farm at Splatford where some of the sequences were shot; others were filmed around Shaldon and Newton Abbot.

We moved further down into Devon. We wanted to be near Totnes and Dartington where we knew so many people at the school. Quite by accident we found a most secret place called Hazard Kiln. We were walking along a narrow, leafy lane one morning, and suddenly there was a gap in the thick hedgerow—wide enough to let a caravan through, and then we were in what appeared to be an enormous cave open to the skies.

---

78 Note: Cynthia Pughe is a phantom haunting the history of the BBC. Little is known of her, or rather, there isn't much of an official or public biography— yet in searching the archives, she is singlehandedly responsible for adapting hundreds of plays and stories for radio broadcast during her long career.

Massive rocks towered around on all sides, and strangely the ground surface had been covered with tarmac as if it was to become a car park (the old kiln—hard ground). There were few cars anywhere, of course. The farmer who owned it let us pull in. It remains one of my favourite pitches. It was like being in a brigands' lair. The hedge parted as we went in, then closed again when we were through. No one suspected there was anything or anyone there.

A legend grew up that the place was haunted. The lane led nowhere, so no one ever walked that way. But people who walked along the Totnes road told stories of hearing distant music. At nighttime I used to sit on the steps of the wagon and play my harp. The rocks echoed the music so that there was a great resonant sound, like an organ. It could be heard all the way to the Totnes road, but no one knew where the sound came from. Hence the legend. I liked that! But soon it was back to Wales again with the caravan. The BBC had switched over to television and wanted Jim to make a documentary film about the road in Wales, similar to the series we had done with them for radio.

A farmer towed us up into mid-Wales and we based ourselves beside Raglan Castle near to the Brecon Beacons. Once again we had a wonderful few weeks touring the Welsh countryside courtesy of the BBC.

When the film was finished we decided to take the wagon back to Cornwall. Leaving Wales, we pulled in near to Hereford beside an ancient manor, a place like an old illustration from Thackeray. This was the home of Major Hereford, Sufton Court, Hordiford, Hereford of Herefordshire. A person with those kinds of credentials doesn't need a family tree.

While we were there, Sydney Box decided that he would like to publish a collection of Jim's underworld stories to be called *Men of the Underworld*, with a view also to making a film. Work kept pouring in. A string of small TV films for Newcastle studios—ditto for Glasgow. We were making lots of money. Sydney Box paid us well for the *Underworld* book. Our feet were getting itchy for the continent. We got someone to tow us to Allington in Cornwall and once there decided that Europe was a must.

1966
NOTE

AFTER A LIFETIME OF SMOKING, JIM DEVELOPED LUNG CANCER. He discharged himself from the hospital against medical advice and went to his son Seamus' West London home. He spent his remaining days confined to bed with Kathleen and Seamus by his side. Kathleen never wrote about these long months of Jim's illness. Her good friend, Grace Jackman, recalls an incident that Kathleen shared with her.

> "He said, 'Listen to me. Repeat after me: I, Kathleen Phelan.'
>
> "I wasn't going to get into anything like that. I just pretended I didn't understand him. I just messed about and asked him if he wanted a cup of tea or a bit of soup or a glass of whiskey.
>
> "He just looked at me and then he said 'Come over here.' I went. He pulled himself up and headbutted me! The guy was dying and he did that; and I respected him for it."
>
> Kath emphasised respected with a hand bunched fingers to thumb and pushed briefly through the air for emphasis.
>
> "I wouldn't say the words. I wasn't getting into any of that but..." As Kath talked she would make a characteristic shake of the head for emphasis, almost as though she were shaking her hair back, a shake of the head in wonderment at the guy's willpower.
>
> Kath never did say what sort of promise he may have been intending to extract. Really I don't think she cared. She'd make no promise to the dying, no matter how dear they were. She was going to be free—that's the gypsy way—one dies, the belongings are burnt and the one that is left moves on.
>
> She loved him and revered his work but she would never enslave herself.

FROM ENGLAND TO THE HIMALAYAS

WHEN JIM DIED, I WALKED OUT OF LONDON, AND FOR TWO WEEKS, I hitched blindly all over England. It was November, so the weather must have been pretty bad. I have no recollection of where I went, or where I stayed, or much of what I did.

Philosophy

Life's like a poker game
Some get a bad hand
Some have the aces
Secure from the start.
More curse the dealer

And play with a mad hand
Our kind are glad
We're allowed to take part.

Win we, or lose,
We receive but one sole break
All cards bring gain
If you play them aright.
Only the non-player
Loses the whole stake
So up and get moving
It's burning daylight.

One day I hitched a car, and the motorist had given Jim and myself a lift some years previously. I cannot remember what I told him, fact or fiction. I had a little tramp book about the road which Jim and I had written together, and which I was selling. I know he bought one and gave me much more money than I asked for. But that is all.

I had no time to worry about Jim having died. On the road, whatever happens, one still has to cope with the everyday problems of survival. My sense of survival has always come first. Rule one: Stay alive.

My main preoccupation was reshaping my 'line of guff.' I needed a new story, and I'd better write it quickly. It would have been bizarre reading if any of the motorists who gave me lifts during that time had put my "tales" side-by-side as each received it.

Sometimes I said I had been recently widowed, not too recently, of course— I did have the sense not to say that my husband had died the day before! Sometimes I said he had passed a long time ago. There were further variations, either I had never been married at all, or I had just left him somewhere else and happened to be hitching alone that day. Somewhere out of the barrage of questions, I must have managed to formulate a reasonably plausible tale, because I survived without being charged with vagrancy or being committed to a lunatic asylum.

Then one day, I hitched a car travelling south out of Bristol. Somewhere along the road, in a field, I saw a small caravan. I suddenly remembered that was where I lived. I got the driver to drop me off and went into the field.

Some weeks before Jim was ill, we had borrowed the caravan so that he could finish a book he was writing. This was customary ever since we had given up the horse-drawn wagon. Some friends had lent us their trailer whenever it was time for Jim to write a book. So, I was put down at my own doorstep as it were.

I went inside the caravan and took out everything except my own clothes, some letters, and scripts. Then I made a bonfire in the corner of the field and burnt the lot. I telephoned some friends who were relieved to know where I had surfaced, and they sent me some money.

Then I hired a man with a Land Rover and got him to drive me and the trailer to a remote part of England near Glastonbury, which I hardly knew. A friendly farmer let me park the wagon in the corner of the stack-yard, a snug place for the wintertime. I paid off my driver—or more correctly, did not pay off the driver, as he refused to take the money; and I settled in.

Everything that had gone before was a distant dream. In typical tramp fashion, I had hurried away to the next place.

I started to reorganise my life. First, there was work to be done. The page proofs of *Nine Murderers and Me*, a book which Dents were bringing out, had to be corrected. The final script of another book, *Meet the Criminal Class*—already sold and the money spent—had to be typed and sent off to the publishers.

I had to work fast. Apart from the fact that both books were overdue, I was determined to leave England for anywhere. There was no time to sit around moaning.

Working on the books for four or five hours in the mornings and spending the afternoons in the betting shop "playing the horses" (my balm for all sickness), I managed to achieve a trance-like existence for a couple of months. At last, the books were ready and off to the publishers, and I was prepared to go the road out of England. When I told friends about my plans, they helped me by giving me some money, and I went to London for a few days.

My road life was going to be different, that was for sure. The first difficulty was that I had a few commitments in future dealings with Jim's publishers, which meant carrying weighty scripts along the road. Also, I was not sure what my new role was going to be.

Hitherto I had been a vagabond, certainly. But I had also been the vagabond-girl of that famous tramp author, Jim Phelan. Ever since we had married, I had used my own name, Kathleen Newton. It had always been a rather shameful thing that I had married even if it was only to "keep the papers tidy" for the bureaucrats during our moving around—especially under wartime and postwar restrictions.

But I had never told anyone I was married. Now I promptly adopted my married name, Kathleen Phelan. I was working on the adaptation of my new line of guff. Whatever my new identity was going to be, I knew that I would have to carry those scripts along the road. I was painting a lot too. There were my easel and oil paints. If I was planning to walk around the Mediterranean and leave England in January, I would need heavier clothes; Northern Europe can be very chilly until April. I had no idea how I was going to carry all the gear. I was the young mug of all young mugs—after all my years on the road! Then one day in Chelsea, London, I looked in a shop-window and saw my solution. It was the centrepiece of a display—a basket on wheels. Not just an ordinary basket on wheels, like one of those little supermarket push-carts—this was the basket to end all baskets. It was enormous.

Roughly the size of a wine barrel, it was about four feet high with two good-sized rubber tires and a long walking stick handle. I did not hesitate for a second.

I walked inside and bought it. In ten minutes, I was out on the sidewalk pushing it through Chelsea to where my friends lived.

Looking back, I must have been quite insane. The bigger the pack, the more you can find to put in it. With my easel tied to the walking stick handle, my scripts, books, clothes, sleeping bag, and even a small tent in the basket, I staggered out from my friends' house. Pushing the basket in the direction of Victoria station where I was to board the boat train for France.

My friends stood outside their door, shouting, "Young mug, young mug!" as I marched down the street out of sight.

1967

FRANCE

IT WAS EARLY FEBRUARY OF 1967 WHEN I STARTED OUT. THE crossing to Dieppe was calm; there were only about twenty people on the boat. I travelled with a young student from Brighton, Jane Carter. She was returning to Paris, where she worked as an au pair. The first night in Dieppe was warm but wet, so I spent some of my precious francs and stayed in a cheap hotel. The weather was going to be a problem in northern France. I might have to sleep "in" rather than "out," and France was *very* expensive.

However, I consoled myself with the thought that I wouldn't have the problem for long—I had so little money I'd be broke in less than a week. That made me feel better—things would be back to normal—and Spain would be cheaper anyway, my lack of money would go further there, and in Morocco, I could live off the land all the time. And how had Morocco crept into the itinerary? I slept.

It was still raining as I left Dieppe the following morning. I got lifts a couple of times in small trucks but walked a good deal as well. In the early evening, I arrived in Rouen—a lovely old city—where the basket containing all my gear was a sensation.

I was walking around, nibbling a baguette, when a young man approached me and asked the way to the bakery. He was a university graduate and had lived for a time in London. He invited me to dinner and found a room in a very cheap hotel. He wanted to stay. I got rid of him by using the excuse that my husband had died recently. That was a mistake. Perfect! It made everything simpler from his point of view. But he left.

It took me hours the next day to get out of Rouen. I crossed the massive bridge spanning the Seine and kept on walking all day. The days continued to be sunny—and even hot occasionally, but the temperature dropped swiftly at sundown. I slept in all the clothes I could put on and awoke each morning with my tent frozen to the ground. My bones ached for warmth. Every morning I set off early—in the darkness—when I couldn't handle the cold any longer and just kept plodding along through the enormous, heavily wooded farmlands of Normandy.

There were a lot of freaky characters around. I must have been considered as one of them! It was like hitching through Epping or Sherwood Forest. I think some of the types hiding in those French woods hadn't left them since the Crécy. I kept mostly to the side roads—very lovely and very lonely.

Speaking as a professional tramp, the farmers in Normandy were a pretty hostile lot. Every farm was guarded by three or four Alsatian dogs. I didn't know whether it was me or the basket that sent them crazy as I passed along. One day I started walking up one of the farm lanes when one of the dogs went into a frantic fit, and the farmer hurried along to remove it. He then removed *me* pretty quickly by aiming a shotgun at me. The traditional hospitality of La Normandie!

Moving on, I kept seeing signs for a place called Fouqueville. It was well named. Invisible people lurked in the woods alongside the road. Whisperings floated across with the breeze, "P-pssst—fouquie, fouquie," and there would be a waving of hands from behind tree trunks holding what looked like money. On closer inspection, it turned out to be toilet tissue.

Fouqueville was in the wilds. There was a vast truckers' café—and the biggest truck park I had ever seen. It looked like the Yukon might have looked in the Gold Rush days, and there was a wild, uncivilised feel to it. French lorry girls came and went. Lorry girls are prostitutes with a difference. They were girls who couldn't stay in one place but roamed up and down the roads with truckers. They were the professional girls of the road.

A lift in a laundry van took me well south of Chartres, and late in the afternoon, I was put down in the pouring rain outside of a poverty-stricken hotel. The owner of the place was standing outside. She took one look at me and decided she was closing up for the night. It was five in the afternoon. She slammed the door, shouting. "Seven miles up the road, you'll find one!"

I regretted not stopping in Chartres. By six o'clock, it was pouring rain, and I had walked twelve miles on a bad road. Eventually, a professional cyclist (driving a car, of course!) gave me a lift and put me down outside of a little hotel in Cloyes. I went in with my basket. A pretty young woman behind the bar sang out, "Ah, la vie bohème!" I was in! What I thought was terrible fortune had turned to good.

This was a Parisian girl who had been running the hotel for a few years, all the while sighing for her native Paris and the Left Bank. She gave me soup and bread and a room with a bath for free. Then she produced a bottle of pastis, saying, "You have no money—I have no money either—but I have a bottle." We drank the lot discussing 'la vie bohème.' I staggered to my room and had the best night's sleep since arriving in France.

The next morning I hoped for a long lift south. The cold was really getting to me. Luckily, it was a beautiful warm day as I drifted down to the Loire valley. I found a fabulous little boulangerie along the wayside. Homemade bread and cakes, lots of café au lait and little plum tarts...

It was *such* a lovely day that I camped out at Pezon, up a side road by a little wooden bridge over a river. I went to bed early. Soon it started to rain and didn't stop for two hours. The temperature dropped, and my tent froze solid. I shivered for the rest of the night. In the light of dawn, I collected my frozen things, heaped them into the basket, and took to the road. No more dawdling around. South it was. SOUTH.

I flagged the first car that came along and hitched a lift three hundred miles to Bordeaux. I was given plenty to eat and drink along the journey. At Poitiers, I had a picnic lunch, and I could feel at once the difference in the weather. The countryside was green, and spring had arrived.

I slept out the next night at what was supposed to be a campsite. It was filthy. The lavatories looked as if the entire Foreign Legion had used them, and no one had ordered latrine fatigues before they left. I fled!

The next few days were spent following the Garonne river and camping alongside it. The Garonne is a huge river, and I walked along the valley for several days. One night I slept in the catacombs of an old walled city near Saint Martory church. The site was used 2,000 years ago by the Roman legions.

There was not a person in sight, but the usual three or four Alsatian dogs barked for hours. I wondered how many drifters of one kind or another down the centuries had done the same thing I was doing.

I was now on the road to Toulouse. I camped at the outskirts of the city alongside a canal where I watched barges glide along to destinations unknown. It was French election time, and I watched the events on TV in a nearby pub.

Toulouse is an old city. It is also a tough city. It used to be the first stop from Algeria for many refugees. The guys in the streets I frequented didn't accost girls to go to bed with them but work for them. There seemed to be hundreds of ponces. They owned the town.

I gave a political speech in one café. I don't know who it was in favour of, but whenever I got stuck for words, I shouted, "Vive la France!" Everyone shouted back, "Vive l'Irlande!" Then we all had another pastis and started again. I don't *think* I was elected.

I got a lift of 150 miles to Perpignan. The trees suddenly became green. I reached my first sight of higher ground—the hills of the Corbières, foothills of the Pyrenees. A big, *warm* wind was blowing, and the mimosa was in bloom. I made camp behind a café on the outskirts of the city. There were two gipsy-looking guys dressed in bright colours in the café. They said they were from Barcelona. All gipsies and tramps come from faraway places and are en route to others even more distant. So I was not surprised when the barman interrupted, saying, "Not from Barcelona. French gipsies with money." They came rapping on the pole of my tent later that evening, inviting me for a drink. They had brought guitars with them. Then they took me to a gipsy wedding.

We went by car to a little fishing village, then transferred to a boat and sailed along the coast. A car was waiting for us near a jetty, and we drove miles up into the Pyrenees mountains. The wedding feast was held at a town hall. I discovered I was in Spain! There was terrific flamenco; the dancing slew me. I was asked to dance a fandango. To me, it was a funny word, not a dance. But boy, did I fandango! Then it was back down the mountain road to the boat, then to Perpignan just before dawn. I collected my gear together, and as the first bird was starting up in the grey of the morning, I started off up the road that leads over the Pyrenees to the Spanish border—a fitting finish to France.

SPAIN

I WENT ACROSS THE PYRENEES TO THE SPANISH BORDER. A BORDER official came up to me. He fingered the easel and said, "Salvador Dali was the last artist to cross the border. He drew me as an ant. Will you draw me too?"

I was in—as a vagabond artist! It is wonderful how people will tell your story for you.

I drifted down the Costa Brava, down secondary roads with appalling surfaces. The wheel and axle had survived—but barely. Everything is transported on carts dragged by horses and mules; it was a miracle that the local carts moved.

I hoped my lovely Perpignan weather would continue as I intended to sleep out in just my sleeping bag. The tent was too visible. Sadly, after an hour in beautiful sunshine, a gale started, and I had never known wind like it. It was even worse than the mistral in southern France. And why did it always hit me head-on? The local people said it was usual for the Costa Brava and it can blow all the year round.

In the evening, I found a bar with some holiday chalets nearby, but they were closed. However, over anise the proprietor said he would let one to me at fifty pesetas a night. I told him this was too dear. He said forty. Again, too dear. He suggested twenty-five pesetas if he and I could be 'muchos amigos.' I said better that he and I be 'muchos enemies,' and I'd be getting along.

I headed out into the tornado. I had to walk another fifteen miles before I came within sight of another building. I'd already covered twenty.

This was a darling little town that did not cater to tourists. I found a tiny hotel down an alleyway and checked in. All my resolutions about sleeping out went by the board. It was a very cheap hotel with breakfast thrown in and the people so hospitable it was almost worth the thirty-five-mile walk.

At nightfall, I found a terraced pine grove high up overlooking the Mediter-ranean. I hauled up my basket and camped. I could see the main road south way below, and peeping through the trees the blue of the sea. The wind was still with me, and the waves pounded the rocks far below. When I woke up the next morning, I watched the sun climb out of the sea into the sky.

I was off on the road again before six o'clock—a beautiful road clinging to the cliff's side. It was impossible to build along these stretches, and a delirium of wildflowers took over, so many I had never seen before.

Late in the afternoon, I saw a port in the distance, a tiny place, nearly oblit-erated by the new buildings, but it glowed in the afternoon sunlight. There was an old ruin on the crown of a hill on the outskirts. A car stopped, and the driver offered me a lift. I pointed to the little place in the distance. "Tossa de Mar," the driver said. He was calling there, then he muttered something about Barcelona and eight o'clock.

We turned down an incredibly dusty street and sped down at breakneck speed. Three dead hens, one near-dead dog, and one possible police summons for dangerous driving later, we arrived at the foot of the hill where the ruin was perched. Now I had walked many miles on a hard road before getting the lift. It was late in the afternoon, and I was getting a little preoccupied about where I would spend the night—and then I realised we were only visiting the place for my benefit.

My driver got out, flung open the door at my side, saying the equivalent of "We'd better get going," then marched off swiftly to the hazardous stony track which wound its way up to the ruin. What could I do but follow? It took exactly an hour to reach the top and roughly the same time to get down—but Spanish hospitality was satisfied.

My driver then announced that he was going to Barcelona and although it would be dark when we arrived there at about half-past eight, I was welcome to the lift. I accepted.

I had heard of only one place in the city, the Ramblas. I had no idea what the Ramblas were, but everyone I asked knew about them. Straight on, straight ahead... and so they were—all of five miles later. Of course, in Spain, no one gives directions. They come along to be sure you get there—or if that's really where you want to go! By the time I was in the centre of the city, I had a mob with me. I had not really intended to march into the red-light district and vice district, but it was pretty apparent that's where I was. I chose what looked to be the best of the hotels and walked in with my basket. My mob followed!

It was dark, the streets were poorly lit, and I had difficulty with the basket. I was walking through an old part of the city with cobblestone streets, and the rubber tires of my basket wheels fitted precisely into the spaces between the stones. It was torture. The roads got narrower as more and more people attached themselves to me. The Ramblas were long tree-shaded walks near the old city centre, where everyone met up to gossip in the evenings. To either side were narrow dimly lit alleys, reminiscent of Soho in London. By now, I had a goodly procession behind me: beggars, street musicians, idle prostitutes and thieves, all the rag-tag and bobtail of the slums, who needed diversion.

A place to stay? Of course. The leader of the gang pointed the way to a reasonably good hotel. I went in, and my mob followed. Luckily the manager spoke good English and was quite excited by my arrival. I do not think many foreigners turned up there. I asked for the cheapest room, and he said 150 pesetas. I wondered aloud where a vagabond storyteller who had walked all the way through France and Spain would get 150 pesetas for a room. He laughed, and my mob cheered. We bargained, my crowd helping to get the price lower and lower.

At last, the manager compromised. I could have a room free if I agreed to have my photograph taken with himself, my street friends, and the basket. It seemed a pretty good bargain. My basket disappeared into an elevator, I went with my friends into the nearest tavern and drank wine till dawn. I got a beautiful room with a bath, had my breakfast brought up in a special lift, after which my mob returned to the foyer, and we all had our photographs taken.

I thought that would suffice for Barcelona, so the following morning, I headed out of town. As I started out, I was part of a procession. A mule loaded with pottery, led by a small boy, a man with a small hand cart waving a leather bottle filled with wine, taking a swig every now and again, a scissor grinder, a bootblack, a shoeshine boy, and three heavily laden carts of market produce. The police stopped all traffic to let us pass.

Soon Barcelona was behind me, and I was back by the sea once more. I collected, en route, two young girls who were hitch-hiking. They said they were medical students from Paris at first, but as they spoke no French, I discounted this claim. They confessed they came from Barcelona, which explained why every truck driver had hooted at them, calling them by name. They then told me that they were in the sanitation branch of medicine, which sounded useful. My feeling was that the nearest they would come to either medicine or sanitation would be a V.D. test. A couple of lorry girls. They were filthy, and they were fun. They decided to accompany me out of the town. However, the road took us past the Army barracks. A soldier called out, "Hi, niñas," they hurriedly explained that he was an 'amigo' and disappeared inside. I left them to the French truckers and the Spanish army.

The next day I followed the road to Sitges. A beautifully scenic route, thousands of flowers. After I had crossed the Pyrenees into Spain, I asked many people if there were any mountain ranges to cross, and was told 'nothing until the Sierras.' But for two days I hadn't seen a flat piece of road. There was nothing *but* mountains! Anything under 4,000 feet didn't rate a mention.

Sitges was delightful, but there were hundreds of English tourists, and everything was geared toward them. I camped outside the town in a pretty orchard. The man who owned it let me have a little room with a washbasin and lovely balcony, which was lucky as I wanted to stay a week and paint.

The weather was gorgeous. I painted one of the little streets in Sitges, Carrer de la Carreta. There was great excitement every day amongst the locals. I got to be friends with almost everyone in the street. One old woman came every day to ask where her house was in the painting. I explained the difficulty—she lived up the road away from the direction I was painting. That was no excuse. She became a holy terror—she didn't organise a funeral to upset me, but every darn thing else, including the fire engine, and part of the Palm Sunday procession!

I developed a routine: Walk each morning into the town, paint till late afternoon, then back to my orchard to clean up, and back to the town mid-evening.

That was mildly unpleasant in the dark with "Lobos"[79] in cars following me along the road, turning and driving the car straight at me—I found this to be a common Spanish pastime. Every morning the big fat cop on point duty said to me out of the corner of his mouth, "Okay?" I mutter "okay" back at him. I don't know what I am okaying...

Eventually, I took a lift from Sitges to Tarragona—another beautiful place. Spent the whole day just wandering around. A lot of the buildings there were from Roman times. Late in the afternoon, I found a spot along the road to camp. To avoid people who follow me out of towns, I usually turn smartly into a lane as if I live there and hope for the best. This time it worked out perfectly. A beautiful mansion was at the end of the path, completely deserted, so I walked round to the back. A grassy patch made an excellent site. There was an ornate fountain playing, with water gushing out both sides—one sun, the other shade. Hot and cold! Only ten yards from the main road and except for an old peasant who passed with his mule, I didn't see a soul.

The next evening in a little bay of the Med, I saw an old house being repaired. It looked suitable for sleeping in the garden. I found a caretaker—there were half a dozen workmen on the job, and I knew they'd knock off at six—and he said I could sleep there. Better still, he showed me a little room, very filthy, with a bed and mattress. I spread out a lot of newspapers, set my groundsheet and sleeping bag on top, and waited for the workmen to depart. There's always one whose motorbike 'won't start,' so I watched carefully. Sure enough, there was. He started tinkering about with it, but as I had the key to the filthy room, I wasn't too bothered. Presently he came over and explained that for a little while, he would be my vigilante. Did I understand? He made a small circle round his eye with his thumb and forefinger showing me how he was going to look up at the sky, round the corners—everywhere, to make sure no nasty people were about. I certainly understood! So I went in and locked the door, then peeping through the shutters I watched him do his vigilante act.

Just as it was getting dark, back he came and knocked at the door. I opened it a little. He tells me it would be much better if he does his vigilante act inside the room with me. I look down and see his foot wedged in the door so that I can't close it. He looked down as well and saw my hand poised directly over his foot with my knife open. He hastily withdrew. I closed and locked the door, then propped a loose plank against it. He waited a long time, then in the darkness, I

---

79 Note: Spanish for wolves. In this usage, Kathleen uses it as slang for young men on the prowl.

heard the engine of the bike start up, and he drove off. A couple of hours later, I heard it coming back down the track. Then he drove the motorbike full-pelt against the door. My plank held. He did this three or four times, then gave up. The bike roared away into the night. I was afraid, but I put down my sleeping bag and slept soundly. I left early the next morning.

To be on the road along the coast and watch the sun come over the ocean was a joy. Many nights I slept on the beach, and this too was wonderful. I sat and watched the sun rise up from the sea. Some days the road wandered inland, and I never lost sight of the olive trees.

Dotted among the olive groves were small stone buildings that reminded me of the sheep fields of Cumbria. This is where the olives were brought when they are harvested, but they are quite deserted at this time of year. One evening I turned down the dusty tracks to one of them—a darling place. There was a sandy flat area in front of the little stone shed, just right for sleeping. I sat down for a long time looking out at the landscape. I could see for miles. There was nothing but olive trees covering every hillside. The lovely grey-green of the leaves turning to silver as a little breeze stirs them. Far away, I could hear the roar of the Mediterranean, the tinkling of the mule bells nearby on the road as the peasants drove home.

The next morning the olive groves were left behind, and I entered the orange grove country. Here there were acres and acres of trees loaded with the

lovely fruit. I was dragged back to times gone by. The methods of agriculture were most primitive, but nonetheless effective.

Heading towards Valencia, I saw a wayside café in front of an orange orchard and turned to find a place to camp. A small boy saw me and ran into the café to tell his mother. I explained what I wanted, and she said, "Sí." She walked me to a patch of wasteland where they threw the shit and asked if that would do. I thought she must be joking. She wasn't. I said, "No, no, further back from the road—on the grass underneath the orange trees." By this time, several old women and young children came to join us and commenced heaving everything out of the basket. They were helping, I presume. I had to scream at them to make them stop.

They silently formed a half circle and watched me set up the tent. When the tent was fixed, the oldest woman came up to me and said she had never slept in a tent, and she was sure it would be better for me if she shared it. I thanked her but shoved in all my baggage showing her that there was really only room for one. A pity—but there it was. She nodded yes and shrugged her shoulders, then added, "A very great pity!"

It was getting dark quickly, but I took a walk around the place to see what it was like. At the back of the café there was a long table with about half a dozen men sitting around it as their families hovered nearby. A family party was in progress, and the men were very drunk.

I went back to the tent and turned in. About midnight the fun started. The first thing I heard was something pelting against the canvas and voices murmuring. Whatever was being thrown was very soft.

"Christ, they're moving the shit-heap over here," I thought, "and it's quicker to throw it!"

Next, the stones started, and I was bombarded for a quarter of an hour. I began to collect my things together inside the tent. Then the gang arrived. They surrounded the tent, calling, "Señora, señora, I'm sure you must be cold in there. Wouldn't it be better if some of us came in?"

They groped around, trying to find how to get in, saying, "Dónde está la puerta?" They kept trying to push their hands underneath the sides of the tent. I sat frozen to the ground. They stayed around for the best part of an hour. I kept thinking if only they would go, I would get up, pack up, and beat it. Eventually, they disappeared, but they loosed two Alsatian dogs and sent them over to prowl the tent. All night long, those dogs circled round and round. I lay down and drowsed, what else to do? Every time I made a movement, the dogs sprang at the tent and growled savagely.

128

At the first hint of dawn, the dogs disappeared. Nothing stirred at the house. I got out of the tent, packed up, and took off down the road. Lots of the stones they had thrown were all round the tent; the soft stuff was not shit but oranges. I collected every orange in shite—I mean sight—and put them in my pack. It's an ill wind...

Somewhere along the road south of Valencia, I stopped at a café run by a girl who had lived in Golders Green. She fed me. An elderly man with only one eye kept popping over to my table to give me cups of coffee and cigarettes. Each time he came to the table, he unfolded his no-eye-lid and said, "Look—only one eye—result of accident." Then he would drift away again. A horrible thing it was.

When he heard I was on the road, he offered me a lift to Seville. I kept thinking, "My God—one arm, one leg, if necessary one ball, or preferably a eunuch after some of the people I'd had lifts with—but one eye?—never."

I could just see him, at every crossroads or hold-up, turning away from the wheel, saying, "Look—only one eye—result of accident."

Further and further down into the orange-scented air. An orange grove, the most beautiful I have ever seen, with lush green grass between the rows.

I plunged straight up a little lane running up the middle and darted in amongst the fruit trees. It was still early evening, the trees grew so close together I had difficulty getting the basket in. Branches laden with blood-red oranges— the sweetest of all. Heavily ripe on the trees and a mass of blossom at the same time. The scent was overpowering as I moved towards the centre of the orchard. Not a thing moved. An evening blackbird sang its head off, and there was the occasional soft thud as an over-ripe orange hit the grass. The branches were so low that as I lay in my sleeping bag, the oranges rested upon me.

Presently there came the friendly tinkling of the mule bells and the attractive tap-tapping of hooves as they went along the road. They didn't sound quite so friendly this time, but rather hostile and a bit fearsome. I listened to each cart coming along the main way, dreading it would come up my lane, bringing an angry owner and a savage dog. I heaved a sigh of relief each time the cart passed the end of the road without turning in, and the bells and hooves faded into the distance. Soon there were no more sounds, and I was safe. It was a hot night. I sat looking out at the orange world. A big rock mountain in the distance, orange trees all around, and nearest me, the blossoms. Incredibly beautiful. I watched the moon come up—the same moon that I have watched rise so many times in so many beautiful places, thousands of miles apart, and as the air grew cooler, the scent became heavier, and acting like an anesthetic, put me to sleep. Nirvana.

In the morning, I threw away all the oranges I was carrying and filled up with the pick of this crop. I continued south for Calp and Benidorm. On the way there, I passed a little market where the only thing for sale was baskets. The woman who owned the shop saw my easel and asked me to do a painting on her wall. Of what? A basket, of course!

On the outskirts of Calp, I passed a peasant dwelling. A man was digging amongst his vines. He invited me to go in and meet his wife and three small sons. They pressed me to stay the night as it was cold and damp outside. I slept in my sleeping bag on the stone floor. It was an L-shaped room, and I slept round the corner of the "L," giving us each some privacy. There was an enormous open fireplace, and every now and then, the father threw a hedge on to keep the fire going. We had fresh fish for supper. One by one we threw them into the fire; when they sizzled, we drew them out with a pair of tongs, put them on the hearth, cut off the heads and tails, and gobbled them up. Delicious. I played the harmonica for the children, and we all had a game of football later. It's so convenient when houses are not cluttered up with possessions. A wonderful party feeling prevailed.

Whenever I couldn't understand the patois the woman spoke—which was all the time—she got up from her seat exasperated, and shaking me violently by the shoulders as if I was a half-wit she repeated the sentences one word at a time, making me say each word after her as if that would help. I just hadn't a clue.

I may have been a great success with the kids, but the mother just threw up her hands in despair at the fact that when God sent them a visitor, it had to be a moron. I loved it.

Moving on, I found a little bar not far from Alicante. I hung out there a lot of the time. It was run by two ladies from Belgium. One of them had had to clear out of Leopoldville in the Belgian Congo when it became independent— with nothing and by road, so we got on very well. They fed me sandwiches and cakes and ice cream and drinks all the time and got their customers to buy me coffee. The weather became very windy; hanging out on the beach became uncomfortable, so this was a real haven.

I did one painting at Alicante of a bare rock mountain behind the town with an olive orchard below. Soon after, I met an English family, and the guy took me out to drinks and dinner and bought my painting for one thousand pesetas.

It was pouring with rain as I left Alicante. Luckily, I got a lift to Elche, where I slept in a grove of date palms. Elche is a little desert island in Spain with the largest date palm grove in Europe and is quite delightful. There was a beautiful municipal park with exotic flowers—and of course delicious fresh dates.

A man followed me out of Elche and in bad English kept muttering something about me and a pair of garters and would I go with him. This reminded me of a night at the pub in Gloucestershire, many years previous. A man in the bar brought me a present. When we opened the box, it was a pair of old-fashioned stays—from his dead wife's old corsets! Jim 'interviewed' the guy in the lavatory later...

However, back to Elche. I had no intention of being taken by a Spaniard to be measured for a pair of garters—especially as I was not wearing stockings! Then I decided perhaps garters were something else in Spain. So I stopped and asked him.

He pointed to my sandal, which I had strapped to my foot with a rubber band and string because the sole had broken loose, and he said, "What you need is a strong pair of alpargatas—rope-soled sandals." I bought a pair for fifty pesetas. I had a lively time purchasing these. There's no right or left foot, you put 'em on either. Of course, I looked at them in the shop and thought they'd been put into the wrong box and took the whole stock to pieces looking for a left foot. Meanwhile, the shop girl kept saying, "No, no, señora, unico, unico," which presumably means any old foot will do.

From Alicante and Elche onwards, the land becomes much more arid and rocky, which is given over mostly to vines and olives. I left Elche on a beautiful sunny morning. It was sweltering, and neither vines, olives, nor date palms afforded much shade.

The countryside was mostly uninhabited save for a few herds of sheep or goats. Late the first evening, I found a grove of almond trees. The shepherd whose flocks grazed the surrounding land came over to talk and brought his thirty black goats. They were beautiful!

The next morning I started trekking back towards the coast, heading for Cartagena. Everyone told me it was horrible, but I wanted to see it. A place which has been a port for over 3,000 years must have something as interesting as the high-rise buildings along the Costa Brava.

Darkness fell suddenly that evening, and over towards the mountains, I saw flashes of lightning and heard thunder. Farms were few and far between—no agricultural land, and strange-looking places they were.

Each one was a large house with a courtyard, very Moorish-looking, surrounded by a wall three feet thick and twenty feet high. I wonder what they were protecting. Must have been defensive places of old when the Arabs were here. I hurried towards one of them and wheeled my basket up a lane and round the walls, which made a complete circle around the house. There was not a sound. A chilly forbidding place indeed!

When I eventually came to a gap in the wall, something jumped clear over me and my basket, nearly knocking me off my feet. It was two dogs on thick chains about forty feet long. I was petrified. I pulled out of range, stood within sight of the house—but out of view of the dogs—and waited. Nothing stirred.

Gradually it got darker, and the storm came nearer. I had two alternatives. Wait and see if a farmer turned up, but let the storm arrive plus the torrential rain and be drowned and blown away. Huge gales accompany these storms. On the other hand, I could get my tent set up and sit inside the doorway and confront an angry farmer. They hate you camping even in a storm without permission.

I decided to set up the tent and was glad. The terrific storm broke, so I zipped up my tent and waited. Suddenly there was a lash on the tent pole at the back, sounds of hundreds of pattering feet, and someone shaking the tent fit to pull it down. Then me screaming, "Momento, momento!"

In the middle of the storm, the farmer had arrived with a forty-foot lask (used for the herding). That was it hitting the tent pole, and hundreds of sheep trotting by. I heard the clanging of their bells, and I at once thought of a story called 'Bellwether' about a man getting smashed to bits as hundreds of sheep trampled over him.

I managed to scramble out into the storm, and the farmer strode off laughing. Screaming hysterically, I crawled back inside the tent. An hour later, the tent shook again, and the farmer was shouting above the thunder for my passport. I gave him my camping carnet or Youth Hostel card or something—he couldn't read, so didn't know the difference and went off with it saying he would return it in the morning. The storm lasted all night. It was the first time I had slept out in a really wicked one, and it was quite exciting. It stopped suddenly at dawn. I started to pack up at once. When I looked out, there was an enormous lake of water; another hour and I'd have been drowned. I looked over towards the farmhouse; the whole family was at the gap in the wall looking at the lake, the tent, and me. The farmer gave me my passport, I said "Gracias," he said "De nada," and I left for Cartagena.

The storm clouds were still hovering, and ere long, the rain swept in again. I walked through a horrible place called La Union, where everyone screamed and jeered at me. But leaving the town, I popped into the last café and had a coffee, some bread, and a plate of anchovies. When I asked how much, the barman said "Nada," someone had already paid for me. I get this often—they say "Mucho valiente" or something and pay my bill. This is quite something in a country where work is so poorly paid that it is hard to believe the money they get is wages.

Outside of Cartagena, in the pouring rain, the spokes of the nearside basket wheel buckled, and that was that. I had to wait an hour in the rain for a suitable car to stop. When one did, the driver took me right to the centre of the city. He ordered a man to carry my gear into a nearby café and further ordered him to find me a hotel and disappeared. I left my gear in the café, and then, the thug leading the way, we marched around Cartagena with no luck. Only the biggest hotel was left. I told the thug I would go in that one alone. I bargained for a room for myself—a super place. I was disappointed that I had to do this, but my basket had to be fixed at a workshop. I had to stay three nights, but I found someone to fix it. My vocabulary was considerably enlarged by the episode—I now know lots of things about repairs, workshops, and wheels in Spanish.

It was wonderfully hot but liable to heavy showery gusty periods. I hitched a lift to Aguilas. The road went right along the coast, and the scenery was superb.

Later I was walking along the road when a man on a bicycle overtook me. He asked if I was walking far and pointed out a farm where he and his wife were caretakers. He hurried on ahead so that tea would be ready by the time I arrived. They had a lovely house and were looking after a much bigger one for some English people. The couple was delightful.

They continually kept a lookout for hitch-hikers and had them in for a meal. They insisted I stay on for a day or two. It rained the first day, and they were thrilled. Water was a severe problem for them. It was the first rain for four years! Just three days before they had paid five hundred pesetas for water—and then the rain came. We spent the whole day filling every receptacle in sight.

On leaving them, I hitched on to Almería. The countryside was breathtaking—but the road surface was awful, and one of the tires wore through completely. I had to travel at a snail's pace, and the road got worse and worse. Unending mountains and the way went up and up in a series of hairpin bends. There was a village at the top, and the air was so clear and still that I could hear every sound coming even though it was at least a couple of miles away. The whole village was out watching me crawl along the road—very embarrassing for me, but very entertaining for them. They kept shouting, "Bur-ro! Ar-ria!"—the call the men make to keep the mules moving. I saw at a glance when I arrived that there wasn't a hope of sleeping out anywhere, and as it was coming nightfall, I hoped I wouldn't be delayed. I needn't have worried. They lined the street, watched me walk right through the village, and never spoke a single word. Eerie!

On the outskirts of the village, as I was despairing of ever getting a lift, a truck pulled up, and a young boy hopped out and offered me a lift. He looked about ten years old but said he was the trucker's friend and was seventeen. He might have been twelve—but I doubt it. We drank wine and smoked and talked right across the Sierra Nevadas to Almería. It was a great way to cross that mountain range—and a lucky one for me. The cab was so high I had a splendid view. It would have taken days on foot if it was even possible. Because there was nothing but magnificent mountains... range after range. Totally stark and arid. Not a house, barn or blade of grass, just sheer snow-capped rock. Over three hundred miles of it!

Almería was a colourful town with very gipsy-looking people. I had to buy new tires, so I spent two days there. The night after I left, I stayed beside a farmhouse in a pleasant valley. The children came to sit around my fire and teach me Spanish.

I got a lift into Motril, a port on the Med, where all the sugar cane is refined. It is so different from the north. There are no cars on the roads! None of it looked real. There was a narrow mule-track running alongside the road, and the mules staggered along under loads of sugar cane. Sometimes a tribe of tinkers passed by, all sitting atop one mule. It was a most paintable region. I would like a studio and huge canvases and oceans of paint!

Setting out for Granada, I hitched a car with Canadian plates—Philip Hahn, the Canadian consul in Madrid. He took me to Granada, and we owned the road. He invited me to spend the day with him, and we went to see the Alhambra and the Generalife gardens, the art gallery, lunch—a wonderful day. He found me a place to pitch my tent and invited me to Madrid. I can have a room at the embassy—for life. The vagabond life!

The next morning I went into the city to buy a canvas. There I met Simone Shartin, a well-known Spanish artist. I loved her work—she had painted all the famous toreadors.

Simone found me a place in the Albaicín district just two minutes from her own studio. I had a bedroom, a little writing room, another room to paint in, and a short flight of steps leading to the roof. I could see the whole of Granada, the Alhambra was just opposite to me, and the Sierra Nevadas loomed in the distance. It was glorious.

Simone took me all over Granada. She had dozens of relations and artist friends to visit with. We climbed the mountains all around the city and took picnic lunches and our sketching pads. I finished a painting of the Albaicín during my stay and left it with Simone when I (reluctantly) headed out of Granada.

134

The road down to Málaga was beautiful. I stayed one night in Torremolinos and had a lovely evening with a couple of English hitch-hikers and a guy from Holland. We drank anis[80] most of the night. I turned in about 3 a.m. and was up again at 6 as I wanted churros and coffee. So I hitched back into Torremolinos and straight into the first bar. I walked into a terrific welcome. A crowd of flamenco dancers were there with whom I had become great friends in Granada. They were well away on anis too! They set a bottle in front of me—or rather pushed it into my hand—shouting "Finito!" We did. Over and over again. Then we all staggered out and bought hot churros from the pans in the street, ate them, and went off for coffee. I sat with the dancers for a couple of hours and then hitched to Fuengirola, down the coast for Gibraltar and Algeciras. I didn't know when, how, or why I was crossing to Morocco.

MOROCCO

THE SHORT TRIP FROM ALGECIRAS TO CEUTA WAS TRANSPORTATION to another world. There were unbelievable sights on the road. It was lovely, I thought, to have arrived in Morocco on a Festival day. I walked along slowly pushing my basket along the smooth wide road running between two hills. It was early May and already the countryside was bare and brown from the burning sun. But the road was a rainbow splash of colour, curving away into the distance.

After arriving on the boat in Ceuta, I had not stopped there, but had taken the road to Tetuan at once as there was a checkpoint a little way out of the town. Until I had passed it, I was not officially in Morocco. I was surprised to see so many people on the road but the passport formality was very brief—a smile of welcome and a little bit of banter about my basket. I was obviously bound for the fair and festivities with all the other people.

---

80 Anis is an anise-flavored liqueur that is consumed in most Mediterranean countries, mainly in Spain, Italy, Portugal, Turkey, Greece, Albania, Lebanon, Cyprus, Israel, Palestine and France. It is colourless, and because it contains sugar, is sweeter than dry anise-flavored spirits (e.g., absinthe). The most traditional style of anis is that produced by means of distilling aniseed, and is differentiated from those produced by simple maceration by the inclusion of the word *distilled* on the label. The liqueur is often mixed with water or poured over ice cubes because of its strong flavor.

The road was thronged; nearly everyone was travelling in small groups, mostly family parties. I had never seen such colourful clothes, many of them silks or satins in bright reds and yellows, purples and lime greens.

A group of women who were walking just ahead of me squatted down suddenly. Sunburnt faces and barefooted, they were all dressed alike. Each one in a bulky white-hooded robe with a red and white striped blanket over the shoulders. Each wore an enormous straw hat decorated with four brightly coloured pom-poms and plaits of wool stretching tightly from the crown to the brim keeping it on. They looked like the chorus of a West End musical.

Their children sprawled around them, dressed in equally bright-coloured silks and satins in vivid hues of red, orange, yellow and lime green. True, the clothes were a bit raggedy, but so are the fancy dress costumes in England as they are dragged out year after year for a party. The little girls wore knee-length pants with a dress on top.

A man riding along on a bicycle in djellaba and fez balanced at least twenty thin pieces of wood, at least fifteen feet long. He steadied them with his right hand while they swayed up and down and guided the bicycle with the other hand. He travelled with a fair lick of speed.

Another man walked the street proudly in ragged torn clothes as if he wore a Savile Row suit. One trouser leg reached to the ankle while the other was raggedly torn off at knee length. A moth-eaten mantle is slung around his shoulders. What elegance and grace!

At the first town from the border I saw a little café. The men outside waved to me to come and drink tea. It was my first glass of mint tea—how many hundreds since? It was very very very sweet. I stopped at a café for mint tea. One man spoke French very well and explained that everyone was very pleased to see me as they had never had a woman in their café before. It would be unthinkable for a Moroccan woman to go there, and tourists never went to visit a café like that. There was no question of my paying for the tea; I was the guest and when they realised I had walked from Ceuta and was now heading for Tetuan they could not believe it.

Meanwhile the men outside of the café were happily playing with my basket on wheels, trying it out along the road. A big car slowed down to look at it, so I rushed out hoping for a lift. At once I saw that it was crowded, but the driver got out calling to me to come over. Fortunately the car had an enormous boot so we put the basket in and left the lid open. The man told me to get inside with his family as they were going to Meknes and would drop me off at Tetuan.

And so about six in the evening, feeling I had been in Morocco for years—that's how it is on the road, so much happens in one day that time has no meaning—I stood on the main road beside the walled city of Tetuan, watching the car vanish into the distance.

My heart sank. I was standing at the foot of a flight of stone steps which went up and up and finally disappeared through an archway in the city walls. I looked at the steps and then at my basket—it looked impossible.

From nowhere, several youths rushed forward and, lifting my basket high into the air, climbed the steps with it and I followed after, up and up and through the archway into a narrow street into another world.

My 'bearers' walked slowly along the street, jostling their way past little shops and booths and stalls. The vendors stared. There were stalls piled high with fruit, gleaming copper-ware, hanks of brilliantly coloured wools hung across the streets—the eyes were dazzled with colour enhanced by the afternoon sun. And the music wailed.

At the end of the narrow street we emerged into the main thoroughfare. A central square built entirely of mosaic resembling the one at Algeciras with tables and chairs, fountains and stone seats. Ringed around by buildings, every one of which appeared to be a café or tea-shop, all crowded with people drinking tea. One or two larger buildings looked like palaces or mosques. Then, booming and echoing across the square, the muezzin from the mosque called the people to prayer.

I passed a big café filled with men playing chess. I went in and stood to watch a game. After about ten minutes one of the players asked me if I understood the game, which seemed an odd question. When I told him yes, I played, there was a buzz of excitement and exclamations of total disbelief. I was invited to have a game. A table beside the open windows was made available. In less than ten minutes the street was thronged with people, they were almost coming through the windows as they stood on one another's shoulders for a better look. Not to watch the chess—the majority of them hadn't a clue about chess—but to see a woman actually moving those bits of wood around was unheard of.

One of the guys, a teacher, invited me to stay at his house. He had a beautiful wife named Zora. I stayed for a couple of weeks. It was only an hour away from Spain, but it seemed like another world. Europe had certainly arrived here though.

Zora and her husband lived in a modern apartment block. Modern, that is, from the outside. Inside it was a typical Moroccan household. Piles of cushions of red velvet decorated with silver were stacked to make divans. Only part of the house was roofed. The rest was open to the skies and three white doves fluttered in and out. Zora was beautiful and spoke only Arabic. She usually wore long silk pants, harem pants we would call them, and a silk chemise on top. She never left the house without her djellaba and veil. One day, Zora invited some of her friends to tea. They arrived as mysterious strangers concealed by their long robes, but as soon as they were inside the house they threw them off and turned out to be friendly, outgoing people looking like any chic Parisiennes in short skirts and T-shirts. So much for the romantic mysterious Orient!

A young girl of about thirteen years also lived in the house. She came from one of the poorest families as a servant. She slept at the foot of my bed which was on the balcony, open to the sky, and if I made the slightest movement in the night I heard the tinkling of the silver bracelet she wore around her ankle as she made me a glass of mint tea.

I played chess in the evenings and explored the casbah by day. I never heard an English voice, only French and the strange Arabic language which meant nothing. I lived in a dream world, and lost all sense of time. Until one day I met two American guys and their girls. We talked about books and films and Morocco in general. They were nice folk and they were very interesting, but it broke the spell of Tetuan. A good thing—I might have been there yet. I knew it was time to be on my way.

At midnight I returned to the lovely Moroccan apartment and told Zora I'd be leaving the next morning. After she and her husband went to bed, I packed the basket, and as it was then 2 a.m., I didn't turn in. It was a hot night and I

sat in my 'room' drinking mint tea, watching for the first streak of light over the mountains. I crept out with my basket; there was not a person in sight. Early mornings in Morocco are stupendous, so the magic of Tetuan held. I hit the road for Tangier.

At dawn, a car stopped and by 6 a.m. I was in the dazzling white city overlooking the sea. Tangier was a beautiful, dreamy place completely fouled up by tourism. I was there for three weeks. I stayed in a small hotel in the casbah just off the Petit Socco called Hotel Widad. My grotty little Hotel Widad was once a palace. It was quite beautiful. From the rooftop I could reach out and almost touch the tower of the oldest mosque in the casbah. I looked out to the twinkling lights of the port and beach only five minutes' walk away. My view over Tangier Bay was exquisite. I would climb up onto the flat roof in the early hours of the morning to listen to the prayers. The chanting floated out across the town, no less wonderful for being recorded!

The Petit Socco is a small square in the centre of the casbah in Tangier. It was always a lively place. The main café was called Café Central. To one side of it was a little alleyway where a man stood every morning making sfeni, the hot doughnut-like buns which people eat for breakfast with their coffee. Sfeni resemble the churros of Spain or Mexico in consistency but not in shape. I preferred those of Spain.

A man sidles up to a newcomer at the tobacco stand and mutters out of the corner of his mouth "Buy keef? You wanna buy keef?" just as in Piccadilly before porn ejaculated onto the market, a man would sidle up and say "Filthy

pictures?" Times change. The man offering the keef was of course, it should be unnecessary to say, a cop.

Central Square was always busy. Each morning, at seven o'clock a man brought his herd of goats into the square and anyone wanting milk was served on the spot. Direct from the goat. You could even choose your goat!

Kathleen intensely focused on her chess game.

One morning all conversation ceased in the cafés around the square. A Moroccan man came walking down the alley. He walked very slowly and with great dignity. On his head he wore a little red skull cap. All eyes were riveted on him, but he walked across the square looking neither to right or left, heading for one of the myriad alleyways. No one so much as murmured as he made his way across. Fascinated, they watched him disappear out of sight, a small serious man walking slowly—with not a stitch of clothing on him save his little red cap.

One morning I decided to leave. Everyone spoke of Marrakech and the south. I set off on the road again...

The route from Tangier to Marrakech is roughly the distance from London to Carlisle. I hitched it there and back at least a dozen times. Of course it takes much longer than London to Carlisle—Moroccan roads are different! It was like travelling through scenes from the Old Testament. I stopped to watch the oxen trampling out the corn—only a quarter of an hour's stroll from Tangier—and that was the civilised part.

On the skyline outside of Tangier, a string of camels walked proudly along. There were many women with their feet and hands dyed red and their faces painted blue. There were more camels, but this time with baby camels playing alongside. Who ever thought of baby camels? I delight in my ignorance—I always get such wonderful surprises. Now there are more cars on the road and a lift is easy. I cannot walk all the time. It would take too long.

My next lift put me on the side of the road beside an enormous pile of ripe melons. The farmer told me to take whatever I liked. Another lift gets me to Rabat, then another to Casablanca.

I had a room in a small hotel in Rabat. A very pretty young Moroccan girl occupied the one next door. One evening she invited me to her room to have supper with her. When we were both inside, she locked the door and put the key in her pocket. "Men," she hissed. "Too many men outside."

We had supper. Then the girl threw off her djellaba, and she had nothing on underneath it. She threw herself on the bed and invited me to massage her stomach. Oh, dear—not my scene at all. She had left the key on the table, so I slipped out.

CASABLANCA

CASABLANCA IS A MODERN CITY WITH WHITE HOUSES (AS THE name suggests) and wide boulevards. I found the casbah and stayed in a dirty room for only half the night—with good reason!

First, a man climbed with incredible agility up to the fretwork to look down at me. He must have done this often. No one could have got up there so successfully and expertly without a lot of practice. Next, I looked at the bed. It was moving slowly up and down. It was a solid mass of bugs! Every bug in Morocco must have gathered there. The hotel was perfectly quiet. I called out loudly for the manager. There was no answer. I raised my voice louder.

"If you think I am shouting," I screamed, "this is nothing. I haven't even started. Do I have to open the window and let everyone in Casablanca know about the bugs in this hotel?"

That worked. The manager appeared. I pointed to my hand. "Give me back my money," I demanded. After a second's hesitation, he hurried to get it. I went out into the street and started walking out of town.

SAFI

I ARRIVED IN SAFI IN THE LATE AFTERNOON, JUST AS THE CHILDREN were leaving school. A group of them run to me. They want to know where I come from. I'm sure they will never guess Ireland.

"Sweden!" calls out one of them. I say no.

"Denmark? America? England? France?" without success. Then one little girl clapped her hands and danced up and down in glee, sure she has the answer.

"From Touriste!" she calls triumphantly.

The mountains from Tiznit to the High Atlas are glorious. Bright reds with deep orange, ochres, golds, and dark, dark browns. Les Couleurs vivants. I came down from the mountains as the sun was sinking, turning everything into a blazing fiery redness. I arrived at Marrakech.

It was too hot to sleep. I travelled in the night like the locals, as the days were blazing. Now and again, I saw a miniature sandstorm go dancing across the road. I drowsed most of the daytime away. Everyone assembled in the courtyards after dusk to smoke and talk and drink refreshing mint tea. There was the sound of music—drums and guitars everywhere.

I made a delightful discovery in Marrakech. On my passport, I usually give my profession as 'Storyteller,' claiming that all tramps and vagabonds are like the bards, minstrels or troubadours. We sing for our supper, as it were. In Morocco, that made me something quite unusual, and turned out to be very lucky for me.

When I was in Marrakech, I was staying in a little café in the casbah. My first day there, I had asked the little Moroccan lady who kept it, if I could sleep

141

the night on the floor in my sleeping bag. She was enchanted and would not let me leave. In my second week there, I sat on the floor one day, sharing lunch with the family in the traditional Moroccan style. That meant the couscous, the staple meal of the day, was served on a big dish, and we all sat around it on the floor, cross-legged. A large pitcher of water circulated for us to drink from, and as we ate with our fingers, each one of us had a little finger bowl of water to wipe away the grease.

There was a commotion outside in the street. A calèche, a horse and carriage, had stopped at the door, and a man came inside the café. He was dressed in a bright blue uniform and wore a kind of helmet with a long feather in it. He asked if I was the lady who walked along the road and called herself a vagabond. I assured him that this was so. Then he explained that he would like to offer me some alternative accommodation. As I had been sampling a lot of the pot on offer and as he sounded very official, I wondered if he meant the jail. So I hastily thanked him and said I was doing great just where I was and learning a lot about Morocco!

He suggested that I should see what was on offer before I refused. So, telling the family I would be back shortly, I climbed up beside him in the carriage, and we drove off. We crossed the big square and presently, after driving through a maze of alleyways, came to a massive wooden door set in a stone wall as high and thick as those of Windsor Castle. The driver gave me a huge key and told me to open the door and go in.

I was in fairyland. Red geraniums were growing everywhere—there was a courtyard surrounded by palm trees with necklaces of bougainvillea hanging from every wall. In a corner was a house or what looked more like a studio—made almost entirely of glass. The door was open, and the shutters were thrown back. I went in. There was one large room and an anteroom with white-washed walls.

"You are now in the gardens of the Palace Bahia, which belongs to King Hassan," said my guide. "I am authorised to offer you this place to stay for six weeks."

I couldn't believe it. When I asked why, he told me that any visiting celebrities such as artists and writers visiting the country should have a pleasant place to stay. I insisted there must be some mistake as I was neither a writer nor an artist. "No," he agreed, "but you are a storyteller, and storytellers are honored in our country." So—I moved house. In a way, I had been much better off in my café in the casbah, because although I now had the most beautiful place to stay, I had no money and no food.

But my little café lady brought me a bag of charcoal for my small stove—which was a present from some of the Berber women I had met in the Atlas mountains. Every day, we wandered the market together shopping for the café, and she always made sure that some extra bits were added for me. In the evening, she would join me for supper and teach me Moroccan cooking.

For a while, this was great. But one day I decided to pull out of Marrakech and go to Ouarzazate, a desert town. I got a lift to the outskirts of the city. A strange thing happened: without warning, the town disappeared from view, and I could not see a thing except for sand, sand, sand. I was in the middle of a sandstorm, which seemed to have come from nowhere. I'd never been in one before. A typhoon is a picnic compared to the desert blow-up. I looked for a café where 'les pauvres' are allowed to sleep on the floor for free and found one without any trouble at all. A veritable doss-house. A largish room with about thirty men sitting or lying around in the last stages of degradation. No women, of course.

My Arabic was improving, so I was able to ask for sleeping space. The patron of the café showed me a small recess in the wall, threw down a straw mat and indicated that was my place. What a night. The place was like a train station waiting room—the dirtiest in the world and then some. I had better sense than to ask for a lavatory. What? With all that floor-space going begging? I must be mad! I lay down on my straw mat that reeked of urine. I thought of leaving, then remembered the sandstorm raging outside. So I stayed.

The men had little stoves and made coffee and tea in filthy cups, which they offered me throughout the night. I am a quick adapter and take on whatever my surroundings as my normal environment, so I happily accepted their hospitality. Enteritis, dysentery, leprosy—I thought I would collect them all. About 6 a.m., the sandstorm abated. I hit the road out of town without a second glance at Ouarzazate.

I walked all day. There were few vehicles and sometimes I went for hours without seeing anything but camels, donkeys and mules. I possessed a tin of jam, a tin of sardines, cigarettes and a bottle of orangeade in my pack. Now and again I glimpsed a distant farm, so I knew I had no real problems. The farms were difficult to distinguish because the buildings are made from the earth all around and cannot be sorted out from the surrounding scenery. Once some children spotted me from far away and when I arrived near their farm, they were there with hands outstretched offering me a date palm leaf on which were arranged fresh figs and pomegranates and whatever else was growing.

143

In the evening, I got a lift to a little hamlet called Boumalne Dades. There was no hotel or café, but a policeman came to my rescue and gave me a cell in the gendarmerie. I ate my bread, fruit and sardines and slept like a log. At least the floor was spotlessly clean!

On again the next day towards the Algerian border. The countryside was beautiful—palm trees everywhere. Occasionally, I passed a grove of pomegranate trees. Barbary figs and peaches were in abundance.

About midday, I came to a small village and the road ended. The countryside had changed utterly. Leading out from the village was a cart track—much worse than any cart track I had ever seen, and to either side of it was not desert, but land that was just one stage ahead of it. Vast acres of rocks and stones, and the track winding its way in and out. There were indications that a big road was soon to be made, but they hadn't got it ready for me. I waited.

I knew I might have to wait for days. Occasionally a truck came along filled with men who were working on the road, or with tons of gravel or dirt. Impossible to flag one down. There I sat, penniless at the edge of the village with at least forty miles of *nothing* to cross. The fact that I had no money was immaterial. It would have been quite superfluous with absolutely nothing to spend it on.

I waited many hours in that no man's land for a lift. Ever the optimist, I just hoped that whatever it was would arrive before the vultures decided to swoop. At last a jeep came and stopped.

The young driver said he was going halfway across the wasteland—about twenty miles, but that when he put me down I would be in the middle of nowhere in the isolated scrub desert, no village, not even a house. I took the lift just the same. I figured I could walk the other half the following day. I'd deal with that problem later. The driver was working on the road job. He was a Moroccan tramp-navvy, and when we stopped, I found myself in the middle of a tramp-navvy camp. Just like home!

I set up my tent alongside all the others. More accurately, the tent was set up for me. A dozen young workmen hurried over to do the job, while I sat and watched. They brought me coffee and bread and butter. Then they arranged a hurricane lamp in the doorway of my tent—it was quickly falling dark—so that I could read or write. I settled in. About eight o'clock, my driver came and invited me to dinner in the navvies' camp. One huge tent served as their dining room. Neat and clean, it had a long table down the length of it. Twenty to thirty men were already seated. A place was reserved for me at the head of it.

They had prepared a delicious meat stew with vegetables, a luxury couscous, a huge bowl of tomatoes, grapes, peaches and pomegranates. Wine and cigarettes. A real feast out in the scrub desert in the middle of nowhere! Conversation flowed as we talked of books and plays and movies. Countries I had visited and those I had not. We reorganised the world in dream and fantasy and talked far into the night.

Next morning breakfast was brought to my tent. Afterwards, the gang packed up my tent for me and then came the big surprise. The manager of the outfit had organised a truck to take me the remaining forty miles across the wasteland. Just before I got into the cab one of the men handed me an envelope, 'something for the journey.' He made quite a speech, apologising for the state of the road and promising that they would have the new one made ready for me before I returned.

Just as suddenly as the wasteland had started, it ended. And I was back in the beautiful oasis country. A lovely river, date palms, fresh green trees... Women were doing the washing in every little stream. I stayed to talk with some of them while doing some of my own washing, while the children pulled clusters of the fresh dates for us to eat.

Next morning I took to the road again. A lift took me to a sizable town, Ksar es Souk (now called Errachidia). Ksar es Souk was a town roughly the size of Ripon in England. I pitched my tent on a patch of sand outside the police station.

I found a little restaurant in the casbah and had a meal, courtesy of my tramp-navvies' envelope. I had a fight with a truck driver I'd hitched with. The driver and his mate tried to blackmail me for some money. In Morocco, all Moroccans hitch and are expected to pay for the lift. Most truckers wouldn't dream of asking a foreigner—which is odd when you consider who is likely to have the most money. But not this one. There was loud shouting on either side—myself and the driver in the middle of the road with half the population gathered around and cheering me on. Needless to say I didn't pay. I can shout very loudly when necessary. He was very lucky that he didn't have to pay *me*. When he had gone I settled down comfortably in the main street to sleep for the night. Survival is tough sometimes.

The next day, I turned south towards lovely mountain country, where there is skiing in wintertime—a little Switzerland.

ALGERIA

I EXPECTED DIFFICULTY ENTERING ALGERIA. IT WAS A BIT DICEY with the Middle East situation having exploded, but I sailed through with no searching and no awkward questions about money. It was handy to have a fiver, or something to show in any currency. One of the contradictions of civilisation—I spend weeks travelling the road with not a single coin (where it might be useful), and the only place I have money is at the border crossing where there is nothing on which to spend it.

I trotted off down the road, singing. I hadn't gone far when a car coming towards me from the opposite direction stopped and the driver asked me where I was going. I said "Maghnia," which was the first small town. There were two men in the car, and the one who was the passenger asked me where I came from. "Why?" I asked. "Police," they said.

Well, I was in a different country and didn't know what an Algerian cop looked like so I merely replied, "How do I know? Show me." They hadn't been asked that one before, but they showed and they were.

The man driving said, "Wait here, we will be back soon and we will drive you to Maghnia." It was just falling dark but he also added, "Do not stop an auto," so I waited. After all, they were border cops and I didn't want to get off to a wrong start. Darkness fell, the dogs from the farms barked around me, an occasional stroller wanted to know what I was doing—of course, I was hesitant about saying "waiting for the cops." I got madder and madder.

After what seemed like hours of waiting the car arrived. I got in. They explained they had been detained. I said they should have come and told me. I was so furious I sounded off. Was it right to leave a woman standing by the side of the road in the dark? It was all right by me, I was used to travelling alone at all hours of the day and night, but, I added in an admonitory tone, next time they met a woman in similar circumstances they should act differently. It was quite a speech. We had a very quiet drive.

As we approached the town I asked them to drop me at a hotel. There was no way I was staying in a hotel, but I thought once they had driven off I could skip around a corner and disappear into the night.

But the driver said very meekly, "I'm very sorry I asked you to wait by the side of the road but I wanted to invite you to meet my wife and baby, have supper and stay the night. We have never had a foreign lady walking across our country before."

146

I gladly accepted. He was a frontier guard, looking for people entering the country illegally, carrying drugs, guns, guerrillas, etc.—the usual thing. He had fought in the revolution and knew the wilder parts of the border. Also, he proudly showed some of the poems he had published. Quite an evening, and great to know it was the same old road, with the same law of hospitality. Every lift came with an invitation to stay in an Algerian house.

I left Maghnia early the following morning and got a lift to Oran in a van loaded with produce. I got out with a dozen apples and a couple of melons. My fiver from Morocco was quickly getting depleted, so after a night in Oran I decided to belt on a bit across Algeria—it's a vast country. I turned towards the coast road, pining for a sight of the Mediterranean again.

I started walking down the road to the coast as the sun comes up. I hope I'm well ahead of the hue-and-cry. A van stopped to give me a lift and carries me the forty miles down to the main road.

Algeria was very different from Morocco. There was lovely green countryside, and the grapes were being harvested. I must have eaten hundreds of pounds of them. Every cart that passed me stopped to hand me two or three bunches. They were growing right up to the roadside and I could eat all day long. I'd no idea there were so many grapes in Algeria! The vineyards stretched right across the country from west to east. I walked through them for days.

I hitched a lift in another market van, and the driver invited me to his farm. Since the revolution, all the big houses had become farms run by the government, with the Algerians in charge, sometimes as many as five or six families. This man's family had been farming way down in the south of the country, but after the war came up to the coast.

We sat on cushions on the floor to eat. An enormous dish of couscous, everyone digging in with their hands or scooping the food up with hunks of bread. Everyone keeping to their own portion of the dish, nothing changed for hundreds of years.

My next stop was Oran. Finding no place to sleep there, I went to the public library. When it came closing time, I asked the librarian if I could sleep on the floor inside for the night. He said certainly, but he would have to lock me in. Seemed like a good idea to me. He went off and brought me a carton of milk and some fruit and bread. I slept comfortably there until he came in the morning to let me out.

Yet another market van took me to Algiers. These were always good lifts—among the fruit and vegetables. I was deposited in the middle of the afternoon in the equivalent of Covent Garden. I've often stood in Marseilles, down at the

Vieux Port, and looked across the Mediterranean, dreaming about Algeria. A far-off, distant place where I knew the names of the streets by heart, and the twists and turns in all directions. For me, Algiers meant Cervantes arriving in chains, Barbarossa, and Ibn Khalid. I knew where I wanted to go first. I couldn't stay long in the city without money.

It was four in the afternoon and I decided to stay up round the clock. I headed straight for the little back streets leading down to the waterfront. First, I parked my gear in the nearest all-night café. I asked the man in charge if he'd look after it while I walked around the town.

What better place than Covent Garden? No problems with picking the basket up early in the morning! What luck to be dropped off there.

I took my shoulder bag, with passport and coins, and disappeared into the night. I wandered for a succession of days through all the little fishing ports, money dwindling rapidly, and hard on the tap for my food.

Every morning down at the quaysides, I'd go begging for fresh sardines or roughy—the little red fish, so delicious, but so full of bones! Then it was around to the market for a lemon, down to the boulangerie for a quarter of a loaf of bread, then, squatting down anywhere—beach, quayside, street—to cook my breakfast.

Small children on their way to school came along to talk and share my food. Veiled women came to watch and ask questions, the men joked and laughed, and I handed out a bit of what I was cooking. Inevitably someone popped out of a shop to give me something, to make up for what I gave away.

A long hitch—400 km—in a huge car took me inland to Constantine. We had lunch en route in a lonely Arab restaurant way up in the mountains and arrived at about four in the afternoon. I am constantly astounded by the mountain country. So different from the mountains to which I am accustomed—the green of Ireland or the white of Switzerland.

Here they are so bare and savage, and sometimes quite frightening. Great rocks with nothing growing at all. I've often walked alone at night across some of the mountain ranges and it is overwhelming. The man who drove me to Constantine knew the town well. It was quite a splendid place.

He took me on a tour. Constantine is built on two sides of an enormous gorge and it would have taken me days of walking to cover the same amount of territory. I had no idea where I would stay, had no money, and needed luck.

Unfortunately, at eight o'clock, my companion said, "And now we will go to my apartment."

Poor me. 'Twas good luck, not bad I wanted.

So, I was pitchforked out once again onto the side of the road—except that it wasn't the side of the road but a deserted area in the stony streets of Constantine. Casanova, fortunately, disappeared into the night, cursing me. Good.

Towns in North Africa were very badly lit. This was no exception. Except for a main street in the distance, it was absolutely black darkness and there were holes and trenches and implements lying around everywhere. It was quite dangerous to walk about! But I have a way of coping, quite simple and very exciting. It is an adaptation of a game we played as children called "knocky-nine-doors." As kids we would run up a street and at the ninth door, knock on it fit to break it down, then the next ninth until, by the time we got to the end of the street we could turn the corner and peep round to watch the wrathful householders appear.

When stranded, I knock on the door of the first house in the street that has a light showing and wait to see what happens. After that the road takes charge. If you crave an adventurous life, I recommend this as a very simple method of getting it. You just don't know what's coming. I don't seem to have developed much since childhood, do I? Playing at living, you see. And so that night there was a light in a window and I knocked.

It was a large house—very large, with a sizable garden, and lights in many of the rooms. The door opened, and a pretty young teenager stood there looking at me inquiringly. I asked her if her mother was in. She said no rather dubiously and waited. I started to talk. "I'm from Ireland," I told her, "and this is my first time in Constantine and I'm not sure where I am. Can you help me?"

"I speak a little English," she said, "please come in." I entered. You see how simple it is. Just tell the truth. Probably the only important maxim on the road.

Well, this house was a boarding school, run by Norwegians who had been there before the revolution. And being Algeria, there are thousands of children who were orphaned and homeless after the war. The Algerian government had done marvellous things to provide for such children and many people who were not Algerian but were sympathetic stayed to help. I was made welcome!

As I said to the woman in charge, "I'm not exactly an orphan, but I'm certainly homeless." They invited me to stay for as long as I liked. I was there for about a week, and had a wonderful time. They gave me a beautiful room and I had my meals with the kids and helped cook and wash up and clean. There were little Arab babies who had been picked up in the mountains. Although the war was long over, there were older children who had been there since they were small. A few of them were teenagers who had overcome some traumatic experiences and difficulties when small and were now doing courses at university and college. It was a girls' school and I loved my stay there. How wonderful it would be to revisit some of these places and people and see what course their lives have taken since.

After a week I hit the road for Annaba. This was called Bône when the French were there, but in Roman times it was the old town of Hippone, and it was 50 km closer to the Tunisian border. I hoped for a farm or a wood on the outskirts of the town, intending to stay one night and prowl the town the next day. As I walked along the main street I spotted a building marked 'Jeunesse des Sports.'

Anything to do with Jeunesse (the young people) had been good to me, so, leaving my gear in the care of the Commissaire, asked for the Chief. Luckily he was free and I was ushered in. A sort of board meeting was in progress. I explained that my gear was downstairs and did they know anywhere cheap I could stay for the night or a day or two. Everybody wanted me. I chose a young Algerian couple. They whisked me off to their house where they lived with mother, father, grandparents, and countless children, and after a plentiful supper we all slept up on the roof under the stars.

The next day they took me back to the office and a young French woman who lived alone allowed me to stay in her apartment. I had a slight touch of dysentery (all those grapes!) and though I was not really feeling ill, I had lost an alarming amount of weight, and badly needed a rest and proper food. Because of the dysentery, I had stopped eating. It was the only way to survive. So this haven came at just the right time. Marie-Louise, worried by my thinness, asked me what was wrong. When I told her, she dashed out to a pharmacist and bought loads of expensive medicaments and said, "You will stay here and take these, and not leave until you are quite well again." She was utterly marvellous. I seemed to be eating charcoal tablets for a week, but they worked.

I was in Annaba for at least a couple of months. Time to read, listen to the latest discs, all the things I had been missing along the road. Movie houses were showing Algerian, Egyptian, Russian, and Indian films, and one night there was a theatre gala of all the top artists in North African songs and dances. A wonderful show. One of the painters I met gave me lots of paints and a couple of canvases. I did a painting of Marie-Louise's sitting room for her as a present. It was a pretty room, with long French windows, a balcony with a view out over the mountains, and palm trees in the foreground. Now she'd have her Algerian apartment with her forever! The ruins are splendid and cover a huge area. I spent a lot of time there.

I went to an Algerian wedding during this time. Also a christening—really a fête for the arrival of a newborn babe. All fêtes are celebrated by processions of cars containing the guests winding their way through the streets, everyone very happy, with loud honking of horns until you want to scream aloud from the noise. Meals and general entertainment are held as usual up on the rooftops. The area is divided by a huge curtain of blankets strung together. Men on one side, women on the other. We women spent most of our time throughout the evening peeping through holes we cut in the blankets, watching the men sing and dance to the music of the tambourines. That is, in between ministering to our lords and masters of course!

One day before I left, Marie-Louise and I made a trip to a little fishing village not far from Annaba. Every year a fête was held in this village, and in the afternoon Marie-Louise was to make a speech and present prizes. So we dressed up in our best frills and furbelows.

She suggested that we go very early in the morning so that we could lounge around by the harbor for a few hours. We arrived at about eight o'clock. It was a most perfect day. We sat on the rocks by the sea and watched countless little boats chug-chugging around. The occupants waved and called out to us. A happy scene.

Suddenly, Marie-Louise confessed that she had never hitch-hiked anywhere and how much she would love to do so. Excitedly, she said "We could hitch one of these boats!" And before I could say a word, she was on her feet and waving her thumb wildly at anything and everything in the water. A small boat chug-chugged towards us and without bothering to say a word, Marie-Louise scrambled down through the pools and over the rocks—in all her finery!—and hurled herself into the boat, urging me to follow. I did.

Now, I am not a lover of boats. I do not swim, and although I will take a chance with anything on solid earth, boats and the sea petrify me and always end in disaster. I am forever swearing that never again will I be led onto water. But there I was.

Marie-Louise said they would take us for a little trip around the harbor. Oh yeah? We did sail around once, but then disappeared through the gap into the open sea and in ten minutes there we were in this boat which was only a couple of inches above water in the middle of the Mediterranean with nothing in sight. There was a fair amount of water in the bottom of the boat, but the two guys just handed us a couple of cans to throw it out. Great!! We went on and on, far out to sea, then the boat stopped. We were asked to stand up, as we were sitting on huge coils of rope. By this time I was unconscious of anything that was happening. True, I was there and responding, but I closed off my mind, waiting for the end. The truth dawned. We were in a fishing boat and the guys were setting lobster pots for the day's catch. It took a very long time. Eventually, we got back to the little port, too late for any fête or indeed anything. But Marie-Louise was delighted. Me, I vowed *no more boats*. But of course there were. Experience teaches me little or nothing.

Marie-Louise gave me some money when I left so that I could get as far as Tunis. She wanted me to stay for the winter! But I was quite recovered from dysentery, had regained some weight, and was anxious to get on.

During the winter season, there were few people travelling the North African roads. Within each country, there was plenty of traffic but few vehicles actually crossed the borders. When I reached the Tunisian border, the guards on the Algerian side told me it would be better to wait at the border post and they would find me a lift. I was at the border at five in the morning and had to wait until early evening for the first car. There were only two cars during the whole day: the first one crowded, the second a couple of Libyans who drove me to the small fishing port of Tabarka, where the coral comes from, and where I stayed the night.

TUNISIA

I HAD HITCHED A TRUCK THAT I THOUGHT WAS GOING RIGHT INTO Tunis. Instead, it stopped in the pitch darkness about twenty miles short of the city; I was left stranded on the unlit Route Nationale. There was no moon, and I was unable to see anything at all in any direction. And the main roads in North Africa are *not* like the M1.

Eventually I got a lift to within four miles of the city centre, which I had to walk. I seem fated to walk the last few miles into any city in pitch darkness no matter how I try to plan it otherwise. Something always cuts in to prevent this and at midnight I am walking along old cobbled streets, not a clue as to where anything is, with a crowd following me. Somehow I cope.

I found a cheap hotel on the edge of the casbah. I stayed in the hotel for two weeks, did a largish painting of a mosque in the casbah—and then had no money. I tried to talk the hotel proprietor into accepting the painting in lieu of money for the hotel bill to no avail. I left there without a copper coin and sold the painting to the first little shop that would buy it, for a pittance. Terrible. But I was heading for the open road and had to take whatever was offered.

I found a wood about twenty kilometers on and explored it. It was near the ocean and when I got out the other side there was a beach and a deserted campsite. It had little shelters built all over it and on entering one of them I found they were spotlessly clean with stone beds cut into the wall—so I decided to stay there for a few days. I threw down my sleeping bag and slept soundly. I woke at dawn when I felt something wet licking my nose and woke to find an enormous Alsatian dog staring at me. A man was attached to it on a chain. He explained that the site was now closed for the winter but said that if I went back into Tunis to the Ministry of Sport, they might give me an authorisation to stay there for a while. This I did, but by the time I got back it was nearly midnight and I hesitated to try going through the woods alone. I found it better to stay in an all-night café than prowl around looking for my particular 'chalet.' Hedi Otir was the name of the Minister who had given the authorisation for me to stay there, and he had telephoned the warden to tell him to switch on the electricity and the water for me.

Then the first of the winter rains started. The weather was beautiful really, quite hot during the day, occasional storms, but warm. Like an Irish summer. Two nights ago there was a real storm and my chalet was flooded. I searched around and found a little stone building in the same wood, a lovely place only two minutes from the Mediterranean. At least I had a roof and shelter from the rain. Each day I hitched to Tunis to look for mail and spent the day and evening in the town. I'd hitch out at night, as late as possible. I made a few friends in the town, so I got an occasional meal or coffee. It didn't seem the least bit strange to walk to the edge of Tunis in the middle of the night and flag a lift to my "sleeping out" place.

My Arabic lessons continued. They started strangely. One day while I was sitting in a café in Tunis, a young boy came to talk with me. He asked if I would like to see his school. We made an appointment for the next morning. Naturally, I imagined this to be the place where he studied. But he led me down into the very poorest quarter of Tunis, past a market, and down an alleyway.

We went into a little room. There were twenty little desks and chairs, a blackboard, and twenty little five-year-old children! I too sat at one of the little desks. This young boy was teaching the market men's children how to read and write. I joined in. Carefully, he wrote one of the beautiful Arabic characters on the board and said the sound. We slowly copied it into our exercise books and repeated the sounds.

Gradually, we began to build up words—the equivalent of 'the cat sat on the mat' etc. For five weeks I attended this class and left with a wonderful grounding in the language. From there, I went on to learn it properly. But what a way to learn—as a five-year-old child! I remember later standing beside a signpost in Libya and carefully deciphering the weird-looking letters which came out as 'Casa Blanca, Magic.' As I cannot remember learning to read as an infant, I had no previous knowledge of how wonderful it was to suddenly understand something.

One evening, I was sitting in an all-night café outside of Tunis. The proprietor of the one and only hotel offered me a room at an outrageous price—or for free if I slept with him! A young, well-educated young man proposed I sleep with *him*; he said it would be a good opportunity for him to practice his English. His friend was just hoping I liked the look of *him* better. Then, a big fat man who looked like a trucker put down a handful of sunflower seeds and tells me he knows I have refused three men, but he can give me a good meal (more sunflower seeds, perhaps?) and if I don't want him, he can find me a woman to sleep with instead.

A student at a commercial college was playing it quiet. He thought he'd be elected by being intelligent and nice. I clung to him like a leech. Yet another produced his card, showing that he was a respectable employee of the Ambassador at Tunis. He was very drunk. The doc card looked genuine! It probably was, but I doubted *he* was though. He was going to take me to see some photographs of Bulgaria. I told him I'd seen Bulgaria, I didn't need the photos. None of them looked to have my staying power—I bet they had all fallen asleep before two in the morning!

One morning I packed up my gear and headed for the road. The night before I left, I stayed in a Bedouin camp in the ruins of Carthage. At Nabeul, I got a lift halfway down Tunisia with five men in a large car. They were on their way to Sfax. It was a most curious drive. One of the men asked me if it was really true that in England it was possible to use something to prevent their wives from becoming pregnant. He said 'wives' but I think that may have been a euphemism. So I spent most of the journey giving a lecture on contraception!

SFAX

ON ARRIVING AT SFAX THE DRIVER ASKED ME IF I WOULD LIKE TO stay for a few nights with his family. The first evening we all sat around talking. The second evening I became one of the household, in as much as at five o'clock we women were locked in a room because the husband was going out, and only released when he came home.

After this happened a couple of times, I decided to find a way around this. I discovered a chess club and told the husband he need not lock me in, as I was going to play chess. After some thought, he decided that that was okay. So at five o'clock the whole family, some nine of us, got ready to go to the chess club. At the door, the husband went in alone, then came back and said that would be all right. But we shall return in an hour for you, he said. And they did. At seven o'clock on the dot, there was the family waiting to pick me up. I left the club. I also left the house the following day.

Sfax is the second largest town in Tunisia, roughly the size of Sudbury, Suffolk. I spent a lot of time down at the harbor. Especially in the early hours to watch the sunrise. I'd have coffee in the sailors' café there. The weather was beautiful—chilly at sunrise and sunset, warm sunshine during the daytime.

I was in Sfax for the month of Ramadan. The festivities to end the religious period lasted three days and nights. It took me a further three days to recover. Many of the people I became friendly with were students, they refused to observe the rules of Ramadan as a protest. But they kept the festivity part. Rebellion is only comparative. Many of the students told me in hushed tones that they *ate pork*.

Some friends from Algeria went mad and drove all the way to Sfax to visit. We went by boat to Djerba, Circe's isle. A most beautiful place, like a South Seas island with palm trees and sandy beaches. I stayed for a while with a French guy who had taught school in Copenhagen and in Brasilia. It was a lovely house to stay in, hundreds of books, discs, a piano, and a sports room with table tennis. Two or three weeks of luxury before I hit the hard road for Libya!

One day in a mad moment I accepted a lift in a boat to the Isles of Kerkennah. A fascinating place. But the weather started to deteriorate so the boatmen decided we had better get back to Sfax. The trip had begun well. It was windy but pleasant, plenty of sunshine. We got a quarter of the way back when a tempest got up. This was the sirocco, a miniature sandstorm. Everything—sky, sea, land, and wind—turned bright red and the visibility was nil. The sand was blowing right out to the middle of the ocean from the desert behind Sfax. I'd never been upside down in a boat before, but I travelled most of that journey on my head. The waves were colossal.

Fortunately, I do not get seasick, although I must say I am terrified of the sea and can't swim a stroke. All the other passengers went below except for myself and a young sixteen-year-old Arab girl. We just clung to the side of the ship as it heaved and hauled. A magnificent, splendid experience, which I have no wish to repeat. I drank most of a bottle of brandy when we reached land.

Back in Sfax, I found a tiny hotel in the casbah and took a cheap room. A small courtyard surrounded by teeny rooms on three sides. Nine altogether. No women, only Arabs up from the country or the desert for the market stayed there. The rooms were so small that when I stepped in the door I found it was almost up against the farthest wall. There was a single bed and that was all. No windows. And as the walls were made of stone, absolutely bitterly cold. I had a small charcoal stove and I decided to light it to give me some warmth. About two o'clock in the morning, I woke up suffocating and unable to breathe. I managed to hurl myself from the bed and open the door a crack, screaming for help as the smoke from the charcoal fumes filled the room. Then I passed out.

I was practically naked, and it was something of a shock to wake up lying on the bed with an unending stream of men coming in and hurling buckets of ice-cold water over me. It took me a day or two to fully recover. As I was going out the following morning, the hotelkeeper, a pleasant little man, said with a twinkle in his eye, "Madame, are you going to light your stove and close your door again tonight so that we can come to rescue you?"

It was moving-on time once again. As ever, my heart was broken as I left Sfax. I'd been there six weeks, but nothing save divine intervention can keep me off the road.

LIBYA

FROM TUNISIA, ON AND ON INTO LIBYA. ONE OF THE HIGHLIGHTS there was my stay in Tripoli. A car had deposited me in the town about 10:30 at night, and the driver had given me a postal order for a pound so I could have a bed for the night. I knew I must find lodgings quickly because it simply isn't done for a woman to be alone on the street at night in such places. I looked around for a small hotel but I couldn't see one. There were only enormous luxury hotels near to hand—so I thought I might as well just walk into the largest!

I asked for the manager and showed him my postal order: "Have you a small room you could let me have for the night for one pound? I will cash this tomorrow."

He said it would actually cost £2.40, but I didn't have to pay now and I could go to my bank in the morning...

"But you don't understand," I said. "This is all I've got in the world."

He was amazed. "But how..." he began and was at a loss for words. I told him of my journey across North Africa and when I had finished, he said "You may have the room for a pound."

It was a huge double room, beautifully furnished and with a private bathroom. I hadn't been there five minutes when there was a knock at the door and a waiter came in with a four-course dinner on a tray. Oh heavens, I thought, he really doesn't understand I've only a pound, so I rushed downstairs and said to the manager, "Is the meal included in the pound?"

He nodded, "Of course. I thought you might be hungry..."

The next morning I cashed the postal order and returned to the hotel prepared to pay and depart. The manager wouldn't hear of it. "We are not busy at this time of the year. I shall be pleased if you will stay a week in that room. I was in England a few years ago and the people were kind. This can be my way of saying 'thank you.'"

Well, he told everyone in the hotel about me and they were particularly fascinated by my wandering life because they were very rich oil people. To them it seemed an incredible existence. Every day they would come up to me and say, "Madam, you must come and see this place or that place"—they took me everywhere in great limousines and we ate in some of the finest restaurants.

A young couple on holiday at the hotel asked me how I was going to cross the desert to Benghazi and I told them that I understood there was a good road and I should, as always, set out and see what happened. They were appalled.

"You can't do that. We're returning to Benghazi and we'd be happy to buy your plane ticket if you'll come with us."

It's marvellous how one moment you have nothing and the next you are offered something like this. I thanked them warmly but privately I thought: I haven't hitch-hiked all the way here from Casablanca to look down at the desert from a plane. I should be frustrated all the way wondering what it was like down there.

So I explained and they gave me their address in Benghazi "if you ever reach there," they said doubtfully. The next day I set out to cross the desert. After two days' walking, I came to a little oasis, and there met two Bedouin families who were going south with their camels. They immediately suggested I accompany them and offered me one of the camels to ride. We travelled together for five or six days and it was out of this world. In my mind now, I can recall those glorious nights under a sky full of stars and the breathtaking sight of the sun coming up. They took me about halfway to Benghazi. I then managed to get a lift on a large convoy coming up from one of the oil wells.

It was a most enormous convoy—about twenty lorries, a benzene truck which "tanked up" the lorries across the desert. The crew consisted of fifty Libyans, twenty-five Italians, a couple of English, one New Zealander, a Canadian, an Austrian, the chief, and one woman—me!

We camped about four o'clock every afternoon, way out in the sandy scrub waste, huge tents, and bivouacs. I was given a little mobile caravan to sleep in. The desert was covered with tiny flickering fires over which we cooked supper, talked, and drank to the wail of Arabic music. A thrilling sight. The flickering fires, millions of stars overhead, now and again a camel train showing on the distant skyline, sometimes tracking across to us and the drivers coming to drink tea and gossip. Each morning, we were up in the grey of the dawn with the aroma of coffee floating in the air, stronger because of the hint of frost. The lorries pulled out one by one in a long procession as we headed across the sand to meet an enormous red sun coming up over the horizon. Something to remember.

I travelled with a Libyan driver. The first night he said, "Anybody come bother you, tell me and I beat them up." Nine feet high and as strong as an ox, he could lift all my gear with one hand. Nobody bothered me.

I had a few books with me—some of Jim's. The guys who could read English bought them all from me. I went into the Sahara with no money and came out the other end with about twenty-five pounds. Selling literature in the desert! They dropped me at a little place called Ajdabiya and I managed to hitch rides for most of the remaining distance to Benghazi. I had crossed the desert and I was looking forward to visiting the couple who had doubts as to whether I'd ever reach Benghazi. After a little while there, I thought, it's Egypt for me!

In Benghazi, I met an American married to a Swiss girl with two nice kids. They had a beautiful house, so I had a glorious shower, lovely food and drink, and a chance to relax for a couple of days.

It was still another 600 km to the Egyptian border from Benghazi on an atrocious road. I got a lift in a truck to the new town of Al Bayda, still in the process of being built. The truck put me down on the outskirts—of course— and I walked along in the middle of the road towards the centre. Huge crowds lined either side of the street. I knew they couldn't really be for me—I hadn't known I was going to Al Bayda! As I neared the centre, a cop came up to me and suggested he would appreciate it if I and my basket pulled over to the sidewalk—to make way for the Turkish President!

One of the cortèges stopped as he was passing and said if I waited till the ceremony was over, he was going to Tobruk and would give me a lift. This was about 300 km. He made a great detour to show me the Greek ruins on the coast road. It used to be Cyrenaica.

I stayed the night in Tobruk, of Second World War fame, which looks like it never recovered. A horrible place, the port for all the oil exports. I shared a room—but not a bed—with this Greek guy. He was furious. Kept waking me up all night and telling me to stop the noise. I was snoring my head off!

EGYPT

A HUNDRED THOUSAND WELCOMES. I DID NOT ARRIVE IN EGYPT in an airplane, or by boat, nor even by train, bus or automobile. I came on foot right across North Africa, because that is how I prefer to move around.

I follow the road. Few people travel that way nowadays, for time has become a most precious commodity. But for those few who keep the nomadic way of life, time is what one gains. I knew that would be seeing life in Egypt as few people can.

The next day I made the frontier and crossed into the U.A.R. at El Salloum. As usual, no trouble at all. I stayed at a small hotel in a tiny frontier town. The next day, I got a free ride in a taxi for 200 km. It was 600 km from the border to Alexandria, and nobody told me that it was still all desert! I couldn't afford a map, and every sign was in Arabic. I hadn't a clue where I was coming from or going to. I kept making strange sounds which I hoped might be mistaken for Arabic from another country. Some of the people thought they could speak English, but perhaps they were only making queer noises too!

I had passed a signpost leaving Tunis which said 'Cairo—3000 km.' It had seemed such a long way off, but there I was one morning in late January, crossing the border at El Salloum. In large white letters painted across the road was 'U.A.R.' I walked up and down the U and the A and the R like a child playing a game. I was in.

There were, of course, the formalities of having passports checked out some couple of miles further on. That was over swiftly, and "Welcome to Egypt!" was shouted from everyone around me. The words became a refrain during the whole of my stay. As I walked along the road it was good not to be burdened with too many heavy things to carry. My basket was much admired, especially by border guards—they all wanted to come along.

El Salloum is a small village in the desert by the side of the sea. A huddle of houses, a few shops, an ancient water wheel. It cannot have changed much in centuries. I walked up the little street in the general direction of Alexandria. At a checkpoint outside the village, the man in charge offered me tea and said he would get me a lift—if there was a vehicle! After a couple of hours of tea and cigarettes, a taxi bus came along full of Libyans; they took me as far as Marsa Matruh. For three or four hours we crossed the desert, sharing food and drink and talk. Marsa Matruh was my first Egyptian town. I bought some bread in a desert baker's shop and took it along to a café to eat with a cup of tea.

I was refreshed. One does not need much on the road. I decided to walk through the town and have a look around. Hopefully, I could find a place to sleep.

A huge truck brought me to El-Alamein, only 100 km more to Alexandria. El-Alamein is a touristy place. Outside of a tourist restaurant, I saw three buses. Surely, I thought, they must be heading for Alexandria. A group of students were talking animatedly nearby. I asked if this was so. "Yes," a young man said, "but not until this evening."

He added that the buses were private—this was an outing of the students from the commercial college. They had come to have a party in El-Alamein.

I asked if I could join the commercial college just for one day and go back to Alexandria with them.

"Of course," he replied, "but you must come to the party first."

There was lots of food, dancing and singing, poetry reading, and drama. A good act about telephones and the King of Yemen. A belly dance by a guy. Then I gave a talk about myself. We climbed into the buses and left for Alexandria. It was a two- to three-hour journey, by which time I had recounted most of my life story.

The lights gleamed in the distance and soon the bus halted in the centre of the city. I got out accompanied by loud cheers and good luck messages—and some money the leader of the students' union handed me in an envelope. "A small gift from us all to make your stay in Alexandria easier." Two pounds. I was rich.

I threaded my way in the darkness—lights were minimal—across the tramway lines to a row of hotels. I left my basket in one of the cafés, had a glass of tea and went looking for a room. Hard to find in the casbah, as there were no signs. But I knew the set-up, and when I saw a door leading into a passage with about two hundred stairs up, I knew I had found one.

I stayed five days in Alexandria. The chief of tourism took me to meet a famous painter and the director of the theatre—the latter took me to see *Medea*.

He also gave me an introduction to a guy who did a program called *The Voice of the Arab*. When I met this man, he took me home to a lovely lunch with his wife and twin daughters.

From Alexandria, I got a lift with a guy who had actually been to Ireland. He gave me a pound for the road. Then I got a ride to the centre of Cairo in a fast car with a young, Eton-educated Egyptian! He put me down right beside the Nile. What a great thrill. I spent the first day at Radio Cairo, fixed up to do a talk—I'm something of a knockout when it comes to talking. Any prizes for the Modesty stakes? I recorded a ten-minute interview for the European section and two longer programs for the Arabic section.

Pajamas were high fashion in Egypt. I came into my hotel one day and was stopped by a man who was very well dressed and spotlessly clean—in his pajamas. He was standing at the door of his room.

"Come and have some tea," he invited. Having tea with a man in his pajamas is something different, even in the weird hotels I have lived in. So I declined, saying I was just going out. I expected him to go back inside his room and close the door. However, he stepped out of his room, locked the door and walked down the stairs behind me, following me into the street. "Ha, ha..." I thought. "I was right. He is a lunatic."

I hurried after him to see what would happen. I thought at first the hotel was on fire and no one had told me, because the street was crowded with people—all in pajamas—at four in the afternoon in broad daylight. Good God! It was their walking-out clothes! Somebody must have told them it was European dress. They wore them like suits of clothes. Many of them were trousers and jackets but many of them flowing night-shirts straight off the counters of Marks and Spencers.

An *actual* madman offered me an empty room on the roof of a house. He had pieces of string tied in patterns on the floor, and I had to walk about the room in a careful design to avoid evil spirits. He would bring books for me to read, saying "Look at page so-and-so," and when I did, there was a five-pound note in between the pages. That was the kind of magic I approve of!

I soon found out that my madman had only just been released from the lunatic asylum when I met him. Those strings were to ward off the vibes from my next-door neighbours who might harm me. I was not to touch them. I didn't. Particularly as I *had no next-door neighbours*—there was only one room on the roof!

Then he took me to meet auntie, an ill old lady. He instructed me to sit down while he took her pulse. Around his wrist he had a leather strap which he unfastened and put on her wrist; attached to it was a long piece of flax cord with a plug of cotton wool at the end. He put this in his ear and started counting. I was a little worried, but fascinated. When he got round to wanting to measure the size of my feet with one of his bits of string, and started to crawl round the room on his hands and knees looking for my third foot, I fled!

When I think of all the people I have casually and trustingly shared rooms with (not beds), my mind boggles.

I found Egypt much stranger than fiction. All that 'thousand and one nights' stuff is as dull as the *Financial Times* compared with reality.

I made two recordings for the BBC. One was a talk I gave at the Cairo Women's club, and the other at a school on El Gezirah island. The kids were great. I also spoke at the Asian Women's group. This was lovely. The hostess was a beautiful woman from Ceylon embassy. Actually they were all the wives from the different embassies. India, Indonesia, Pakistan, Philippines, Ceylon, and Burma. They all wore their native dress, and they each brought along a national dish for a buffet lunch. I received invitations to all their countries, and they gave me a lot of money.

My radio show with Abdulwehab[81] was a great success. He taught me the words of one of his songs—in Arabic of course! We sang it together on the show

81 **Mohamed Abdel Wahab** (March 13, 1902 – May 4, 1991), was a prominent twentieth-century Egyptian singer, actor, and composer. He's best known for his Romantic and Egyptian patriotic songs. He also composed "Ya Beladi" (also known as "Libya, Libya, Libya"), the national anthem of Libya from 1951 to 1969 and again since 2011. He also composed the national anthems of Tunisia ("Humat al-Hima") and United Arab Emirates ("Īsiy Bilādī"), and many Egyptian nationalist songs.

while he accompanied us on the oud, an instrument a bit like a lute. I was also invited to be the celebrity on a Jazz program. All I needed was an invitation to perform a belly dance naked and I'd have won an Oscar!

On an evening walk, I met a guy who had been in jail for a long time. He said he had been inside every prison in Egypt. He was on the run in Cairo for two years, and he took me around the casbah showing me all kinds of secret entrances and exits to cafés and houses where he did his 'hop skip and jump' bit. This information seemed handy in case I had visa problems, and certainly would be an asset in the small hours when I was drifting in the city—a great way to avoid the hassle. One minute you see her, the next you don't.

I was trying to improve my Arabic further after my stint in Tunisia. This was the first guy in Cairo who started to teach me. He introduced me to all the salacious swear words, and the program of the Communist Party for the Freeing of South Vietnam. I tried out a few words each day at the local grocery store. In the evenings, I would buy a little butter there. It melted almost at once, so I bought only a very small quantity at a time. Each time I asked for it, the shopkeeper's eyes lit up. "Madame, I love you," he said.

It seems that the word for butter sounds rather like the word for cunt! I'd been going in and asking for a little piece of tail...

My next hotel in Cairo was bizarre as well. There was a family living in the next room who kept bringing in animals. First it was hens, then two turkeys. They slaughtered, plucked, drew and quartered the first turkey very swiftly. The bathroom landing looked as if a massacre had taken place. The second one lived in the bath for a week, but mostly liked to sit on the lavatory seat, where it would get angry and try to push me off. I couldn't complain, they were relatives of the management and the nicest people imaginable. They gave me some of the turkey.

Before I left Cairo, I did an article for *Al Ahram*, complete with a photo and one word in English—'vagabond.' I hoped it might be useful somewhere along the route as it was in Arabic.

I was anxious to get to Lebanon. Sitting in a café late one night, I suddenly went mad to be off on the road again. I said "Cheerio!" to all the people there, picked up my pack from my hotel, and walked straight out of Cairo—heading south. By dawn, I was well clear of the city along the banks of the Nile.

I met a crowd of crazy truck drivers and travelled with them for a couple of days. Slept out in the middle of a town called Quena—it was so nice to be able to crash in the middle of a city in front of the mosque alongside the river.

These guys had their cooking gear with them, so we cooked breakfast by the riverside around five in the morning.

Somewhere near Luxor, I met a vanload of young Germans and they took me to Aswan. Aswan was a perfect wintering place. May through June the temperature is 100, but in wintertime it's around 75–80. Sometimes it rains twice in one year! I went to see the Aswan High Dam. It was magnificent, but I remembered they had to flood the whole of Nubia to make it. The Nubians had to scatter and resettle elsewhere.

I also met a nice guy who took me out in a felucca[82] during the daytime, and wined and dined me in the Abu Simbel Hotel in the evenings. The hotel was modern, beautiful, and overlooked the Nile. I flew with him to Luxor, and we took a sailboat across the Nile in the moonlight to the ancient temple of Karnak, then back to Luxor where I hit the road south again.

Several times I rode on donkey carts with at least ten other people. One was carrying sacks of flour. The flour covered the desert dust, so I was clean again. They'd just been grinding corn. It took days to get the flour out of my hair and clothes. The group had two lovely young camels as well, and several who were fully grown. We went to a huge camel-market—hundreds of them for sale. What a sight!

I hopped a train for the last hundred miles. I got in via the guards, armed with a packet of cigarettes and the biggest melon I have ever seen. My contribution to the free journey. I passed through to a third-class compartment, like a huge cattle pen with slatted wooden seats, and crowded is an understatement. There are doors, but nobody uses them—they won't open. When the train stops, half of the people who are inside jump straight out through the windows (no glass!) onto the platform, and another lot from the platform hurtles in. Babies, hens, hampers, melons, old men and young women are just thrown in wholesale. Hilarious. I loved it! It is the same in the city with the buses. There are bus stops, but there is no need for them. Half a kilometer from the stop, people just start to jump off into the middle of the road. I don't know how they managed to escape being stomped to death underneath the horses' hooves.

---

82 A felucca is a traditional wooden sailing boat used in the eastern Mediterranean—including around Malta and Tunisia—in Egypt and Sudan (particularly along the Nile and in protected waters of the Red Sea), and also in Iraq. Its rig consists of one or two lateen sails. They are usually able to board ten passengers and the crew consists of two or three people.

1968

LEBANON

LEBANON IS VERY BEAUTIFUL. I DID A BROADCAST FOR RADIO
Beirut, plus a TV program, and they put me in the news bulletin. Something
about the UN, then Nasser trotting up the steps of the Kremlin, then me! *Le
Jour* did an article about me—I wasn't sure why—maybe they thought I was
someone else.

I was famous when I got here. A glossy magazine published a photograph
of me with Mohamed Abdulwehab. The editor said, "Don't you know he's the
most famous musician in the Middle East?"

"Oh well, I'm the most famous vagabond, so that makes us equal!" I was
getting to be a regular show-off. No sentence passed without the pronoun 'I'
plus a superlative adjective somewhere adjacent!

I hitched to Tyre and Sidon. Tyre was terrific—such incredible ruins. A guy
gave me a lift there, took me to lunch and around all the mountain villages,
and then back the 100 km to Beirut. I couldn't decide whether he was a security guy or organising papers for refugees from Palestine. No concern of mine
whichever—it was a pleasant and interesting day. I know we were very near
the Israeli border.

He took me to a nightclub he owned, where I stayed all night watching the
show, then went back to my sleeping bag on a ping-pong table in the University
sports ground. I decided the guy must have been on some kind of a fiddle—
hence the nightclub as a cover-up. Of course, that could be security too. I must
have had a fair dossier by now. The Uni sports ground was a nice place with a
bar and restaurant, showers, all sorts of facilities. The tennis coach arrived at
5 a.m. every morning to give me an hour's lesson.

On Saturday I had only thirty piasters left (about 9p), so I stowed my pack
at the sports place and hit the road with my sleeping bag. I'm the reverse of
city people. They hit the road with some money and when they run out head
back home to the city. I hit a town with some dough and when it's gone, head
back home to the road.

I went off on the road to Baalbek through the mountains. The grapes were
still sour and the locals kept giving me handfuls of them with salt. I hated them.

I passed a big hall with the doors open and people inside playing ping-pong.
They're crazy about table tennis here. I plonked down my things, walked in
and asked, "Like a game?"

They were so astonished when I beat everyone one after the other. Without saying a word more I walked out again, picked up my sleeping bag and continued along the road!

I think Baalbek was perhaps the most stupendous ruin I have ever seen. Situated over near the Syrian border among the high mountains, still snow-capped, hints of desert here and there, but also a fertile strip nearby. The whole setting was awe-inspiring. The small village no longer exists. Here, according to the Bible—or *somebody's* Bible—is where Adam lived. Abel was killed in the valley; Cain probably founded the town, Noah and his sons reputedly were buried in the area. True or false—who cares? I loved it! The temple had many incarnations. First Baal, then Jupiter, on to Roman times—truly wonderful! I rank it along with the Colosseum in Rome as one of my favourites.

Umm Kulthum[83], the famous Arabic singer, was giving one of her rare concerts at Baalbek. I had met her briefly in Cairo, and Abdulwehab had written so much of her music. I was her 'honored guest'—meaning I got a free seat.

I met a man on the grounds of the ruins during the day who said "Follow me quietly." I love mad people. So I did. Well, he started to scale a bloody wall—a mile high, truly! I followed, actually scared out of my mind. But I had to see where he was going. He kept calling back to me explaining that he wanted to go into the theatre for nothing and this was the only way he could do so without being seen.

Well, if you can imagine two people climbing the walls of Windsor Castle at midday without being noticed—that was us. As I climbed I kept wondering how I got into such daft situations. And me with a ticket for the thing anyway! We landed safely in what the guidebooks describe as the temple of Bacchus! I sat and read a book for some hours while my madman paced up and down, deep in thought.

Late in the afternoon, he came along to me and told me I'd have to hide for a while because the police will be making a thorough search of the place.

---

83 **Umm Kulthum** (born Fāṭima ʾIbrāhīm es-Sayyid el-Beltāǧī, December 31, 1898, or May 4, 1904 – 3 February 3, 1975) was an Egyptian singer, songwriter, and film actress active from the 1920s to the 1970s. She was given the honorific title *Kawkab al-Sharq* ("Star of the East"). Umm Kulthum was known for her vocal ability and unique style. She sold over 80 million records worldwide, making her one of the best-selling Middle Eastern singers of all time. She is considered a national icon in her native Egypt; she has been dubbed "the voice of Egypt" and "Egypt's fourth pyramid."

They had to make sure that no one came in unauthorised, especially with Umm Kulthum here. And where did he hide me? In the catacombs!

There's an excitement of wondering what the situation is leading up to, hence I floated into the catacombs. There were eight guys there already; they had bottles of whiskey and brandy, cigarettes, sweets, and fruit for the vigil which lasted a couple of hours in pitch darkness.

It was a great party. Baal and Bacchus would have loved us. I couldn't help thinking of the thousands of people who must have hidden there over the centuries and probably still do, with their lives at stake. The madman let us out at nine o'clock and we were given wonderful positions up on the stone columns to hear Umm Kulthum. The concert lasted for five hours with only two short breaks. At this time she must have been about 70, looked marvellous on stage, and had a stupendous voice.

It was a long way from that first week in Morocco when I heard her voice coming over the radio every day—and what seemed like all day—and it meant nothing to me whatsoever. The Arabs go crazy about her. It's a weird show. Seems very serious, but every now and again everyone went berserk like in a Camden Town music hall. Everyone screamed, clapped in a hypnotic rhythmical fashion, got up and danced individually. It was utterly mad and intoxicating, and in a way, very Irish.

After everyone had left the temple I hid in the ruins and spread out my sleeping bag.

I left reluctantly the next morning and hitched back to Beirut. Met up with the young Nabil Mattar again. We went to meet a newspaper editor and ended up by doing an article and a talk for radio as well. Must have been quite something. I spoke in French and it was translated into Arabic. Happily, like so much of this nonsense, I will never hear or read it—only spend the money!

This place used to be Canaan, flowing with milk and honey; now it feels like Wall Street, flowing with silk and money. Very expensive compared with North Africa!

The fruit and vegetable market was a wonderful sight, tons and tons of every variety. There didn't seem to be even one grape bruised. It was only a peach stone's throw from my hotel in the old quarter. No Europeans in those tough, colourful little streets—reminiscent of the alleyways in Soho just behind Piccadilly. I had a room on the roof. I wouldn't call the place clean. There was a wash-basin—no water came from the taps, of course. I thought it might be a porcelain basin, but as it had never been cleaned it looked more like black marble. But the view was good and the breeze was heavenly. No other woman

in the place—I got great service! As I arrived here with only a fiver, I knew I'd
be moving out soon, to God knows where.

Someone had pinched one of my bags at the quayside when I arrived in
Beirut. The one containing every single item of clothing, and personal things.
I arrived with nothing except what I was wearing: a pair of thin sandals, pants
and bra, skirt and blouse—and a silk scarf. These were my oldest things because
of the long boat journey, and I was sleeping on deck for two days and nights.
I had to sit naked every morning waiting for each item to dry. Of course there
was nothing to do except laugh. I didn't bother to tell anyone. A nice Danish
girl, Berit Jacobsen, gave me a beautiful dress—she had three, and was hitching
home quickly so didn't need them. It's things like toothpaste and needles and
thread which were in the bag, which I find tiresome.

An artist I met in Alexandria turned up unexpectedly and brought along
a fellow painter, Nabil Mattar[84]. He was twenty-seven years old, and had won
a prize in Italy for one of his paintings. He held an exhibition in Beirut three
weeks ago, and both he and the canvases were seized by the authorities. They
put him in jail on anti-Christian grounds! They let him go a couple of days later
but kept his work. He did manage to get them back, so I was able to visit his
studio to see them. He was in the same magazine as myself—we recognised
one another in a restaurant from our photographs.

I went off along the road through miles of banana plantations. Went to
Tyre, Nebuchadnezzar's old stomping ground. It was in the military zone, and
I had to surrender my passport for the time I spent there. There was a range of
mountains not far away, and on the other side, Israel.

It was quite ridiculous to find myself back in Beirut in a nightclub several
hours later having a rest and a rethink! There I was, sitting having a bath in a
strange man's apartment, getting ready for another night on the tiles. It was
fun and I didn't leave till 6 a.m. when he drove me to my tent. I decided it was
too late to turn in. So I'd been twice around the clock without sleeping. Then I
remembered I was due on TV that very day—I must have looked great!

Off to the mountains again. That's what is so lovely. From the Med straight
up to the peaks in thirty minutes. A croupier gave me a lift and invited me to a
casino. I refused. Even I need sleep sometimes. Back to the ping-pong table it
was. I threw in my cards and booked a plane to Adana, in Turkey.

---

84 Note: There is mention in an English-language Beirut newspaper of Mattar
    winning an Italian art prize, but no other mention of him appears in the modern
    press. Another of Kathleen's acquaintances lost to time but not to her memory.

TURKEY AND IRAN

I WASN'T SURE WHAT I WAS DOING THERE. EXCEPT THAT WITH MY Alice in Wonderland reasoning, it's cheaper to drift east than to drift west. I had escaped from Beirut by taking the plane to Adana, and I had an address to go to and stay for a few days. Turkey was so beautiful—and so huge. It was 1000 km to Istanbul. I went right around the Mediterranean and Aegean coast, called at Tarsus and Troy and such places, Izmir (Smyrna) was very lovely, and nearby Ephesus—a wonderful ruin. Eventually I got to the Marmaris Sea and took a steamer across to Istanbul, which I always thought of as Constantinople. It was very beautiful too, but a very tough city. I slept on the roof of a hotel with fifty other hitch-hikers. My friend Rita arrived from Athens, so we moved into another part of the city and shared a room. While there, I got a visa for Iran and had a weird evening with the consul.

I hitched from Istanbul to Teheran via Ankara and the Kurdish including the Armenia plateau and snow-covered Mount Ararat (no ark available). Appalling roads, very beautiful, very wild, and very hard going. Sometimes a long-distance coach picked me up, gave me a lift and fed me, and I stayed in some very weird places. I think it was about 3,000 km to Teheran from Istanbul. I arrived at Teheran with enough money for a couple of nights' sleep at a cheap hotel here. Teheran—enormous modern city with Oriental flavour—quite fascinating but not to be compared

Downtown Teheran, 1968

169

with Istanbul, Marrakech, or Cairo. I met an English journalist and did an article. He had a huge apartment in the centre of the city and invited me to stay for a few days. An Australian girl was there too, so I had a chance to relax and clean up for a few days before leaving and going east for Afghanistan, Pakistan, and Kashmir via the Khyber Pass. I thought I might as well go the whole hog. I was now travelling very light and getting lifts whenever I could instead of walking—too many challenges with the heat, the dryness, the great distance between towns in wild open country, and of course the appalling roads or lack of them. The Khyber Pass loomed ahead.

I left Teheran early for Afghanistan. Soon I had a lift with an army doctor. He was delighted to have someone to travel with, and when he realised I was from England, he was doubly delighted to have someone with whom he could practice his English. After a few miles, he enquired if I had breakfasted. After telling him I'd only had a cup of coffee, he invited me to join him at a restaurant where he always ate upon leaving Teheran.

I very rarely bother to look at a map of the countryside, and know only vaguely the names of towns I might want to pass through. So imagine my dismay when after a couple of miles there was an important fork in the road. The driver didn't even ask me but drove swiftly straight ahead while I looked out of the corner of my eye and saw a name on a signpost which I knew was on the road to the Afghan border. But what could I do? Here was this man, so happy to be speaking English (which I could barely understand), but who had also just treated me to a lavish expensive breakfast. I just said nothing. That was about six o'clock in the morning. At ten in the evening, I was some three hundred miles due north of Teheran on the shores of the Caspian Sea. Too bad!

I'd always wanted to see the Caspian Sea, but it took me days to rejoin the main road. I drifted along this sea road for two or three days. A mountain range separated me from the main road I had left behind, but one day, seeing a passable road-track, I decided to see if it led over the mountains.

A young woman, accompanied by two children, came trotting along the road on a mule cart. She reined in and patted the seat beside her, so in I hopped and we drove along all day. She lived in a little hamlet at the top of the mountains and invited me to stay. She, her husband and several relatives were all going to go to a town on the main road in a few days' time and I was welcome to stay with them and travel down to set me on my right road. So good luck comes—I had a wonderful sojourn because I had no plan!

Afterwards I went across the Great Salt Desert. I never knew there was so much desert lying about the world. It goes on forever. One wonderful evening

I arrived at Neyshabur, the birthplace of Omar Khayyam. Outside of the town there was a wonderful memorial to him—an enormous shrine set in a rose garden. The marble walls were covered with all the quatrains of the Rubaiyat—a sensational mosaic.

The road forked after this for Mashhad, the Islamic religious and cultural centre, and after it the waste track that led to the Afghanistan border. Once or twice a bus stopped for me—nothing to pay of course. The roads were terrifying. Not roads at all, like ploughing through layers and layers of dust which formed tracks. Often the bus hung over the side, and occasionally we all had to get out to right it. Tires fell off. My expertise was welcome!

After I left Teheran, there had been a terrible earthquake just to the south of the road I was travelling. One day a jeep came along carrying several doctors and nurses to Mashhad. They had been attending the wounded at the site of the earthquake. Now they were relieved to have a few days' rest. The government had arranged a hotel for them so they took me along. It was a beautiful city, with an incredible mosque, gleaming gold cupola outside and inside all mirrored.

I stayed in a hotel with the doctors and nurses. Next morning they insisted on buying me a coach ticket to the Afghan border. Passengers on the bus were equally divided. One half Afghans, the other half mostly travellers of one sort or another from all over the world. The road was appalling, the heat was stifling, and we changed buses at least a dozen times for no reason that I could see. Often people's luggage was left behind, other times it was thrown around. We had shouts, fights, arguments—a wonderful twenty-four hours of total chaos.

A miracle of tramp-talking had gotten me a visa at the Afghanistan embassy in Teheran. When I arrived at the embassy, I discovered I had to show proof of possession of at least $500. A very large lady handed me a form to fill in. In the space to be filled in with the amount of money in my possession, I simply wrote 'five dollars,' thinking it was better to simplify things, and as that was all I had. The woman took the form when I handed it to her and without looking at it said, "Come back tomorrow and you will get your visa."

Not wanting to waste valuable days, I said I think you had better look at the form now. When she asked why, I explained that I had only five dollars, that was the way I travelled. Could she let me know right away if I could expect to get the visa? Telling me to wait for a few minutes, she disappeared. A little while later she returned and told me the consul would like to speak to me. I went in, and after being given a cup of coffee, the consul commenced to interrogate me in the nicest possible way. I had said on the form after writing 'five dollars,' "I hope you don't want to see it."

So, I confessed I only had three dollars. A long talk ensued. The consul seemed quite delighted. He pressed a bell after about half an hour and said it was okay for Mrs. Phelan to have her visa. The woman told me to come back the following morning. "No, no," said the consul. "You must give it to her now. If we wait until tomorrow, she might not have even five dollars to start the road with."

So, several cups of tea and the autobiographical talk, and the visa was mine.

AFGHANISTAN

AT THE BORDER WE WERE KEPT HANGING AROUND FOR EIGHT HOURS in the middle of the night. We lay around on carpets and rugs, drank tea, talked endlessly, smoked and slept—very strange and otherworldly. At 2 a.m. we crossed the border and made for Herat. We arrived at sun-up.

Herat was strange and lovely. There was no mechanised transport. I saw a total of three cars! So many wonderful horses and carriages—lively high-step-ping ponies just spanking along, decorated with brilliant colours. The roads were extremely dusty and the heat was excruciating—about 100F. I loved it. The living standards were so low that anyone with a fiver was a millionaire. The grapes were the best I've ever tasted, and the watermelons were colossal. The people were kind and extremely polite. I left Herat with 500 km of desert to cross to get to Kandahar.

I left rather hastily, having had a slight contretemps with a man who had invited me to supper the night before. When he arrived to pick me up—in one of the carriages with two horses—I had not realised we were going to the out-skirts of the town and beyond where he had a villa. Having gone through the usual routine of the drink (vodka), the music (the stereo), and the invitation to dance, leading up to the swooning into bed—I left! Unfortunately he had locked us in, and as the only way out was through one of the windows, I deftly smashed it and fled back to the town. To leave early the next morning seemed a prudent thing to do.

A long-distance bus stopped to give me a lift for free. This was common everywhere in Iran, Turkey, and now Afghanistan. The journey took about a day and a half. I liked the wayside halts—inside of cafés with tea and coffee for refreshments, and we stopped frequently at wayside stalls and drank!

Kandahar was filthy—perhaps the filthiest place I have ever been in. Camels roamed the streets. Having no place to stay, I waited until night fell and then having seen the one and only hotel which was surrounded by a garden and high wall, I scaled the wall and dropped down into the garden and went to sleep. When it was daylight I went to see if I could get coffee at the hotel; I think I had a couple of dollars. The hotel entrance was pleasant and clean, several people were sitting having breakfast. I was ravenous! A waiter passed me carrying a tray, on which reposed a poached egg on toast. It had been so long since I had seen anything which remotely resembled food as I know it. I tugged at his arm, and in a voice much louder than I had anticipated, I shouted, "HOW MUCH DOES THAT COST?!"

It was something less than a couple of dollars, and I could not resist ordering the same. After I had eaten it, I asked for the bill. "Nothing," said the waiter. "The man over there has already paid for you." He pointed to a corner nearby where three men were sitting. I collected my things and said to the man he had pointed out, "Thank you very much, but *why* did you do that?" He said, "When anyone comes into a hotel and screams out for the price of a simple poached egg on toast, I thought you might not have enough money..."

He turned out to be a delightful person. He said his name was Fernando and came from Bolivia. Well, any name will do, and who knows who comes from where? He managed to get me a little room in the garden. A haven!

I enjoyed Kandahar. One person I met was an engineer and had studied at Moscow University. He was the proud possessor of a Land Rover and eventually drove me all the way to Kabul! I played a lot of chess in a café in Kandahar. I ate nothing though. There were cakes on the tables, but they were almost invisible because so many flies settled on them. The chess was great though. My Moscow man also took me up into the Hindu Kush mountains and to Bamiyan, the stupa outside of Kabul. The Hindu Kush overlooked the city, and the Khyber Pass was just down the road, leading to Peshawar and Rawalpindi and India.

PAKISTAN
(September 27, 1968)

MADE IT TO PAKISTAN FAIRLY QUICKLY. KABUL WAS GREAT, BUT VERY dirty. I was without money, and cities—unless one has good luck—are impossible without a few coins. Some French people gave me a lift to the Pakistan frontier, then I lived in the Khyber Pass for what seemed like weeks over some mix-up at the border.

I kept running up and down to Kabul, and slept out several nights with the tribespeople. I could talk perfectly with them by using all the gipsy words

I knew! Eventually, a taxi took me for free all the way to Peshawar, ignoring the border. The authorities apparently didn't like foot passengers. Something about after 6 p.m., tribal law prevailed, whatever that may mean. It must be that same old story about rape, robbery and murder...

The road was closed between the two borders between sunrise and sunset. I liked being locked in between the two! The officials were very skeptical about the fact that I could go through Pakistan and India on such little money. But, when I explained that I had crossed North Africa with less than that, and *surely* the Pakistani people would be as hospitable as the North Africans, they saw the point.

From Peshawar I got a lift with a crowd of office workers from a factory in a small town. They took me to see the steelworks and gave me breakfast. You might think I know nothing about steel, but Jim once did the script of a documentary called *Steel Goes to Sea*, which started in John Brown's shipyard in Glasgow and ended with a big liner pulling out for distant Ophir. Those factory workers thought I was an expert!

Later that day a man and his wife took me to a famous beauty spot for lunch, where the Kabul river meets the Indus. A great thrill. The man was a senior advocate in the law courts at Lahore, and knew Jim's jail books. They gave me money for a couple of nights' stay in Rawalpindi. Rawalpindi was not a bit like a city. So green, like one huge garden. It reminded me in some vague way of Hereford.

Islamabad was even more beautiful, but not yet finished at the time. It is situated at the foot of the mountains. I had an introduction to the Ambassador of the U.A.R. in Islamabad. I met his sister in Cairo. Unfortunately, he was just departing for Karachi when I called. Again, I was recognised from the photos in *Al Ahram*. I could not stay at his house, but he gave me enough money to last a week. I'm glad I worked hard at learning Arabic. There are lots of similarities between it and Urdu, so I could prattle my way about there!

I was twenty-five miles from Delhi on October 1st. I came via Lahore, stayed overnight in the university. I crossed the border at Hussainiwala without a cent. No dollars, pounds, traveller's cheques or Indian rupees. "What have you got?" they asked. I answered, "Two Pakistani rupees. Could you exchange them for Indian rupees?"

This they did, and gave me a meal, and put me on a bus free of charge to a place called Moka, in Karnātaka. A Sikh begged a room for me in a place resembling a coal shed, up on a roof, where a lot of cooking was going on. The place was *black* with soot. The next morning I read a notice outside which said 'Grand Hotel.'

I hitched a car the next day with a member of the Government, complete with a servant and chauffeur, and had a VIP's-eye view of many small places on the route. I was offered a car with chauffeur for the rest of my trip—but declined. Got to Delhi just in time for a post office strike!

NEW DELHI
(October 20, 1968)

I WAS LYING ON THE VERANDAH OF A LITTLE BUNGALOW, ALONGSIDE a canal just as the sun was coming up. Not quite awake, but I lit a cigarette and closed my eyes, trying to remember where I was. When I opened them again, I still wasn't sure. It couldn't be "after-grass" I was having—I hadn't been smoking—but what were those two groovy-looking guys doing standing there, staring and grinning? One in a little orange skirt with his black hair done up in a top-knot on his head and a flower stuck in it. And his pal, very brown, with long black hair down his back and only a little towel around him. Must be hotel Gülhane in Istanbul... but no, they closed that and threw out the hippies. And that one standing in the background looking like Jesus—or more like his uncle Moses... I remembered seeing him last night... Oh, that's right—I'm in India!

There didn't seem to be any individuality in India. The family is the unit and is *everything*. Grown men and women obey the dictates of their parents. Men of thirty tell me they cannot do such and such because their father or mother won't allow it! Women have no say at all. India was such a culture shock. Different from anything I had imagined. I thought they would be more "enlightened" and advanced than the Muslims. It must have been all that high-minded philosophy I used to read. Nothing could be further from the truth.

To me, it was a sad country and a sad people. It had nothing to do with poverty—there had been poverty everywhere I'd been, from Spain to Nepal. I was unhappy in India. There seemed no love in the country. The Arabs gave the impression of loving, and demonstrated it constantly with their incredible generosity. There was great generosity in India too—but there was also a chilliness.

I didn't even scratch the surface of New Delhi, let alone Calcutta, Bombay, Madras, Hyderabad... Superficially, I knew the north of India like the back of my hand, having hitched all over dozens of times to Kashmir, all over the

Punjab, down to Rajasthan (the desert province), the Himalayas-Kathmandu, all around the Ganges.

I'd like to have gone across to Thailand. A crowd of people I met were stranded in Laos. Everyone was making for there from Bangkok, then one day the Thai authorities put the bar up—and the only way out from Laos was via Thailand. But I'd get through. It was mostly the hippies they were stopping. Reminds me of the time I slept out in Paris in a little garden near Boulevard Saint-Michel with a crowd of drifters. In the early morning, the cops rounded up everyone else and ran them in. Except for me, I was respectable! The only genuine tramp in the park!

It was time to hit the road for Nepal. I made it as far as Shimla in the Himalayan foothills the first day, and spent the night at a girls' boarding school.

HIMALAYAS

ONE OF THE TIBETAN BORDER INTELLIGENCE PEOPLE WAS AN honors grad in English from Calcutta University. I met his physicist wife and three children, and was taken to lunch in a lovely rest house with a superb view over the snow-capped mountains. When I left them, I was well and truly stranded in the Himalayas (oh gorgeous feeling!) because there was no longer any road inland to Mandi. The only thing was to return to Shimla or chance my luck walking across this stupendous mountain pass. I tried that.

The first night I slept in a little café in a beautiful valley, *very* conscious that the night was *very* cold. The next morning I started climbing the pass from Luhri to Ani and then to Jalori crossing which is 10,000 feet up. Met a family of Tibetan refugees travelling with forty ponies across the mountain, so I joined up with them. They strapped my pack to one of their horses. Then, in a small café in the top of Jalori, it was wonderful to sit around a blazing fire coming through a hole in the ground, eating fierce curry and gazing down at the high snow-capped peaks.

We went on from there down to Kullu Valley where a festival was in progress. The whole valley was a kaleidoscope of colour. Every village sent its idol, carried by the local people who did a kind of dervish dance with daggers drawn. What a scene!

I spent quite a while up in Kashmir. It was so ethereally beautiful. I went to a miraculous festival in Kullu Valley with two families of Tibetans and forty ponies. We had been picking potatoes! Crossed the road at Jalori, ten thousand feet. Also went on a pilgrimage by accident to some Hindu goddess three days over the mountains. Shades of Lourdes or Croagh Patrick! Kathmandu was fascinating. I visited lots of the Buddhist temples. Stayed in a house nicknamed 'the Matchbox,' looking straight across to the Monkey Temple. Gongs and trumpets and chants floating across the valley—all very Sam Goldwynesque. Nepal was great, but overrun with tourists—mostly the hairy-legged variety, and millions of Peace Corps types. Of course Kathmandu is ruined, but it was wonderful to see it all.

I was standing at a signpost which said 'Tibet—12 miles.' A little old man hurried towards me. He was about five feet high, had a merry twinkling face, and he wore a long blue robe. On his head perched a little red hat. He was carrying a large wooden box on his chest. I thought it might be a musical instrument, such as a piano accordion. But when he came right up to me I saw that it was exquisitely carved. It was like a little cupboard.

He spoke to me in English, and invited me to a cup of tea in a nearby café. I was delighted as I hoped to find out about the box on his chest. As we waited for tea to arrive, an old man came to the door of the café and looked across at my companion, asking him a question. Up to that moment, my man with the box had been very jovial. Now he took on a very serious air and nodded affirmatively to the ancient at the door, who walked slowly towards us.

With white hair hanging down his back, and a long white beard, he was naked except for a little orange sarong and a string of orange marigolds round his neck. He had a staff in his hand, looked about a hundred, and probably was. When he was right in front of us, my man pressed a little button on the side of the box, and two little doors sprang open. Inside was a beautiful carved image of Buddha sitting lotus-fashion and in front of him were emblems of the Buddhist religion.

A prayer meeting started between the two men. When it was concluded, the ancient with the beard took a coin from his clothes and popped it into a slit cut in the wood in front of the Buddha—rather like putting money into a church collection box, and left the café. As soon as he had gone, my man nudged me and winked. Pressing a button underneath the box the coin fell into his hand and he paid for our two teas. I travelled with him for two or three days—selling Buddha to the Buddhists!

One day I was in the jungle in India. It was late at night and an old bus stopped. The passengers got out for refreshments. There was a Scots boy amongst them; he was as surprised to see me as I was to see him. I discovered his name was John Smith, which seemed hilariously funny. As he got back onto the bus I heard him whistling "The Skye Boat Song."

I was swept down by an overwhelming bout of nostalgia for the Hebrides. When the bus drove away, I turned round in my tracks and started to head back for the West Scottish Highlands and the Isle of Skye in particular.

I left Quetta, in Pakistan, on a train which was going two hundred miles into the desert on the start of a long trek across southern Pakistan to Iran. I had not purchased a ticket, but had jumped the train. I was in a fourth-class compartment and hoped no one would want to check up on me. I went as far as the train would take me. I hoped to sleep the night in the train but a train checker explained it would be return-ing to Quetta very shortly.

When he discovered that I was hoping to hitch the remaining 1,500 miles along the dusty road running alongside the railway line, he offered me a place to sleep for the night. He lived in a tiny room about a mile across the desert in a tiny village.

When we went into his room, there were two men sleeping on the floor, so he kicked one of them say-ing, "We have a visitor, make some tea," and excused himself for a few minutes. I sat down on the floor in front of a wonderful coal stove. It was the end of November, and had been bitterly cold outside, near freezing.

In a very short time my host was back, bringing with him two more men. The room was now very cramped, there were six of us, five of them and me.

"Care to smoke?" asked one of the men, rolling a joint. I was in no mood to get stoned, but not wishing to be stand-offish, I had a couple of hits as the joint circulated. I was really hoping to get some sleep, and was mainly preoccupied by the sleeping arrangements.

There was a small bed alongside one wall so getting out my sleeping bag I asked where I should sleep, on the bed or on the floor.

"Oh, on the bed of course," said the train checker. He watched me as I unrolled it, examined it carefully and said, "But, it's only for one?"

"Of course, I am only one," I replied.

"Then how do we make love?" he wanted to know. When I told him that was not on the program, he was outraged.

"You accept my hospitality and won't make love?!" he shouted.

"That's right," I said. Then he had an idea.

"I am a gentleman..." he went on.

"How do you mean?" I wanted to know.

"You do not have to make love with the other four, only with me!" he said proudly.

Alas... I shook my head. I could already feel the icy desert wind.

"In that case, I'll go," I said.

"Yes, you go!" he agreed. After collecting my gear, I was ejected into the desert.

Happy to get out so easily, I made my way back to the railway line. I knew there was no more chance of a passenger train but that occasionally there was a goods train, but no one knew what kind of goods. I put down my sleeping bag and went to sleep.

I was awakened in the early hours of the morning by a loud crashing and banging. Right alongside me a goods train had pulled in. I got my things together and went to see what it was. I didn't care where it was going as long as it went forward and not back to Quetta. A long line of wagons stretched backward and forward along the line as far as I could see. Each wagon had one word written on the side of it in large capital letters. WATER. It was the desert water train. Each wagon had a small ladder running up the side. Without thinking of what I was doing, I took my gear and climbed the nearest ladder. I put down my things on the top and lay down to see what would happen.

As the sky began to lighten I saw that I was lying on a perfectly flat place and around the sides there was a ledge; it would be impossible for me to fall off. In the middle was a large hole. I lay down again in case I was seen. I lay for a very long time, until well after sun-up, terrified I might be seen and brought down. Then suddenly the train started, with those funny little bumps and jerks and stops and starts of motions that all freight trains go through. The first thing that happened was that with the bumps the water leaped out in spurts from the big hole quite near to me and I was drenched. But I didn't care. It was the desert water train and I was going somewhere. I was on that train for something like forty-eight hours. I had a couple of hard-boiled eggs and a few oranges some people had given me in Quetta, and of course there was no lack of water.

The train snaked its way across the desert, day into night and night into day. Every now and again it stopped and I peeked over the side and saw water being siphoned off into a tank outside of a desert village similar to the one I had stayed beside. We were delivering water across the desert. After two days and nights we stopped but instead of a desert hamlet there was a large modern cement construction with one or two vehicles standing near and a platform leading from the railway to it. I decided that this was my stop.

I climbed down the ladder and made my way across to the building. A group of people rushed out. If I had been a Martian I could not have been a greater sensation. A very official-looking person came up to me. He wore a peaked cap and lots of gold braid.

"I have worked here for thirty years," he said, "and I have never seen anything like this happen before. A woman!"

They ushered me inside the office, brought me food and tea, let me wash up, examined my luggage and passport and wanted to know how I'd got up there. That seemed a daft question. These things always seem so straightforward to me. I just go along and along, and things happen and I cope in the simplest possible manner. Then I wanted to know where I was. The Iranian border—I'd made it. On to Iraq!

I was in Baghdad at about the time the Beirut airport was bombed by the Israelis. I was not sure then which route I was going to take back. Turkey I rejected, I had had enough of Turkey on my way out to last me for a while. Syria was impossible. No transits were allowed. The only place left to me was Jordan, which from any standpoint seemed pretty insane. However, Jordan was elected.

So there I was, sitting outside of Baghdad with still more desert to cross to get to Amman. About a day's journey, I reckoned. Until this journey I had never realised there was so much desert in the whole world. Now I began to wonder if there was anything else. There wasn't a thing on the road. I sat for hours. It occurred to me that there couldn't be much reason for anyone to go to Jordan except myself. Then I saw clouds of dust in the distance. A truck was coming. Not one, but several, very slowly. Then as the line of vehicles came nearer, I saw they weren't trucks at all—but buses. Buses?

The oldest buses I had ever seen, with no windows and looking very unsteady on whatever they had for wheels—and they were full of soldiers. The first one stopped and I got in. I was travelling with the Iraqi army, going to the war! It was a long, tedious journey of over twenty-four hours with many stops because the engines would overheat. The icy wind blew across the bus; everyone huddled together as we crept in the black darkness over the desert. I was not sure that the whole thing was happening. Where had I got to this time? We crossed the border into Jordan and then, a few miles from Amman, a wheel came off the bus. I don't know what happened to the army, but I was put into a taxi and carried along to Amman. Reality had long since gone from my life. I was floating along in some weird world, far away from anything I knew. The taxi driver, mindful of his traditions of hospitality, fed me and gave me a drink and then drove me up into the mountains so that I could look down upon beautiful Amman in the night-time. Then he drove me to a small hotel in the casbah where I was given a room for free.

That was lucky. I had not one coin. I'm not sure how many foreigners were in Amman at that time, but they certainly weren't wandering around in the casbah. For two days I roamed at random, trying to figure a way out of Jordan.

I must have been followed many times, but that was the least of my problems. Sometimes the police would stop me and take me in for questioning, but they were always extremely polite and let me go quickly. What my story sounded like, I have no way of knowing. It must have been very easy for them to check on me. There couldn't be too many people who were walking and hitch-hiking from India to Amman. My saver was that I was carrying with me an article and photograph of me from *Al Ahram*, the main newspaper in Cairo, and also a photograph of myself with Abdulwehab from a magazine, *Chabaka* I think, in Beirut. Finally, I decided I must try to bum a lift on a plane to Lebanon.

I went to the airport and asked to see someone in authority. Yes, planes were taking off once more for Beirut—the runways had been cleared since the raid and of course there were seats. Who wanted to go? Well—me! I hastily spread out my newspaper cuttings. Within minutes I had a seat on the plane, was air-bound and a couple of hours later landed in Beirut. So much had happened to me since I left India, the miracles of chance bringing me further and further along the road. I was confident that anything was possible.

The first thing to do in Beirut was to visit my friends and pick up the basket. Then I started to do the rounds of the radio places and newspapers. I was soon in possession of ten pounds. I went to an airline office to find out where I could go for that or less. There was only one place: Cyprus. The next evening I landed in Nicosia.

We landed in pouring rain. I had two pounds left out of my ten, and certainly did not want to waste it on bus fares or hotels. A taxi offered me a lift to the centre of the city, to Ledra Street. Turning up a side street beside a big hotel, I saw a flight of steps leading down to a basement area. I eased my basket down the steps and stood out of sight under the poor shelter the steps afforded. There was a door, and when I pushed it, it opened. It was a kind of storeroom, presumably for the hotel. Bar any accidents, I had my accommodation for the night.

Next morning I was woken by someone clattering down the iron steps. A man opened the door and rushed in. He wore a chef's hat. He gave a small scream as he nearly fell over me and before I could say a word, turned and went out again, locking the door behind him. I sat for a long time waiting for what was going to happen next. There was one small window in the room, and it had iron bars like a jail cell.

There was a tap on the iron bars. The chef was there, and he handed in half a dozen shish kebabs and some bread, but did not speak a word. At least it was nice to know that if I was being kept prisoner, I was going to be fed.

About one o'clock the chef returned, unlocked the door, and spoke to me in perfect English. An English lady worked in the hotel, he said, and he would take me to her. I was out of the basement before he had finished speaking.

Rachel was from England, had gone to Cyprus for a holiday, fallen in love with the place and decided to stay there. She had rented a villa in beautiful Kyrenia. Then she had taken a job in the hotel and the villa was now standing empty. So she gave it to me! Handing over the keys she simply said, "Go and stay there. The fridge is stocked up, the orange trees are loaded with fruit. I'll come out on weekends." What spontaneous generosity! And what a rest-up after the thousands of miles of desert. It was idyllic and gave me time to think. For the fact was that I really was on an island in the middle of the Mediterranean with not a copper coin.

I wrote to a friend at the BBC in England, and reminded him that I had promised to tell wonderful stories about my trip to India if I ever made it back. I added that if he ever wanted to hear those stories, perhaps I'd better have some money on account as I was in the middle of the Hebrides and needed my fare to Athens. Once on the mainland again, all would be well.

The money arrived by return of post. Then of course, immediately I had my fare waiting and everything was made easy. I looked to see if there was a long way round to Athens. After all, Egypt was just over there. True, it was the opposite direction, but how nice it would be if I could take a round trip, a boat to Alexandria, a quick flip to Cairo, then back and pick up a boat at Alexandria again for Athens. There was and I could.

I went to say goodbye to Rachel. She wanted to give me something as a memento of the trip, and decided on a ring which she no longer wore. "Look," she said, "I had this ring valued when I left England and they offered me sixty for it. Please take it and if you need any money don't hesitate to sell it. Do whatever you like with it." I thanked her and put it on. I had never worn a ring before so it was quite a novelty. It was slightly on the big side but not too much so. I now had my security!

On arriving at Alexandria, I boarded a train for Cairo. I had my basket again so I was not too happy to go hitch-hiking when my stay was to be such a short one. The train was crowded, it was very hot and very dusty, and the journey was a long, slow one. I had written to several of my Egyptian friends, including one at the radio place and another who was a journalist, telling them I was making a brief visit back again. They had promised to be in full force at Cairo railway station to meet me. As I was getting out of the railway compartment with my basket, the slightly loose ring caught in the wicker work, and as I pulled my hand free, fell off. I looked down at my hand—the ring was really gone. My friends were hurrying towards me, welcoming the homeless, penniless vagabond. I stepped out of the train, ignoring the loss of my ring. What else could I do? Here was the return of the drifter. I couldn't very well say, "Excuse me for a moment, I just want to find my fancy ring." So it was gone. Too bad.

I stayed a couple of weeks in Cairo, and the night before I left was packing up my gear. This meant emptying my basket completely and repacking it. I turned it upside down to shake out the dust from the bottom—and shook out the ring. Incredible! My security was back.

On the boat to Athens, a funny thing happened. It was an Arabic boat and it is customary for the captain and the crew to welcome aboard all the passengers. When I got on board, the captain recognised me from a TV show I had done the previous year. He said that he would like to talk with me later. It is a two-day journey from Alexandria to Athens, and as I was sleeping on deck I searched for a good spot for my headquarters. In the evening a steward came looking for me to take me to meet the captain. After a few preliminaries, he asked me if I was comfortable, had a good cabin, and so on. He was shocked when I told him I was sleeping on deck. I found myself a little later in possession of a first-class cabin with orders to eat in the first-class restaurant. There I was introduced to a famous ballet company from Paris who had had an engagement in Cairo. The major surprise came at the end of the journey when all the ballet dancers asked me for my autograph!

It was one of the coldest springs in Northern Europe. The roads through Thessalonia to Yugoslavia were covered in snow. Presently I was in Belgrade. My basket was getting sadly tattered and the wheels were very wobbly. In Belgrade,

I tried to sleep the night in the railway station. At midnight the police threw us all out and it was locked. I spent a lot of time sneaking up and down alleyways dragging my basket through the snow trying to dodge a confrontation with the police. I was looking for an all-night café. I met a young man in the street and asked directions of him. He said there was no café, but that he was going to a nightclub and if I cared to go along there with him, I would be able to get something.

The nightclub was down a flight of steps, in a basement. My acquaintance had to go down and give the password or whatever to okay me. Then he explained about my basket. A doorman and the bouncer had to come up and carry the basket down the steps. Then I pushed it into the club. They never had anything stranger.

The club was a very opulent one. There was a singer and an orchestra and people were in evening dress, eating expensive food and drinking expensive drinks. I marched across the floor in my jeans and pullover, blinking from the warmth after the icy wind, and a fair dusting of snow was melting and falling off my hair and basket. It was one of my more unusual entrances. No one knew what it was about and were too well bred to ask. I sat down to a lot of coffee and sandwiches. When the club closed at about four in the morning, my basket was carried out again to the street. I asked directions for the road north, and started off in the snow again.

A few days later I was in Munich, and tragedy struck. I was making for Munich railway station, a most comfortable place to stay for a day or two. Just as I arrived there, one wheel of my basket gave out. Gradually, I had been shedding spokes from it along the highway. Now it caught in a gutter, and with one wrench it was ruined. I managed to get it into the left luggage office. Then I came to a major decision.

Munich is a very lovely city. There are many fine things to see and do, and it attracts a good many tourists each year. I did not do any of those things. There is one area of the city I know very well, though. I can give information on every pawnshop. I spent three days trying to sell my ring—my great security—and I ended up by selling it for exactly eight pounds to the municipal pawn shop. Nobody wanted it.

With my eight pounds, I went to a cheap store and bought a shoulder bag and a small zip bag to carry in my hand. Back at the left luggage place I took my sleeping bag out of the basket, a change of clothes, my easel and a few oddments. Everything else—clothes, paints, bottles of wine from Cyprus, tent, ground sheet, presents given me from friends as far back as India—I put back into the basket, pushed it into the left luggage office again and walked out of the city on the road to Strasbourg and Paris. I neither knew nor cared what happened to it. I made Strasbourg in two days.

At five in the afternoon, I was crouched on the road outside of the city trying to see the registration plates on the backs of approaching cars. I was looking for the number 75, the Paris hallmark; I hoped for a lift directly to the city. I did not have long to wait. A small car pulled in. The motorist was an industrial photographer, and he was going to the centre of the city to his home in Paris. He worked near Strasbourg, and was on his way back for the weekend. It was a Thursday evening.

Strasbourg to Paris was about a five-hour drive, so we had plenty of talking time. I was able to tell him much of my trip from the Himalayas to where he had picked me up. When we were nearing Paris, he asked me where I wanted to go. I suggested the Gare du Nord station saying that I could sleep the night in the station, find out about boats to England, etc., for the next day, and hitch up to whichever would be the most convenient port.

We arrived at the Gare du Nord, and hurrying away ahead of me he went up to the booking office and bought me a ticket for the whole journey—leaving Paris the following morning for Le Havre. By Saturday morning, I would be in Southampton. Then he said there would be no sleeping in the station, and took me to a small hotel nearby. He gave me the change from the note he had bought me the boat ticket with, saying that it should cover my room and breakfast.

The only thing I had to give him in return was a copy of an article in French, from a Tunisian newspaper. Then he gave me his name and address and said that any time I was in Paris, his house was open to me; his wife and kids would love to have me. They don't come any better than him. The next morning the hotel manager refused my money, saying "What he can do, I can do." So, I left Paris in luxury.

It was springtime and the boat was very quiet. There were about thirty people. Another girl, Gracie Jackman, and the rest a party of Frenchmen who were rugby enthusiasts who were going to watch a rugby international match at Twickenham. They brought lots of goodies with them—French goodies. Chickens and salads and lots of good French wine. They invited Gracie and me to share their *very* wild party.

We all bid goodbye in Southampton to go our separate ways. I was hitch-hiking to London, and I was in a hurry. It was the day of the Grand National, one of the greatest horse races in the world, and I wanted to see it televised. I was in London by two o'clock. I dashed into a friend's house, put down my bags saying, "JustarrivedfromIndiagoingtoputtabeton!!" and dashed out again. I went down to the betting office and looked at the list of horses for the big race. I had exactly one pound. Gay Trip sounded like a good omen, and as I had no time to study the racing form I had to go by omens. My pound went on Gay Trip. I dashed back again to my friend's house to watch the race. Gay Trip won at twelve to one. Wealth! And luck!

The Isle of Skye was now within my grasp. I started hitching north to Scotland. First I called at Aberdeen. I had a kind of floating date to do a small TV interview there. It was amusing when my interviewer said, "For heaven's sake, you were in the Himalayas! How wonderful! Why didn't you stay there? What brings you to Scotland?"

To which I replied, "Well, one day I met a guy in the jungle in India whose name was John Smith, and he whistled the 'Skye Boat Song' as he was leaving to get on a bus..."

The next evening I hitched across to Kyle of Loch Alsh. The last ferry boat was just leaving. There was only myself and a lone piper on board. As the boat glided across the water, and the mountains of Skye loomed up in the distance, he piped me across,

Sing me a song of a lass that is gone
Say, could that lass be I?
Merry of soul she sailed on a day
Over the sea to Skye

Billow and breeze, islands and seas
Mountains of rain and sun
All that was good, all that was fair
All that was me is gone

Sing me a song of a lass that is gone
Say, could that lass be I?
Merry of soul she sailed on a day
Over the sea to Skye

I had made it. It had taken me six months from the Himalayas to the Hebrides.

NOTE

KATHLEEN CONTINUED TO TRAVEL THE GLOBE FOR DECADES, corresponding regularly with her friends all over the world. To see more information about her, her travels and friends, we recommend reading her chapter in Ian Cutler's *The Lives and Extraordinary Adventures of 15 Tramps from the Golden Age of Vagabondage*, the previous title in Feral House's Tramp Lit Series. The following is an excerpt from that chapter that describes her later years.

The email below from Jan Yates, then joint owner of the Mayfield Caravan Park in Cirencester, England, includes a summary of Kathleen's final decade and the manner of her dying.

"It was high summer 2005, not long after we'd bought our caravan and camping site that Kathleen turned up at the door to interview us. She wanted to see if we would be a suitable place to bring her caravan for a few weeks. It seemed we were, as shortly after her van was towed in and put on pitch by a gentleman who waved her goodbye as he left her to settle in. Kathleen soon became friends with everybody, including us, and we were often entertained by tales from her past. Frequently we'd be kept from work by how she met her husband Jim on the road: how they'd drunk with Dylan Thomas in London and Picasso in the south of France, then after Jim died, played football with Pele in the streets of Brazil, and telling stories to the Shah of Iran—tales we were to hear more than once! In fact Kathleen's favourite phrase was 'Did I ever tell you about ...?'

Describing herself as a tramp and vagabond, in the true sense of the word, we learned a lot about life on the road, the welcome signs such travellers would leave on people's gate posts, the kindness she found from both rich and poor. She would leave us for days and weeks at a time to hitch a ride—to wherever! Itchy feet meant time to move on and in February 2006 we found ourselves towing her caravan to the next chosen site and pitching it for her before it was our turn to wave goodbye.

Several years, sites and letters later (she wrote beautifully, long newsy letters in her careful script) she once again turned up on our doorstep in October 2009—could she come back "for the winter." Of course we welcomed her back and here she stayed until she passed away asleep in her caravan (as she would have

*wished) in the early hours of Wednesday 26th November, 2014—
two days before her 97th birthday.*

*We have many memories of Kathleen: the way she would
dance everywhere rather than walk; her immaculate dress code;
her carefully coloured hair; her pride in keeping her home clean
and shiny, inside and out; her fierce independence; swapping cigarettes with our regulars; her light burning late into the night as
she painted her little horsy booklets she would sell to raise "a few
bob"; listening to her radio; her dislike of tv, computers, internet
and any such modern contraptions; the friends she made with
people on the bus (when nobody stopped for her outstretched
thumb), at the bookies and, in the last years, the local taxi
drivers (delivered to her door!). But most of all it's her stories we
remember, we begged often for her to write them down—I even
bought her a posh notebook. It was found empty after she died
and returned to me..."*

—*Jan Yates, email to Ian Cutler, August 6, 2019* ❧

ACKNOWLEDGEMENTS

The publisher wishes to thank Kathleen's sister, Elizabeth Holdsworth, for saving and sharing Kathleen's work and memories with us and the world; Ian Cutler for introducing us to Kathleen, his great detective work, and allowing us to reprint a portion of *The Lives and Extraordinary Adventures of 15 Tramp Writers from the Golden Age of Vagabondage*; Monica Rochester for her painstaking transcriptions of the various texts; Grace Jackman for her support and shared memories of her dear friend; and Liam Phelan for his personal and thoughtful introduction of his (step) grandmother.

Finally, we wish to acknowledge all lady adventurers—women that accept their worth and follow their hearts and intellects with empathy and curiosity about the world.

FERAL
HOUSE

TRAMP
• LIT •
SERIES

———

FERAL HOUSE
1240 W Sims Way #124
Port Townsend WA 98368
Designed by Jacob Covey
Footnotes by Christina Ward

———

ISBN 978-1-62731-102-1
Printed in the United States of America
10 9 8 7 6 5 4 3 2 1

Photo of Kathleen Phelan on page 188 by Cherie Westmoreland, 1972.
Cover art by Don Tiller | dontiller.com